KAPLAN pmbr

FINALS
Torts

CORE CONCEPTS AND KEY QUESTIONS

Robert Feinberg, Esq.
Editorial Consultant
Steven H. Palmer, Esq.

KAPLAN
PUBLISHING
New York

Series Editor: Lisa T. McElroy, Associate Professor, Drexel University College of Law
Editorial Director: Jennifer Farthing
Editor: Michael Sprague
Production Editor: Fred Urfer
Cover Designer: Carly Schnur

Published by Kaplan Publishing, a division of Kaplan, Inc.
1 Liberty Plaza, 24th floor
New York, NY 10006

Printed in the United States of America

August 2007
10 9 8 7 6 5 4 3 2 1

ISBN13: 978-1-4277-9645-5

Kaplan Publishing books are available at special quantity discounts to use for sales promotions, employee premiums, or educational purposes. Please email our Special Sales Department to order or for more information at kaplanpublishing@kaplan.com, or write to Kaplan Publishing, 1 Liberty Plaza, 24th floor, New York, NY 10006.

Kaplan PMBR Finals: Core Concepts and Key Questions is a law school preparatory series from one of the leading companies for preparing for the Bar exam. It is designed to provide students with focused study to succeed on their law school exams. Remember that *Kaplan PMBR* is not simply another commercial outline series. Rather each edition consists of several integrated sections. This edition contains a substantive outline, capsule summary outlines, objective law school exam questions, essay exam questions, and fully detailed explanatory answers.

Finals is designed to be used as a pre-exam study aid. You should be aware that most law schools are now implementing objective *and* essay questions on their final examinations. In the past virtually all law school exams were written solely in an essay format. Now the trend is to test students with objective and subjective questions.

Objective questions on exams eliminate the subjectivity of essay grading. They provide uniformity and a basis for reliable grading. Law schools are also recognizing the necessity to prepare students for the Multistate Bar Examination (commonly referred to as the "MBE"). The MBE is a uniform, national, 200-question multiple choice exam covering the six subject areas of Torts, Contracts, Real Property/Future Interests, Evidence, Constitutional Law, and Criminal Law/Procedure.

Finals is designed as a national law school study aid. Many of the questions and answers follow the majority rule of law in effect in most jurisdictions. Many of the rationales and explanations refer to the national norm. This is to make the series as applicable as possible for students across the country.

This edition includes three types of questions of varying difficulty. The true-false questions merely require the student know the black letter of the law. The multiple-choice questions require knowledge of the black letter law and some legal reasoning skills. The essay questions require deep thought and extensive legal reasoning. To thoroughly prepare for your exams, students will most likely want to do a number of each type of question.

Kaplan and PMBR wish you the best of luck on your exams and in your legal career.

I. INTENTIONAL TORTS TO PERSONS, LAND, AND CHATTELS

A. INTENTION GENERALLY.

1. **Intent: Definition.** A person acts intentionally where:

   a. he ***desires*** to cause the consequences of his act, ***or***

   b. the consequences are ***substantially certain*** to result from it.

2. **Types of Tortious Intent**

   a. **Specific Intent** - exists where the defendant acts desiring that his conduct cause the resulting consequences (i.e., the harm defined by the elements of the given tort).

   Example: Despite the fact that John was right in the ball's path, Sam caught Barry Bonds' 72nd home run ball. Sam knocked John down in order to catch the ball. John, furious, wants to bloody Sam's nose. If John socks Sam in the nose and causes it to bleed, he has committed a battery.

   b. **General Intent** - exists where the defendant acts knowing ***with substantial certainty*** (a somewhat lesser degree than specific intent) that his conduct will cause the resulting consequences.

   Example: After Sam sells Barry Bonds' 72nd home run ball for $1,000,000, John is even angrier and decides to play a practical joke on Sam. He therefore goes to Sam's house and holds a toy gun to Sam's head. Sam experiences major apprehension that John is going to shoot him. Even if the gun is not loaded, John has committed an assault because he could be substantially certain that Sam would be frightened.

   c. **Transferred Intent** - exists in certain cases where the defendant intends tortious conduct against one party but the resulting harm is caused upon another party. In these instances, irrespective of motive, the defendant's intent is said to be transferred from the intended party to the party actually harmed.

   Caveat: The doctrine of transferred intent applies only to the following torts - ***assault, battery, false imprisonment, trespass to land, trespass to chattels.***

   Example: John and Sam are at a party. John has a banana cream pie in his hand. Sam sees him and is afraid. John throws the pie at Sam, intending to hit him in the face. At the last minute, Eliza crosses in front of Sam, and the pie hits her in the face. John is still liable for assault.

   d. Minors and incompetent persons are generally held liable for intentional torts they commit, even where they lack knowledge that the consequences are wrong or foreseeable.

   Example: Eliza, who is only seven years old, sets off firecrackers under John's chair. If a firecracker hits John, Eliza is liable for a battery.

B. INTENTIONAL INTERFERENCE WITH THE PERSON

1. Battery

a. An actor is subject to liability to another for ***battery*** if:

(1) he acts ***intending to cause a harmful or offensive contact with the person of another or a third person, or an imminent apprehension of such a contact, and***

(2) ***an offensive contact with the person of the other directly or indirectly results.***

b. There is no tort liability for battery where an actor causes harmful or offensive contact without intent (in other words, where the contact is either ***negligent, reckless, or wanton***).

c. Where a person makes bodily contact with another that is offensive to a reasonable person's sense of dignity, he commits a battery.

Example: Where Simon pulls a chair out from under his teacher as the teacher is attempting to sit down, he commits a battery.

d. If an actor offensively touches anything that is close to or connected to the plaintiff's body or person, he commits a battery.

Example: Helen throws a rock at the car Cecelia is driving. If the rock hits the car, Helen has committed a battery.

e. Causation may be "direct" or "indirect." Indirect causation exists where the defendant sets in motion the harm-producing force.

Example: Jeremy puts poison in Alison's tea. Alison suffers a heart attack and dies. Jeremy has committed a battery.

Example: Alison's sister, angry with Jeremy, sets a giant trap for him. If Jeremy falls into the trap and injures himself, Alison's sister is liable for battery.

f. To commit a battery, a plaintiff need not be aware of the offensive contact and need not prove damages.

2. Assault

a. An actor is subject to liability to another for ***assault*** if

(1) he acts ***intending to cause a harmful or offensive contact with the person of another or a third person, or an imminent apprehension of such a contact, and***

(2) the other person is thereby ***put in such imminent apprehension.***

b. Because intent is required, an actor is not liable to another for causing an apprehension caused even if the act involves an unreasonable risk of causing it and, therefore, would be negligent or reckless if the risk threatened bodily harm.

c. To recover for assault, the plaintiff must feel "reasonable" apprehension. Unlike battery, the plaintiff must have awareness or knowledge of the defendant's act. Where a defendant causes baseless apprehension (sometimes called "apparent ability"), he may still be liable for a battery.

Example: George holds a gun to Zelda's head and tells her to hand over her purse. George knows that the gun is unloaded, but Zelda believes that it is loaded and is very frightened. George is liable for assault.

d. Future threats lack ***imminency*** and are therefore insufficient acts for assault. ***Words alone are insufficient, unless accompanied by some overt act*** causing reasonable apprehension of imminent contact. A conditional threat may also constitute an assault.

Example: Herman holds a knife to Gretchen's throat and threatens to hurt her. He is liable for assault.

Example: Leslie, a bank robber, points a gun into a crowded bank and says, "Everyone lie down and keep quiet or else I'll shoot." This conditional threat is an assault.

Example: Charlie throws a rock at Nancy and misses. He has committed an attempted battery. However, if Nancy was aware that Charlie threw the rock, an assault has also occurred.

3. **False Imprisonment**

a. A person is subject to liability to another for false imprisonment if

(1) he acts ***intending to confine a person within certain fixed boundaries, and***

(2) his act ***directly*** or ***indirectly results in such a confinement*** of the other, ***and***

(3) the other ***is conscious of the confinement or is harmed*** by it.

Exception: A defendant may be liable for false imprisonment if he confines a child or mentally incompetent person, even where the confinee is not aware of the confinement.

Example: James kidnaps Andrea, a seven-year-old, while she is sleeping. As she continues to sleep, he places her in the trunk of his car and leaves her there for several hours. James is liable for false imprisonment.

b. Confinement may result ***due to physical force or barriers which restrain freedom of movement, present threats of force, or constitute failure to provide plaintiff a means of escape*** (where such affirmative duty is imposed on the defendant).

Example: Stuart takes all of Susan's clothes and leaves her in the middle of the woods. Because Susan does not have a means of escape, Stuart has falsely imprisoned her.

c. **Caveat:** An ***unlawful warrantless arrest*** (i.e., false arrest) may constitute false imprisonment, since the resulting confinement is without proper legal authority. Confinement can result no matter how brief a time interval is involved.

d. **Shopkeeper's Privilege:** No action for false imprisonment will lie against a shopkeeper who detains a suspected shoplifter if:

(1) there are ***reasonable grounds*** to believe that a theft has occurred;

(2) the detention is conducted in a ***reasonable manner*** (i.e., no deadly force allowed); ***and***

(3) the detention is limited to a ***reasonable period of time*** to make an investigation.

e. A "bounded" area prevents freedom of movement in all directions by providing no reasonable means of escape. Actual physical boundaries are not required, however.

Question:

Angelina Antonelli, a 16-year-old high school junior, just received her Utah state driver's license. One afternoon she attended a picnic at a campgrounds in a remote area of the Deer Valley National Park. Following the picnic, Angelina was driving through the park when she got lost. As darkness descended, Angelina began to panic because she was driving along a treacherous mountain road without seeing any signs of habitation.

Finally, Angelina saw a roadside cafe that appeared to be open for business. She entered the establishment and was confronted by Stein Erickson, the proprietor. As Angelina tried to explain her predicament, Stein smelled liquor on her breath and demanded her car keys. In fact, Angelina had drunk a small amount of beer at the picnic. Intimidated by Stein's threatening manner, Angelina gave him the car keys. Stein took the keys and said, "Get out of here. That'll teach you to drink and drive."

Angelina left the cafe and spent the night wandering in the woods unable to find shelter. The next morning she was found by a hiker who led her back to town.

If Angelina asserts a tort action for false imprisonment against Stein, she should

(A) prevail, if she suffered harm or injury from being left outside overnight in the mountainous terrain
(B) prevail, because she was confined within a particular area against her will
(C) not prevail, because she was not imprisoned within a bounded area
(D) not prevail, if Stein believed that she was too intoxicated to drive safely

Answer:

(B) This is a very interesting Multistate question covering false imprisonment. In order to be liable for false imprisonment, the following requirements generally must be met: (1) the defendant must act intending to confine the plaintiff within certain "fixed" boundaries; (2) an unlawful confinement must directly or indirectly result; and (3) the plaintiff must be conscious or aware of the confinement. With respect to requirement (1), it is important to note that an intentional tort can be committed in one of two ways, either where the defendant acts intending to cause consequences of his act or where there is a ***"substantial certainty"*** that the tortious act will occur. In the present case, there was a "substantial certainty" that Angelina would be confined within a limited area because Stein took her car keys. Many students will be inclined to choose (C). This is incorrect because **Restatement** Section 36 states that "the area within which another is confined may be large and need not be stationary." By analogy, **Restatement** Illustration 6 points out that ***A is liable for false imprisonment where he restrains B to stay within the boundaries of a city by invalid process.***

4. **Intentional Infliction of Mental Distress**

   a. One who by ***extreme and outrageous conduct intentionally or recklessly causes severe emotional distress to another*** is subject to liability for such emotional distress, and, if bodily harm to the other person results from it, for such bodily harm.

   b. Where such conduct is directed at a third person, the actor is subject to liability if he intentionally or recklessly causes severe emotional distress

      (1) to a member of such person's immediate family who is present at the time, whether or not such distress results in bodily harm; ***or***

      (2) to any other person who is present at the time, if such distress results in bodily harm.

   c. Recovery is allowed where the defendant, ***knowing of the plaintiff's peculiar sensitivities*** (e.g., children, the elderly, and pregnant women), intentionally uses extreme conduct to cause emotional distress. A lessened requirement of "outrageous" conduct applies to common carriers and innkeepers, thus allowing recovery based on insulting or highly offensive behavior.

      Example: Adam, who does not like children, dresses up like a monster and runs into a kindergarten classroom shouting, "I'm going to eat all of you little children!" Adam may be liable for infliction of mental distress if the children suffer severe distress and prove actual damages.

   d. Although ***physical injury*** is not required, the plaintiff must prove actual damages.

Torts Multistate Chart:

Third Party Recovery for Intentional Infliction of Mental Distress

Family Member	***Non-family member***
Presence required	Presence required
Bodily harm NOT required	Bodily harm required

5. **Negligent Infliction of Emotional Distress**

Where the defendant's negligence causes only mental disturbance, without accompanying physical injury, illness or other physical consequences, the great majority of courts hold there can be no recovery.

a. This rule applies to all forms of emotional disturbance, including fright, nervous shock, nausea, grief, rage, and humiliation.

b. **Exceptions:**

(1) **Negligent transmission of a message:** A number of courts have allowed recovery against a telegraph company (and hospital) for misinforming plaintiff that a family member had died. In such cases, there is an especial likelihood that such mental distress will result.

(2) **Negligent mishandling of corpses:** There are a series of cases allowing recovery for mental distress (unaccompanied by physical injury) involving negligent mishandling of corpses (e.g., negligent embalming, negligent shipping of a casket).

c. **Mental Disturbance with Physical Injury:** Where the defendant's negligence inflicts an immediate physical injury (such as a broken leg) accompanied by mental suffering (such as fright or nervousness), courts do allow the plaintiff to recover for the purely mental elements of damage in addition to the physical harm.

(1) **Physical harm is not immediate:** If the physical harm is not immediate, but follows later as a result of the plaintiff's emotional distress over a negligently caused event (as in the case of a miscarriage), generally no recovery is allowed.

(a) **Exception:** Under the so-called "impact" rule, recovery is allowed if there has been an "impact" upon the person of the plaintiff (e.g., a slight blow, electric shock, a trivial jolt, or even dust in the eye).

d. **Third Party Recovery:** Where the mental disturbance and its consequences are not caused by any fear for the plaintiff's own safety, but by distress at witnessing some peril or harm to another person (e.g., mother observing the death of her child), recovery is generally denied.

(1) **"Zone of Danger" Exception:** If the third party is personally within the "zone of danger" and is threatened with injury by the defendant's negligence (as where mother herself is standing in the path of the vehicle), the plaintiff may recover for the bodily harm (and accompanying distress) that results.

Illustration: A negligently leaves a truck insecurely parked at the top of a hill. Because of this negligence the truck starts down the hill. B and C, her child, are in the street in the path of the truck. The truck swerves, misses B, and strikes C. B, who is watching C, does not see the truck coming, and is not alarmed for her own safety, but suffers severe shock and resulting serious illness at the sight of the injury to C. A is subject to liability to B for the shock and her illness.

C. INTENTIONAL INTERFERENCE WITH PROPERTY

1. Trespass to Land

a. One is subject to liability to another for ***trespass,*** irrespective of whether he thereby causes harm to any legally protected interest of the other, if he ***intentionally***

(1) enters land in the possession of the other, or causes a thing or a third person to do so; ***or***

(2) remains on the land; ***or***

(3) fails to remove from the land a thing which he is under a duty to remove.

Example: James is hitting baseballs in his backyard. For kicks, he decides to see if he can hit a baseball into his neighbor Chris' yard, 100 feet away. If he succeeds in hitting a baseball over the fence into Chris' yard, absent Chris' consent, James is liable for trespass.

Example: Chris calls James and asks James to remove a baseball that James accidentally hit onto her land. If James fails to remove the baseball, he may be liable for trespass.

b. **Standing:** Because an action for trespass protects the right to exclusive possession, the plaintiff must have either ***actual possession*** or the ***right to possession*** (i.e., an adverse possessor or a lessee would each be able to maintain a trespass action).

c. **Intent:** The ***intent to enter*** upon the plaintiff's land is sufficient for a trespass action. An intent to trespass is not required. ***Mistake*** as to ownership is no defense.

Example: Henry is out for a walk with his dog, Rover. Believing that he is the rightful owner of a grove of pecan trees near his property line, Henry allows Rover to wander into the trees to "do his business." The trees are actually on Samantha's property. Although Henry was mistaken about his ownership of the trees, he may still be liable for trespass.

d. Historically, trespass required the entry of some tangible physical object. Modernly, courts are extending trespass liability to intrusions caused by microscopic particles and invisible gases, where harm is caused.

Example: Andy manufactures peanut oil on his property. When he is pressing the peanuts for oil, peanut gasses are emitted into the atmosphere. One day, a high wind comes up and blows the peanut gasses over onto Sarah's property. Sarah, who is highly allergic to peanuts, suffers an allergic reaction and must be rushed to the hospital. Andy may be liable for trespass.

e. A trespass may be committed on, beneath, or above the surface of the earth.

Example: Angela loves to climb trees. She regularly climbs a tall tree in her backyard. One day, she climbs high into the tree and out onto a limb that overhangs onto Karen's property. Angela may be liable for trespass.

Example: Sol digs a tunnel to escape from his basement bedroom, where his mother thinks he is sleeping. As he digs, he digs under his own house, under the neighbor's yard. Sol may be liable for trespass.

f. Flight by aircraft in the air space above the land of another is a trespass if, but only if,

(1) it enters into the immediate reaches of the air space next to the land, and

(2) it interferes substantially with the other's use and enjoyment of his land.

g. **Privileged Entries:** In cases involving "public" and "private" necessity, a party is privileged to trespass upon the property of another.

Example: Boris is the pilot of a commercial plane carrying 28 passengers. During his flight, as he passes over Gary's farm, he begins to experience mechanical difficulties. Gary may land the plane on Gary's farm in this emergency situation without being liable for trespass.

(1) **Liability for damage to land:** In such emergency situations, the defendant ***is liable*** for damage to land and property.

h. **Negligent or Reckless Entries:** A person who negligently or recklessly enters the land of another is liable for trespass ***if she causes damage to the land***. Conversely, an intentional entry is actionable without the requirement of damage to the land.

(1) **Nominal damages:** Plaintiff may recover nominal damages for an intentional trespass which causes no harm or damage to the land.

i. **Accidental Entries:** There is ***no liability for trespass for an accidental entry that is non-negligent and unintentional.***

Example: Miles is playing golf and hits a golf ball down the middle of the fairway. There is a tree limb that overhangs the fairway. The ball hits the tree limb and ricochets onto Margo's backyard which abuts the golf course. Miles is not liable for trespass.

2. **Trespass to Chattels**

a. A ***trespass to a chattel*** may be committed by intentionally

(1) ***dispossessing another of the chattel, or***

(2) ***using or intermeddling with a chattel*** in the possession of another.

Example: Vera needs a black evening bag to carry to her sorority formal. Without asking Dorothy's permission, Vera goes into Dorothy's room in the sorority house, takes Dorothy's black bag, carries it to the formal, then returns it to Dorothy's closet the next morning. Because Vera had Dorothy's bag, Dorothy did not have a bag to carry to the formal. Vera may be liable for trespass to chattels.

b. A plaintiff must generally prove damages

(1) in the actual amount caused by the tortious conduct, **or**

(2) in the case of dispossession, by the loss of use.

c. ***The difference between trespass to chattels and conversion is one of degree. The seriousness of the interference determines which tort applies.***

d. Mistake as to the legality of the defendant's actions is no defense to either trespass to chattels or to conversion.

Example: In the case of the black evening bag, Vera mistakenly thought that Dorothy would allow her to borrow the bag, as the sorority sisters commonly shared clothing and accessories. Even if her mistake was justified, Vera may still be liable for trespass to chattels.

3. **Conversion**

a. Conversion is ***an intentional exercise of dominion or control over a chattel which seriously interferes*** with the right of another to control it. In conversion cases, the defendant may justly be required to pay the plaintiff ***the full value of the chattel.***

Example: Marianna sees Keisha's 1978 Volkswagen Bug parked by the curb. Marianna has always wanted to drive a vintage Bug, so she decides to hotwire it and take it for a spin. Seven hours later, she returns the Bug to the same parking spot where she found it, full of gas, in perfect condition. Marianna may be liable for conversion.

(1) Damages are measured by ***the full value of the chattel at the time of conversion.*** Alternatively, the plaintiff may seek recovery of the property itself, in which case the remedy is replevin.

(2) Only tangible or intangible personal property may be converted. Real property is not converted, but it may be adversely possessed or trespassed upon.

Example: Alex builds a house on Alicia's property and lives there for 3 years. Although Alicia may be seriously deprived of her property for these years, her proper cause of action is for trespass, not for conversion.

b. In determining ***the seriousness of the interference*** and the justice of requiring the defendant to pay the full value, the following factors are important:

(1) ***the extent and duration of the defendant's exercise of dominion or control;***

(2) ***the defendant's intent to assert a right in fact inconsistent with the other's right of control;***

(3) ***the defendant's good faith;***

(4) ***the extent and duration of the resulting interference with the plaintiff's right of control;***

(5) ***the harm done to the chattel;***

(6) ***the inconvenience and expense caused*** to the plaintiff.

Multistate Nuance Chart

TRESPASS TO CHATTELS	CONVERSION
1. Intentional tort;	1. Intentional tort;
2. Committed by ***intentionally dispossessing or intermeddling*** with a chattel in the possession of another;	2. Committed by ***intentionally exercising dominion or control*** *over a chattel and* ***seriously interfering*** with the rights of the owner;
3. Defendant is liable for the damage or ***diminished value of the chattel.***	3. Defendant is liable for ***the full value of the chattel at the time of the conversion.***

Examples:

1. On leaving a restaurant, A by mistake takes B's hat from the rack, believing it to be his own. When he reaches the sidewalk A puts on the hat, discovers his mistake, and immediately re-enters the restaurant and returns the hat to the rack. This is not a conversion.

2. The same facts as in example 1, except that A keeps the hat for three months before discovering his mistake and returning it. This is a conversion.

3. The same facts as in example 1, except that as A reaches the sidewalk and puts on the hat a sudden gust of wind blows it from his head, and it goes down an open manhole and is lost. This is a conversion.

4. Leaving a restaurant, A takes B's hat from the rack, intending to steal it. As he approaches the door he sees a policeman outside, and immediately returns the hat to the rack. This is a conversion.

5. A stores his car in B's locked garage. A comes to get the car, and demands it. B intentionally delays half an hour in giving A the key to the garage. This is not a conversion.

6. The same facts as in example 5, except that B delays a month. This is a conversion.

7. The same facts as in example 5, except that during the delay of half an hour a fire breaks out in the garage, and the car is destroyed before it can be removed. This is a conversion.

8. A intentionally shoots B's horse, as a result of which the horse dies. This is a conversion.

9. The same facts as in example 8, except that the horse is merely scratched, and quickly recovers. This is not a conversion.

10. A stores his fur coat with B. Without A's knowledge or consent, B repairs a hole in the lining of the coat. This is not a conversion.

11. The same facts as in example 10, except that B alters the coat by cutting down its size so that A can no longer wear it. This is a conversion.

12. A entrusts an automobile to B, a dealer, for sale. On one occasion B drives the car, on his own business, for ten miles. This is not a conversion.

13. The same facts as in example 12, except that B drives the car 2,000 miles. This is a conversion.

14. The same facts as in example 12, except that B uses the car for the illegal transportation of narcotics, as a result of which it is confiscated by the federal government. This is a conversion.

D. DEFENSES TO INTENTIONAL TORTS TO PERSONS AND PROPERTY

1. Privilege

a. **Definition:** Under certain circumstances, a defendant may not be liable for conduct that would ordinarily subject him to liability.

b. A privilege may exist where:

(1) the person affected by the defendant's conduct consents;

(2) some important personal or public interest will be protected by the defendant's ordinarily prohibited conduct, and this interest justifies the harm caused or threatened by the defendant's conduct;

(3) the defendant must act freely in order to perform an essential function.

Example: Grant looks out his window and sees his neighbor's house on fire. He grabs his hose and goes over to the house, putting out the fire. Grant's entry onto his neighbor's land will be privileged.

c. The defendant has the burden of proof to prove the existence of a privilege and that the privilege was exercised reasonably under the circumstances.

2. **Mistake**

a. Mistake may be a defense where:

(1) a defendant is under a duty to act for the protection of a public interest.

Example: A police officer mistakenly thinks that a felony has been committed, and arrests one whom he reasonably believes to be the culprit.

(2) a person acts in self-defense or in defense of others.

Example: Jim, reasonably believing that he is about to be attacked, hits Bill who is running toward him. As it turns out, Jim was mistaken as to Bill's true intentions.

3. **Consent**

a. **Definition:** Where a plaintiff is willing that the defendant invade her interests, she is said to consent.

(1) **Express consent:**

(a) ***Fraud vitiates consent*** where it goes to a material (versus collateral) matter.

(b) ***Consent induced by duress (present physical force or threats) is invalid.***

(c) Consent given by mistake is a valid defense unless the defendant knew or took advantage of plaintiff's mistake.

(d) ***Informed consent*** (i.e., to a surgical procedure) is a valid defense.

(e) Consent to tortious conduct is invalid where ***incapacity*** exists (e.g., youth, incompetency, intoxication).

(2) **Implied consent:** A valid defense may exist where consent is ***implied by law*** or where consent is ***apparent*** from plaintiff's conduct.

Example: Susanna falls and hits her head, splitting it open. She is unconscious. A surgeon may operate to repair the damage under the premise that she would have consented had she been awake.

Example: Albert, a football player, tackles Andrew, a player on the other team. Because the boys are engaged in a football game, it is apparent from Andrew's conduct that he consents to the tackle.

b. **Intentional torts to property:** Consent is an affirmative defense. It may be ***express*** or ***implied***.

c. **Intentional torts to the person:** In the case of intentional torts to the person, lack of consent is generally viewed as part of the plaintiff's prima facie case, rather than as an affirmative defense.

4. **Self-Defense**

   a. **Reasonable force allowed:** An actor may use force not intended or likely to cause death or serious bodily harm to defend himself against

      (1) unprivileged harmful or offensive contact, ***or***

      (2) other bodily harm which he reasonably believes that another is about to inflict intentionally upon him.

      Example: Henry sees Matthew approaching him in a bar with a baseball bat poised to hit him. Matthew shouts, "I'm going to get you, Henry!" If necessary, Henry may tackle Matthew to the ground or grab his arms to prevent Matthew from hitting him.

   b. Self-defense is privileged even where the actor correctly or reasonably believes that he can avoid the necessity of so defending himself,

      (1) by retreating or otherwise giving up a right or privilege, ***or***

      (2) by complying with a command with which the actor is under no duty to comply or which the other is not privileged to enforce by the means threatened.

      Example: Henry sees Matthew approaching him in a bar with a baseball bat poised to hit him. Matthew shouts, "You'd better get out of this bar right now or I'm going to get you, Henry!" Henry does not have to comply with Matthew's command to leave the bar and may tackle Matthew to the ground or grab his arms to prevent Matthew from hitting him.

   c. If the actor accidentally injures a third person while exercising the defense of self-defense, the injury is privileged as long as the actor's conduct was not negligent or deliberate.

      Example: Henry grabs Matthew and wrestles him to the ground. In the midst of the struggle, Henry accidentally bumps up against Lyle, who is standing nearby. If Lyle gets a bump on the head, Henry will probably not be liable for the injury.

   d. Where the defendant is reasonably mistaken as to the need for self-defense, the privilege of self-defense still exists.

      Example: Henry sees Matthew coming at him in the bar, baseball bat poised to strike. Believing that Matthew intends to hurt him, Henry wrestles Matthew to the ground. If it turns out that Matthew was not actually intending to hurt Henry, Henry is still privileged to defend himself and will not be liable for battery.

5. **Defense of Others**

   a. The actor is privileged to defend a third person from a harmful or offensive contact ***under the same conditions and by the same means as those under and by which he is privileged to defend himself*** if the actor correctly or reasonably believes that

(1) the circumstances are such as to give the third person a privilege of self-defense, ***and***

(2) his intervention is necessary for the protection of the third person.

Example: Layla and Terry are walking down the street. Layla sees Terry's ex-girlfriend, Marian, coming toward Terry with a knife. Realizing that Terry does not see Marian, Layla jumps out and grabs Marian's wrist, wrestling the knife from her. Because Terry could have been injured, Layla is privileged to protect him.

b. **Caveat:** A minority of states still hold that the intermeddler takes the risk that the man he is defending would not be privileged to defend himself in the same manner. In other words, the actor may use that amount of force which would have been available to the person being defended. Thus, a reasonable mistake by the defendant as to the belief that self-defense was necessary would ***not*** be a valid defense.

6. **Defense of Property**

a. **Reasonable force allowed.** An actor is privileged to use ***reasonable force,*** not intended or likely to cause death or serious bodily harm, to prevent or terminate another's intrusion upon the actor's land or chattels, if

(1) the intrusion is not privileged or the other person intentionally or negligently causes the actor to believe that it is not privileged, ***and***

(2) the actor reasonably believes that the intrusion can be prevented or terminated only by the force used.

Example: Nancy owns a home in Jamestown. One night, she awakes to hear someone entering her house. She runs down the stairs and finds her ex-husband, Stanley, in her living room. Nancy asks him to leave, but Stanley refuses. Nancy threatens to call the police, but Stanley will not leave. Nancy finally hits Stanley on his leg, causing him to fall to the ground. She then grabs him by the ankles and pulls him out of her house. Nancy's actions are privileged.

b. An actor ***may never use direct or indirect force capable of causing death or serious bodily injury*** (including spring guns and traps) to defend property ***unless a threat to the actor's own safety*** justifies him to use such force as a means of self-defense.

7. **Recapture of Chattels**

a. **Reasonable force allowed where taking is wrongful.** An actor may use reasonable force against another to regain personal property where the other person

(1) ***tortiously took the chattel*** from the actor's possession without claim of right, ***or***

(2) took the chattel under claim of right but by force or other duress or fraud, ***or***

(3) has received custody of the chattel from the actor and ***refuses to surrender it*** or is about to remove it from the actor's premises.

Example: Karen takes Linda's gold bracelet. Karen knows that the bracelet belongs to Linda, but she really likes it, so she takes it into her dorm room. Linda may go up and grab the bracelet away from Karen.

Example: Karen takes Linda's gold bracelet. Karen knows that the bracelet belongs to Linda, but she really likes it, so she takes it. Linda asks Karen to give it back, but Karen refuses. Linda may go up and grab the bracelet away from Karen.

b. **Peaceful means required where taking was rightful.** An actor may only use peaceful means to retake a chattel where the original taking was rightful (i.e., conditional sale, bailment).

Example: Frannie gives her car to a valet to be parked. When she returns, the valet refuses to give her car back. Frannie may not use force to retake her car.

c. An actor is privileged to enter reasonably upon the land of another to remove a wrongfully-taken chattel. The owner of the chattel is liable for damages caused by his entry only if the land belongs to an innocent party, rather than to the tortfeasor.

Example: Knowing that Sylvester has taken his cage, Tweety Bird enters onto Sylvester's property to get the cage back. Sylvester may not sue Tweety Bird for trespass.

8. **Forcible Entry on Land**

a. An owner or possessor of land may forcibly enter onto that land where another has wrongfully entered onto or remained on the land.

Example: Oliver is a squatter on Annie's land. Oliver has built a fence around the property to keep Annie out. Annie may break through the fence to regain her land.

9. **Necessity**

a. **Public necessity.** An actor may enter onto the land ***to avert an imminent public disaster.***

(1) Even where such entry is not necessary, the entry is still privileged if the actor reasonably believes that it is necessary.

(2) Public necessity is an absolute defense. The actor ***is not liable for either trespass or the damage to the property or chattel.***

Example: Arthur receives information that a bomb is about to go off in a restaurant near his home. Concerned that the police will not get there in time, Arthur enters into the restaurant to remove the bomb. Such entry is privileged.

b. **Private necessity.** In the case of private necessity, the actor will be liable in damages for any harm he causes to the property.

(1) The actor's privilege of necessity will supersede a landowner's privilege to defend his property by use of reasonable force.

(2) Private necessity is a qualified privilege; the defendant ***is not liable for trespass but is liable for the damage to the property or chattel.***

Example: Frank is boating on a lake when his motor boat springs a leak. Concerned that he will sink and drown, Frank motors up to the nearest dock, which belongs to his neighbor, Daniel. He is so nervous that he forgets to turn the motor down as he approaches the dock, and he crashes into the dock, severely damaging it. Frank is privileged to enter onto the dock, but he must pay Daniel for the damage he has caused.

c. An actor is privileged to enter or remain on another's land if it is or reasonably appears to be necessary to prevent serious harm to

(1) the actor, or his land or chattels, ***or***

(2) the land's owner or a third person, or the land or chattels of either, unless the actor knows or has reason to know that the one for whose benefit he enters is unwilling that he shall take such action.

Example: Gavin owns a beautiful Ferrari automobile. He allows Megan to borrow the car for a day to impress her boyfriend. While Megan has the car, Gavin decides to drive by Megan's house just to gaze at his prize possession. Much to his horror, upon his arrival, he sees the car parked in Megan's driveway. Car thieves are in the process of stripping the car of all its tires and parts. Gavin may enter onto Megan's land to prevent harm to the Ferrari.

10. **Legal Process**

a. An arrest under a warrant is not privileged unless the person arrested

(1) is, or the actor reasonably believes to be, sufficiently named or otherwise described in the warrant, ***or***

(2) although not the person named in the warrant, has knowingly caused the actor to believe him to be so.

Example: Umberto poses as Osama bin Laden and tells everyone he meets that he is Osama. He wears a turban and has a long beard and an Uzi. He also hides most of the time in his house with the curtains drawn. If the FBI arrests Umberto, believing that he is Osama, the arrest is privileged.

11. **Arrest without a Warrant**

a. A peace officer, if acting within the limits of his appointment, is privileged to arrest another without a warrant.

Torts Multistate Chart

Arresting Party	Arrest without a Warrant – Felony	Arrest without a Warrant – Misdemeanor
Private citizen may arrest	1. Where a felony is being committed, or reasonably appears about to be committed in his presence, *or* 2. If a felony has ***in fact*** been committed, and he has reasonable ground to suspect the person arrested has committed it.	1. Must be a breach of the peace which is being committed, or reasonably appears about to be committed, in his presence.
Police Officer	1. The same as for a private citizen, plus 2. Where the officer reasonably believes the arrestee to be a felon, ***even if*** no felony has been committed.	1. Must be a breach of the peace which is being committed, or reasonably appears about to be committed, in his presence.

12. **Discipline**

a. A parent is ***privileged to apply such reasonable force*** or to impose such reasonable confinement upon his child as he reasonably believes to be necessary for the child's proper control, training, or education.

b. One other than a parent who has been given by law or has voluntarily assumed in whole or in part the function of controlling, training, or educating a child, is privileged to apply such reasonable force or to impose such reasonable confinement as he reasonably believes to be necessary for the child's proper control, training, or education. A parent may, however, restrict the privilege of one to whom he has entrusted the child.

Example: Nancy is a very strict mother and routinely spanks her children and locks them in their rooms with no dinner. Her religion teaches, "Spare the rod, spoil the child." As long as Nancy does not abuse the children, she may use reasonable force as she feels necessary. However, she may also forbid her children's babysitters to paddle the children.

13. **Immunity:** Based on public policy considerations, the defense of immunity is available in certain situations, even though the defendant's conduct has been tortious.

II. NEGLIGENCE

A. GENERAL PRINCIPLES

1. **Definition.** Negligence is ***conduct which falls below the standard established by law for the protection of others against unreasonable risk of harm.*** It does not include reckless conduct. Negligent conduct may be either:

   a. an act which the actor as a reasonable person should recognize as involving an unreasonable risk of causing an invasion of an interest of another, ***or***

   b. a failure to do an act which is necessary for the protection or assistance of another and which the actor is under a duty to do.

2. **Elements of Cause of Action**

   a. **Duty of care.** The defendant has a ***legal duty to protect the plaintiff*** against an unreasonable risk of harm.

   b. **Breach of duty.** The defendant's failure to conform his conduct to the legally required standard.

   c. **Proximate cause.** The breach of the duty by the defendant constituted the proximate or legal cause of plaintiff's injury.

   d. **Damages.** The plaintiff has suffered ***actual harm*** to himself or his property that is measurable and compensable in money damages.

3. **The Reasonable Person**

   a. For most negligence actions, an act is negligent only if the actor fails to use reasonable care. ***An actor is required to exercise the care that a reasonable person in his position,*** with his information and competence, would recognize as necessary to prevent an unreasonable risk of harm to another.

4. **Violation of statute**

   a. **Negligence *per se* — definition. *Negligence per se is defined as the unexcused violation of a statute*** or an administrative regulation which is adopted by the court as defining the standard of conduct of a reasonable person.

   Example: The state of Utopia adopts a statute requiring people to cut down partially severed tree limbs. The legislature passes this statute stating that it believes that reasonable people will cut them down because they are a hazard. If Richard fails to remove a hanging tree limb, and it falls and injures Tracy, he will be negligent *per se*.

b. **Relevant evidence of negligence.** The unexcused violation of an statute or regulation which is not so adopted may be relevant evidence bearing on the issue of negligent conduct.

Example: The legislature passes a law stating that all people shall wear helmets when riding bicycles. However, it does not state that wearing a helmet is the action of a reasonable person. If Gary does not wear a helmet and his action results in his injury, the fact that he did not wear a helmet will be evidence of negligence (**Note:** this might particularly come up in the area of contributory negligence).

c. **Applicability of criminal statutes.** A criminal statute may be used in lieu of the common law reasonable person standard to establish the duty of care owed in a negligence action. Most jurisdictions find such a violation to be only evidence of negligence not conclusive proof of negligence.

(1) **Caveat:** Violation of such a criminal statute ***only establishes duty and breach of duty.*** The plaintiff must still prove causation and damages.

(2) **Caveat:** Furthermore, use of a criminal statutory standard may not be considered unless the plaintiff proves:

(a) ***that he was a member of the class of persons the statute was designed to protect, and***

(b) ***that he suffered the type of harm the statute was designed to prevent.***

Example: (i.e., plaintiff's car catches on fire and explodes due to fuel leak from gasoline truck driven by intoxicated defendant and parked in a "No Parking" zone - negligence *per se* is inapplicable to establish duty and breach under these facts).

B. PROOF OF NEGLIGENCE

1. Burden of Proof and Presumptions

a. In an action for negligence, ***the plaintiff has the burden of proving by preponderance of the evidence:***

(1) facts which give rise to a ***legal duty on the part of the defendant*** to conform to the standard of conduct established by law for the protection of the plaintiff;

(2) ***breach of duty by the defendant;***

(3) that such breach was a ***legal (or proximate) cause of the harm*** suffered by the plaintiff; and

(4) that the ***plaintiff has in fact suffered harm*** of a kind legally compensable by damages.

2. **Circumstantial Evidence**

   a. ***Res Ipsa Loquitur.*** A plaintiff may establish breach of duty by direct evidence, by demonstrating violation of a statutory standard, or, ***where the defendant's negligence can be inferred using circumstantial evidence, by the doctrine of res ipsa loquitur.*** The effect of *res ipsa* is to permit an inference of negligence by the jury. Where *res ipsa* applies, no directed verdict can be allowed for the defendant.

      Note: The Restatement 2d and modern majority view ***do not require that the defendant have exclusive control over the instrumentality*** causing plaintiff's harm. Rather, the jury must infer that the injury resulted from the defendant's negligence.

   b. It may be inferred that the defendant's negligence caused the plaintiff's harm when

      (1) the event is of a kind that ordinarily does not occur in the absence of negligence;

      (2) other responsible causes, including the conduct of the plaintiff and third persons, are sufficiently eliminated by the evidence; and

      (3) the indicated negligence is within the scope of the defendant's duty to the plaintiff.

C. CAUSATION

1. **Causation in Fact.** Before the defendant's conduct can be considered a proximate or legal cause of plaintiff's harm or injury, it must first be a ***cause in fact*** of the injury. Several tests exist:

   a. **"But For" Test** *(Sine Qua Non)*. Under this test, the plaintiff must show that his harm would not have occurred "but for" the defendant's act.

      Example: Kelly is struck by a speeding car. She will be able to show that she would not have broken her arms and legs but for the negligence of the speeding driver.

      Example: Every morning when Bill puts on his tie, the sun comes up. Because there is no causal relationship, Bill cannot prove that the sun would not come up but for Bill's act of putting on his tie.

      Note: The "but for" test does not necessarily impose liability because other considerations (such as the lack of legal duty or foreseeability) may preclude recovery.

   b. **Substantial Factor Test.** If the defendant's conduct was a ***substantial factor*** in causing the plaintiff's injury, it follows that he will not be absolved from liability merely because other causes have contributed to the result, because such causes, innumerable, are always present.

Example: A defendant is not necessarily relieved of liability where another person was also negligent and caused harm. In that situation, the other tortfeasor may also be held liable.

Example: Mary runs a red light and strikes Lucille, who is riding her tricycle on the nearby sidewalk. At the same time, a skateboarder coming down the walk rams into Lucille's other side. The skateboarder will not be relieved of liability simply because Mary also negligently caused injury to Lucille.

c. ***Summers v. Tice*** **approach.** Where an injury is caused by the negligence of two or more persons, and the plaintiff cannot determine which one caused the harm, the ***burden of proof is shifted to each defendant.*** Each must show that he did not cause the harm. Absent such a showing, all defendants will be liable.

Example: If Lucille's head is decapitated, the skateboarder will have the burden to prove that Mary's car, not his skateboard, was responsible for the injury.

d. **Multiple Causes:**

(1) **Concurrent tortfeasors (indivisible injury).** If the tortious conduct of two defendants concurs and both are causes in fact of plaintiff's injury, ***each is jointly and severally liable for all of plaintiff's damages***. It does not matter that they did not act in concert, or that neither's conduct by itself would have caused the injury.

Example: If the skateboarder cannot prove a divisible injury, he will be liable in full for Lucille's decapitation, even if he only caused a part of her injury. Mary will also be liable for all of Lucille's injuries, even those possibly caused by the skateboarder.

(2) **Concurrent tortfeasors (divisible injury).** If tortfeasors D1 and D2 each cause separate parts of P's harm and the harm is subject to apportionment, D1 and D2 will each be liable only for the portion of harm he caused.

Example: If the skateboarder can prove that Mary caused the decapitation and that he caused only the nicks and scrapes on Lucille's knees, he will be liable only for the nicks and scrapes and Mary will be liable for the decapitation.

2. **Proximate Cause:** In addition to being a cause in fact of plaintiff's harm, the defendant's conduct must also be a proximate, or legal, cause of the injury.

Exam Tip: Not all injuries "actually" caused by defendant will be deemed to have been proximately caused by his acts. As such, ***the doctrine of proximate or legal cause deals with a limitation of liability with respect to (a) persons and (b) consequences*** which bear some reasonable relationship to defendant's tortious conduct.

a. **Foreseeable Plaintiffs.** A defendant's owes a duty of reasonable care only to foreseeable plaintiffs (i.e., those individuals who are within the risk of harm created by defendant's unreasonable conduct). The ***majority (Cardozo) view holds that a defendant only owes a duty of care to foreseeable plaintiffs who are within the "zone of danger"*** (i.e., under the circumstances a reasonable defendant would have foreseen a risk of harm to him). The broader ***minority (Andrews) view*** allows recovery to ***any*** person (i.e., "the whole world") thereby harmed due to breach of defendant's duty of care.

b. **Foreseeability of Harm.** If the defendant's conduct is a ***substantial factor*** in bringing about the harm to another, the mere fact that the defendant neither foresaw nor should have foreseen the extent of the harm of the manner in which it occurred does not prevent him from being liable.

(1) **Rescue Doctrine.** Another highly tested area of proximate causation deals with rescuers. A negligent defendant owes ***an independent duty of care*** to a rescuer. Even where the rescue efforts are done negligently, provided they are not wanton, the negligent defendant will be liable for both personal injury and property damage, whether the rescuer succeeds in injuring himself, the person rescued, or a stranger.

Example: India is driving too fast in a storm one day when she accidentally hits another car. The driver of the other car, Yvonne, is trapped in her car with a broken leg. Sam sees the accident and stops to help. As he is trying to get Yvonne out of the car, he slips on the ice and hits his head. Sam ends up in an irreversible coma. India will be liable for the injuries to Sam, even if she did not foresee them.

(2) **Physical Consequences.** Under the ***so-called "thin-skulled" or "eggshell" plaintiff rule,*** a defendant is liable for the full consequences of plaintiff's injury even though, due to plaintiff's peculiar susceptibility to harm (of which the defendant was unaware), those consequences were more severe than they would have been in a normal person.

Example: Garrett is a hemophiliac. Craig leaves a bunch of papers and boxes lying around in the hall just outside his cubicle. When Garrett walks by, he falls and hits his head on the side of Craig's desk. He begins to bleed heavily. Eventually, he loses so much blood that he must be hospitalized. Craig will be liable to Garrett for the full extent of Garrett's injuries, even if he did not know about Garrett's inability to clot blood.

c. **Restatement Approach.** The Restatement 2d approach to determine legal cause views the harm caused by the defendant's act in ***hindsight,*** allowing liability to be cut off where the court finds ***highly extraordinary the relationship between the defendant's conduct and the resulting harm.*** Alternatively, many jurisdictions extend liability only to ***the foreseeable consequences*** of defendant's negligence. Simply stated, students must determine proximate cause by asking "Was the harm within the risk?"

D. SUPERSEDING CAUSE

1. Superseding Cause

a. **Definition.** A superseding cause is ***an unforeseeable intervening cause*** that breaks the chain of causation between the initial wrongful act and the ultimate injury, and thus ***relieves the original tortfeasor from any further liability.*** By its intervention, the superseding cause itself becomes a direct, immediate cause of the injury suffered by the plaintiff.

Example: Susan negligently operates her auto and strikes Adam, injuring him. Adam, whose leg is broken from the accident, is taken to a nearby hospital. While he is being treated for his broken leg, there is an earthquake that causes the roof to collapse. A section of the roof strikes the Adam on the head, causing a concussion. Because the earthquake is a superseding cause (i.e., an act of God) Susan is not liable for Adam's head injury but does remain liable for the broken leg.

(1) ***Types of superseding causes:***

(a) ***Acts of God***

(b) ***Criminal acts of third persons***

(c) ***Intentional torts of third persons***

(d) ***Extraordinary forms of negligent conduct***

2. Intervening Force

a. **Definition.** An ***intervening force*** is one which actively operates in producing harm to another after the actor's has already committed his negligent act or omission.

b. Whether the active operation of an intervening force prevents that actor's antecedent negligence from being a legal cause in bringing about harm to another is determined by the rules stated below.

c. **Rule of Liability.** As a general rule, ***a defendant will be held liable for harm caused by foreseeable intervening forces.***

(1) **Types of foreseeable intervening causes:**

(a) **Negligence of rescuers.** Because rescuers are foreseeable, the original tortfeasor will be held liable for the ordinary negligence (not gross or wanton conduct) of the rescuer.

Example: Melissa is injured by Don, who is throwing balls around at a playground. Don hits Melissa in the head, and Melissa ends up unconscious on the ground. Casey arrives and tries to resuscitate Melissa. Unfortunately, Casey does not know CPR, and she breaks Melissa's ribs doing compressions. Because Casey was negligent, Don will be liable for both Melissa's head injury and her broken ribs.

(b) **Subsequent medical malpractice.** The original tortfeasor is usually held liable for the ordinary negligence (not gross or wanton conduct) of plaintiff's treating physician or nurse.

Example: When Melissa is hit in the head, Casey does not come to her aid. Instead, an ambulance takes her to the hospital. The triage nurse does not examine Melissa carefully and concludes that she does not need medical attention. The nurse keeps Melissa lying on a gurney in the hallway for 8 hours. During that time, Melissa has a cerebral hemorrhage and sustains irreversible brain damage. Don will be liable for Melissa's brain hemorrhage and for the strike on the head.

(c) **Subsequent disease.** The original tortfeasor is usually held liable for diseases contracted or subsequent injuries sustained because of the impairment of plaintiff's health resulting from the original injury caused by defendant's tortious conduct

Example: When Don hits Melissa in the head, her sinuses are affected. As a result, Melissa becomes much more susceptible to sinus infections. She must go to the doctor frequently and take expensive medications. Don will be liable for both the head injury and for Melissa's sinus infections.

(d) **Efforts to protect person or property.** Defendant will be held liable for negligent efforts on the part of persons to protect life or property interests (of themselves or third parties) endangered by defendant's negligence.

(e) **Subsequent accident.** In situations where the plaintiff suffers a subsequent injury after her original injury (and the original injury was a ***substantial factor*** in causing the second accident), the original tortfeasor is held liable for damages.

Example: Henry negligently fractures Tamika's left leg; while walking on crutches, Tamika trips and falls, breaking her right leg. Henry will be liable for the breaks to both legs.

3. **Considerations Important in Determining Whether an Intervening Force is a Superseding Cause**

   a. The following considerations are of importance in determining whether an intervening force is a superseding cause of harm to another:

      (1) the fact that its intervention brings about harm different in kind from that which would otherwise have resulted from the defendant's negligence;

      (2) the fact that its operation or the consequences thereof appear after the event to be extraordinary and unforeseeable;

      (3) the fact that the intervening force is operating independently of any situation created by the defendant's negligence.

Torts Multistate Chart

INTERVENING FORCES

	Foreseeable	Unforeseeable (i.e., Superseding)
Effect	Chain of proximate causation unbroken; original defendant remains liable.	Chain of proximate causation broken; original defendant's liability cut off for consequences of antecedent conduct.
Typical Examples	1. Subsequent medical malpractice – including aggravation of plaintiff's condition. 2. Subsequent disease or accident – includes all illnesses and injuries resulting due to plaintiff's weakened condition, but not being stricken by a deadly, rare disease. 3. Negligent rescue efforts.	1. Criminal acts and intentional torts of torts of third parties, but only where they are unforeseeable under the facts or circumstances. 2. "Highly extraordinary" harm arising from defendant's conduct, as viewed by the court – includes grossly negligent conduct of third parties. 3. Unforeseeable acts of God.

E. DAMAGES

1. In General

a. A plaintiff must affirmatively prove actual damages. Nominal damages are not available, nor are punitive damages generally allowed.

b. Personal injury and property damages are recoverable. Included are general and special damages past and future pain and suffering, medical expenses, lost wages and loss of consortium, but not attorney's fees. Plaintiff's duty to mitigate damages applies.

c. **Collateral Sources Rule.** Payments made to or benefits conferred on the injured party-plaintiff ***from other (i.e., collateral) sources are not credited*** against the tortfeasor's liability, even where they cover all or a part of the harm for which the tortfeasor is liable.

(1) The rule that collateral benefits are not subtracted from the plaintiff's recovery applies to the following types of benefits:

(a) ***Insurance policies,*** whether maintained by the plaintiff or a third party;

(b) ***Employment benefits;***

(c) ***Gratuities*** (this applies to cash gratuities and to the rendering of services);

(d) ***Social legislation benefits.***

Example: Janet negligently injures Katherine when she sets off firecrackers incorrectly. Katherine has second degree burns over most of her body. If Katherine collects disability or health insurance benefits, these will not be subtracted from the amount of damages that Janet owes Katherine.

Example: Liz is a veteran of the U.S. Army. When Terry negligently injures her and dislocates her shoulder, she ends up in a V.A. hospital for physical therapy. Although this is a benefit Liz has earned, Terry will still be liable to Liz for the damage he caused.

(2) **Exception:**

(a) **Payments made by tortfeasor.** Payments made by a tortfeasor or by a person acting for him (e.g., defendant's insurance company) to the injured plaintiff are ***credited*** against the defendant's tort liability.

Example: Terry's insurance company pays Liz part of her money damages. Terry will be entitled to subtract the amount his insurance company paid Liz from the amount he must pay.

III. JOINT TORTFEASORS

A. GENERAL PRINCIPLES

1. Concerted Action

a. Some torts involve three people, two tortfeasors and one victim. Where another person (not the defendant) harms a victim, the defendant is subject to liability if he

(1) does a tortious act in concert with the other person or pursuant to a common design with him; ***or***

(2) knows that the other person's conduct constitutes a breach of duty and gives substantial assistance or encouragement to the other person to breach the duty anyway; ***or***

(3) gives substantial assistance to the other person in accomplishing a tortious result and his own conduct, separately considered, constitutes a breach of duty to the third person.

Example: Vern is a camp counselor responsible for the care of twelve eight-year-old campers. One evening, he wants to go out drinking instead of staying in the cabin with the campers. He decides to leave camp. As he is walking along the road, George, a friend who is not a counselor, sees Vern walking along. Knowing that Vern is supposed to be at camp, George asks Vern where's he's going. Vern tells him that he's heading to the bar. George gives Vern a lift to the bar and buys him several beers at the bar, keeping him at the bar until the wee hours of the morning. If the campers are injured in a fire that night that Vern could have put out, George and Vern will both be liable for the campers' injuries.

b. The effect of ***joint and several liability*** (i.e., where the tortfeasors may be sued separately or all together) is that each defendant acting in concert with the other is liable for ***the entire amount of the plaintiff's damages.***

(1) The plaintiff is not required to join two or more defendants.

(2) The named defendants, however, may implead the remaining tortfeasors for contribution.

(3) **Release.** At common law, a surrender of plaintiff 's cause of action against one joint tortfeasor (i.e., a release) released all others.

(4) **Modern view.** Under Restatement 2d § 885, "A valid release of one tortfeasor from liability for harm ... ***does not discharge others liable for the same harm."*** Furthermore, "any payment by a joint tortfeasor for a claim involving other tortfeasors diminishes the claim ... at least to the extent of the payment made." This modern doctrine protects the plaintiff from the effect of the harsh common law rule. A plaintiff may also give one tortfeasor a ***covenant not to sue*** and so maintain a cause of action against the other tortfeasors.

2. **Apportionment of Harm to Causes**

a. Damages for harm are apportioned among two or more causes where

(1) there are distinct harms, ***or***

(2) there is a reasonable basis for determining the contribution of each cause to a single harm.

3. **Contribution**

a. Where joint tortfeasors have together caused a single plaintiff a single harm, there is a right of contribution among them, even though judgment has not been recovered against all or any of them.

b. The right of contribution exists only in favor of a tortfeasor who has discharged the entire claim for the harm by paying more than his equitable share of the common liability, and is limited to the amount paid by him in excess of his share. No tortfeasor can be required to make contribution beyond his own equitable share of the liability.

Example: Kendra and Joyce together harm Cecily. Kendra eventually reaches a settlement with Cecily whereby Kendra will pay for all of Cecily's medical bills. Kendra can seek contribution from Joyce to pay for half of the bills.

c. **Note:** A defendant who has committed an intentional tort may not seek contribution, even from a tortfeasor equally at fault.

d. When one tortfeasor has a right of indemnity against another, neither of them has a right of contribution against the other.

4. **Indemnity**

a. If two persons are liable in tort to a third person for the same harm and one of them discharges the liability of both, he is entitled to indemnity from the other if the other would be unjustly enriched at his expense by the discharge of the liability.

b. Instances in which indemnity is granted under this principle include the following:

(1) the indemnitee was liable only vicariously for the conduct of the indemnitor;

(2) the indemnitor supplied a defective chattel or performed defective work upon land or buildings as a result of which both were liable to the third person, and the indemnitee innocently or negligently failed to discover the defect.

c. Whereas contribution involves ***equitable apportionment,*** or sharing, among tortfeasors, indemnification shifts the ***entire loss from the party who was found liable to the actual wrongdoer who was primarily responsible*** for the harm.

Example: Horatio is the owner of a large petting zoo. He sets policies requiring the zoo keepers to allow children to pet only gentle, tame animals. One day, Catherine, a zoo keeper at the petting zoo, lets several small children into a pen with a raging bull instead of the pen with the docile cow. The bull charges the children and gores one of them with his horn. If the parents of the hurt child sue Horatio, he may seek indemnification from Catherine.

Example: Agnes buys a can of hair spray from Wall-Store. Unbeknownst to Agnes, the can contains flammable hair spray that can explode under pressure. The first time that Agnes presses the button on the can, flames shoot out of the can and set her hair on fire, burning her severely. If Agnes successfully sues Wall-Store for her injuries, Wall-Store may seek indemnification from the manufacturer of the hair spray.

Example: Frank borrows Lindsey's car. While driving the car at night without headlights on, Frank accidentally strikes a bicyclist, rendering the bicyclist paralyzed from the waist down. If the bicyclist successfully sues Lindsey, Lindsey may seek indemnification from Frank.

IV. DUTIES OF AFFIRMATIVE ACTION

A. DUTY IN GENERAL

1. Duty to Act for Protection of Others

a. **No duty to act.** The general rule is that there ***is no duty of care for nonfeasance*** (i.e., omission to act). Moral obligation alone does not impose a duty to aid another.

Note: Although under no duty to act, one who begins to act is thereby placed under a duty to act reasonably.

Example: Carl sees Linda injured by the side of the road. Late for an appointment, Carl does not stop to help Linda. Linda bleeds to death. Linda's estate does not have a cause of action against Carl.

Example: Carl sees Linda injured by the side of the road. Concerned that she could bleed to death, he stops and ties a tourniquet around her leg. He then leaves her there, unconscious, and goes to his appointment. Linda dies. Her estate will have a cause of action against Carl.

b. Upon engaging in any human activity, the law imposes a general duty of reasonable care such that the actor is required to act as an ordinary, reasonable, prudent person, as viewed by an objective standard, to prevent any unreasonable risk of foreseeable harm.

c. **Professional Standard.** An individual with ***special skills and knowledge*** in a certain area is required to exercise that knowledge and skill ordinarily possessed by a member of that profession in good standing.

Example: Yolanda is a computer specialist who routinely installs wiring and computers. Yolanda sets up a computer for Danny in his home. However, she negligently fails to ground the wires. One day, Danny is working on his computer when there is a big thunderstorm. Lightning strikes Danny's computer as he types, and he is electrocuted. If a member of the computer installation profession would ordinarily ground the wire, Danny's estate may successfully sue Yolanda.

d. In emergency situations, a duty is imposed to act as a reasonable person would under the same emergency.

2. Special Relations Giving Rise to Duty to Aid or Protect

a. The following people and entities have a special or "higher" duty of care to act for the protection of others. In brief, they ***must exercise a greater amount of care than is ordinarily required by the usual reasonable person standard.***

b. **Common carriers.** A common carrier is under a ***special duty*** to its passengers.

Example: Tracy is a bus driver for Blackhound Bus Lines. One night, Tracy drives the bus in the pouring rain with no headlights on. The bus has no seatbelts. The bus crashes. After the crash, afraid that she will get into trouble, Tracy runs from the bus and does not help any of the passengers, several of whom are badly injured. The injured passengers will have a cause of action against Blackhound and Tracy.

c. **Innkeepers.** An innkeeper is under a ***special duty*** to his guests.

Example: Margaret owns a country inn in the beautiful area of Romantica. Despite the fact that "Spring forward, fall back" is on her refrigerator magnet, she forgets to check her smoke alarms for several months. The batteries run out in the detectors. One night, a guest falls asleep with a lit cigarette and sets the inn on fire. Margaret fails to call the fire department. Because many of the other guests are also asleep, they do not get out in time and are killed. Margaret will be liable to the guests' estates.

Note: Common carriers and innkeepers may be liable for even slight negligence because of the very high degree of care required.

d. **Possessors of land.** A possessor of land who holds it open to the public has a duty to members of the public who enter in response to his invitation.

Example: Nikita owns a karate studio. One day, she holds a karate demonstration. The demo is advertised and is open to the public. If the roof falls in on the spectators during the demo because of rotten beams, Nikita will be liable to the injured spectators.

e. **Custody keepers.** Where a person takes another into custody voluntarily or as required by law and deprives him of his normal ability to protect himself, he takes on a duty of care.

Example: Brian is a police officer. One cold winter evening, he arrests Jeremy, a pickpocket. He handcuffs and shackles Jeremy and puts him in the back of his police cruiser. Brian then drives to the donut shop, where he parks the car and leaves Jeremy inside. Brian goes into the donut shop and drinks coffee and eats donuts for three hours. If Jeremy gets hypothermia, he will have a cause of action against Brian.

B. DUTY TO CONTROL CONDUCT OF THIRD PERSONS

1. General Principle

a. There is no duty to control the conduct of a third person as to prevent him from causing physical harm to another ***unless***

(1) a special relationship exists between the actor and the third person which imposes a duty upon the actor to control the third person's conduct, ***or***

(2) a special relation exists between the actor and the other person which gives to the other person a right to protection.

Example: Joshua is in a movie theater sitting next to David. Joshua and David do not know one another; they just happen to be sitting in adjacent seats. David gets very angry with the usher because the usher tells him to take his feet off the seat in front of him. If David decides to slug the usher, Joshua has no duty to control him.

Example: Joshua is in the movie theater sitting next to his son when Eliza enters. Eliza takes one look at Joshua's son, realizes that he is the kid who bit her child on the playground, and lunges at him. Joshua has a duty to protect his son from Eliza and to control her conduct.

2. **Duty of Parent to Control Conduct of Child**

   a. A parent is under a duty to exercise reasonable care so to control his minor child as to prevent him from intentionally harming others or from so conducting himself as to create an unreasonable risk of bodily harm to them, if the parent

      (1) knows or has reason to know that he has the ability to control his child, ***and***

      (2) knows or should know of the necessity and opportunity for exercising such control.

      Example: Dilly and Erica, two thirteen-year-olds, are building bombs in Dilly's garage. Their parents do not supervise their free time and giggle when they find bomb-making manuals in the house, saying, "Kids will be kids!" If Dilly and Erica bomb their high school and kill many classmates and teachers, their parents may be liable.

3. **Duty of Master to Control Conduct of Servant**

   a. A master is under a duty to exercise reasonable care to control his servant while acting outside the scope of his employment in order to prevent him from intentionally harming others or from so conducting himself as to create an unreasonable risk of bodily harm to them, if

      (1) the servant

         (a) is upon the premises in possession of the master or upon which the servant is privileged to enter only as his servant, ***or***

         (b) is using a chattel of the master, ***and***

      (2) the master

         (a) knows or has reason to know that he has the ability to control his servant, ***and***

         (b) knows or should know of the necessity and opportunity for exercising such control.

Example: Christopher owns Silver Skates, an ice skating rink in Coldville. Ellie is a skating teacher at the rink. Christopher is in the office overlooking the rink one day when he sees Ellie, who is supposed to be taking her day off, doing skating lifts with skaters that Christopher knows to be beginners. Christopher knows that beginning skaters are not ready to do lifts and can really hurt themselves if they do. Christopher has a duty to intervene to protect the students if he is able to do so.

C. DUTY TO AID OTHERS AND SERVICES GRATUITOUSLY RENDERED

1. Duty to Act When Prior Conduct is Found to be Dangerous

a. If the actor does an act, and subsequently realizes or should realize that it has created an unreasonable risk of causing physical harm to another, he is under a duty to exercise reasonable care to prevent the risk from taking effect. This standard applies even where the actor did not recognize the potential risk before he acted.

Example: Annie is a massage therapist. She has been trained in massage therapy and knows that massaging a pregnant woman's ankles can cause her to go into early labor. One evening, Lucy, a woman who is 5 months pregnant, comes in for a massage. Lucy is remarkably fit and does not look pregnant. Annie begins the massage and is massaging Lucy's ankles when Lucy happens to mention that she is pregnant. Annie is under a duty to do what she reasonably can to prevent Lucy from going into premature labor.

2. Duty to Aid Another Harmed by Actor's Conduct

a. If the actor knows or has reason to know that by his conduct, whether tortious or innocent, he has caused such bodily harm to another as to make him helpless and in danger of further harm, the actor is under a duty to exercise reasonable care to prevent such further harm.

Example: Isabel is on her way to the bar exam. She is worried about being late, so she is speeding. As she turns a corner, she fails to notice Ronny on his bike. Her car strikes Ronny's bike and causes Ronny to fall into the road, trapped under his bicycle. Ronny sustains a broken ankle. Isabel must stop and help Ronny out of the road so that another car will not hit him.

Example: Annie is a massage therapist. One evening, Theresa, a woman who is 8 months pregnant, comes in for a massage. As Annie is massaging Theresa's back, Theresa cries out in pain. Through no fault of Annie's, Theresa has slipped a disk in her back. Annie, who is familiar with anatomy, realizes that she cannot let Theresa walk or drive; were Theresa to do so, she could irreparably damage her back and possibly cause harm to the unborn baby. Annie is under a duty to help Theresa to prevent further harm.

3. Duty of One Who Takes Charge of Another Who is Helpless

a. One who, being under no duty to do so, takes charge of another who is helpless adequately to aid or protect himself is subject to liability to the other person for any bodily harm caused to him by

(1) the failure of the actor to exercise reasonable care to secure the safety of the other while within the actor's charge, ***or***

(2) the actor's discontinuing his aid or protection, if by so doing he leaves the other in a worse position than when the actor took charge of him.

Example: Helen is getting off the bus one day when she sees Mabel, an elderly woman with a walker, trying to get off the bus. Helen takes Mabel's arm and begins to help her off the bus. Helen fails, however, to warn Mabel that there is a big step at the bottom. She also lets go of Mabel's arm before Mabel is completely off of the bus. Because Helen lets go, and because Mabel misses the step, Mabel falls and breaks her hip. Helen leaves Mabel there and continues on her way. Helen will be liable to Mabel for the hip injury.

b. **"Good Samaritan" Statutes.** Although liability is generally imposed on an individual who, having no duty to render assistance, nevertheless does so and performs in a negligent manner (i.e., malfeasance), some jurisdictions statutorily ***exempt*** volunteering doctors and nurses from liability for ordinary (not gross) negligence.

Example: Ursula is a doctor. While flying to a conference, the plane that Ursula is on hits major turbulence. Polly, another passenger, is so frightened of the turbulence that she has a heart attack. Ursula comes to Polly's aid. She lies Polly down on the floor of the cabin and begins to give Polly CPR. However, she does not secure Polly, and when the plane next hits turbulence, Polly hits her head and is killed. If Polly's estate sues Ursula in a jurisdiction that has a Good Samaritan statute, Ursula probably will not be liable for Polly's death.

D. LIMITED DUTY

1. Children

a. If the actor is a child, the standard of conduct to which he must conform to avoid being negligent is that of ***a reasonable person of like age, intelligence, and experience under like circumstances.***

Example: Susie is seven years old and is very intelligent. One day, she leaves her roller skates on the front walk. Larry, who is walking down the walk, does not see the skates and slips and falls on them, breaking his leg. If Larry sues Susie, her act of leaving the skates on the walk will be compared to that of an intelligent seven-year-old with similar experience.

b. ***Children engaging in adult activities (e.g., operating an automobile, boat, or airplane), however, are required to conform to an adult standard of care.***

Example: Nine-year-old Cameron takes his dad's motor boat out for a spin. While driving the boat across the bay, he hits Vern, a swimmer, and knocks Vern unconscious. Vern drowns. If Vern's estate sues Cameron, Cameron may be liable for negligence and will not be compared to other children's standard of care.

2. **Mental Deficiency**

   a. Unless the actor is a child, his insanity or other mental deficiency does not relieve the actor from liability for conduct that does not conform to ***the standard of a reasonable man under like circumstances.***

   Example: Angus has an IQ of 75. Angus places a large amount of rocks in the back of his pickup truck but does not tie them down. When he drives his truck on the highway, a lot of rocks fall out of the back of the truck, causing a pile-up accident behind him. In a negligence suit by the accident victims against Angus, Angus' actions will be compared to persons of average intelligence, not to those of other people with mental retardation.

3. **Physical Disability**

   a. If the actor is ill or otherwise physically disabled, the standard of conduct to which he must conform to avoid being negligent is that of ***a reasonable man under like disability.***

   Example: Sydney is in labor. She is waiting in the hospital waiting room for her doctor to call her in to the labor and delivery room. During a contraction, she is in so much pain that she accidentally hits a tray table near her chair. The table falls over and hits Samantha, another laboring woman sitting nearby. Samantha falls to the floor. Her fall causes her to begin hemorrhaging, and her baby must be delivered by emergency C-section. If Samantha sues Sydney for negligence, Sydney will be compared to other pregnant, laboring women.

4. **Duty of Automobile Driver to Guest**

   a. Most jurisdictions impose on the driver of an automobile a duty of ordinary care toward a guest. ***Under guest statutes, however, the driver has a lessened duty, namely to refrain from gross, wanton, or willful misconduct.***

   Example: Frances is driving in her car with her friend, Wanda. Although it is nighttime, Frances neglects to put her headlights on. She is therefore unable to see a tree, and she smashes into it. Wanda is thrown through the windshield and sustains a concussion. If Wanda sues Frances, she will not prevail unless the court holds that Frances' failure to use headlights was gross, wanton or willful misconduct.

   Compare: One who confers an economic benefit to ride in an automobile is considered a "passenger," and is owed a duty of ordinary care.

   Example: Amanda attends preschool on Tuesday and Thursday mornings. Unfortunately, her parents both work, and they cannot pick her up from preschool. Amanda's parents hire Camille to pick Amanda up and take her to daycare. They pay Camille $10 a trip. One day, Camille does not buckle Amanda into her car seat. While they are stopped at a red light, George rear-ends Camille's car. Amanda is thrown from her seat and breaks her neck. Camille will be liable to Amanda for her injuries.

V. OWNERS AND OCCUPIERS OF LAND

A. IN GENERAL

1. Possessor of Land Defined

a. A possessor of land is

(1) a person who is in occupation of the land with intent to control it, ***or***

(2) a person who has been in occupation of land with intent to control it, if no other person has subsequently occupied it with intent to control it, ***or***

(3) a person who is entitled to immediate occupation of the land, if no other person is in possession under Clauses (1) and (2).

Example: Sarah, Owen's tenant, rents Blackacre. She has a one-year lease. She is a possessor of land.

2. Trespasser Defined

a. ***A trespasser is a person who enters or remains upon land in the possession of another without a privilege*** to do so created by the possessor's consent or otherwise.

Example: Agatha wants to see the great view of the Mississippi evident from the top of Blueberry Hill. Blueberry Hill is entirely on John's property. If Agatha hikes up Blueberry Hill without John's permission, she is a trespasser.

3. Licensee Defined

a. ***A licensee is a person who is privileged to enter or remain on land only by virtue of the possessor's consent.*** He enters the possessor's land for his own benefit rather than for the benefit of the possessor.

b. **Example:** Social guests, persons who enter with nothing more than consent, such as loafers, loiterers, and people who come in only to get out of the weather; persons taking short cuts across property or making merely permissive use of crossings or ways; those in search of their children, servants or other third persons; spectators and sightseers; and salesmen canvassing at the door of private homes.

4. Invitee Defined

a. ***An invitee is a person entering premises upon business concerning the occupier,*** and upon his invitation express or implied. An invitee generally serves some purpose of the possessor; however, the majority and Restatement 2d view is that economic gain to the invitor is *not* required for invitee status.

b. **Types**

(1) **Business visitors** – The typical example, of course, is the customer in a store. Patrons of restaurants, banks, theatres, bathing beaches, fairs and other businesses open to the public are included.

(2) **Public invitees** – When premises are open to the public (such as churches, museums, libraries, airports, municipal parks, etc.), those who enter are also viewed as invitees.

Example: Hermione goes into a store to buy a flying broom. She is an invitee.

Example: Ron goes into a hotel lobby to use a pay phone. Although he does not confer any economic benefit on the hotel, he is an invitee.

Example: Harry goes to a free exhibition at the Museum of Wizardy. He is an invitee.

B. LIABILITY OF POSSESSORS OF LAND TO TRESPASSERS

1. **General Rule**

a. A possessor of land ***is not liable to trespassers for physical harm*** caused by his failure to exercise reasonable care

(1) to put the land in a condition reasonably safe for their reception, ***or***

(2) to carry on his activities so as not to endanger them.

2. **Activities Dangerous to Known Trespassers**

a. A possessor of land who knows or has reason to know of the presence of a trespasser is subject to liability for physical harm thereafter caused to the trespasser by the possessor's failure to carry on his activities upon the land with reasonable care for the trespasser's safety.

b. A possessor of land generally owes ***a duty of reasonable care to warn trespassers who are known, discovered, or anticipated of known dangers.***

Example: John knows that Agatha likes to hike up Blueberry Hill to see the Mississippi. Although he has not given her permission to do so, he should warn her if his raging bull is likely to attack her when she goes onto the land.

3. **Artificial Conditions Highly Dangerous to Known Trespassers**

a. A possessor of land who maintains on the land an artificial condition which involves risk of death or serious bodily harm to persons coming in contact with it, ***is subject to liability for bodily harm caused to trespassers by his failure to exercise reasonable care to warn them of the condition if***

(1) the possessor knows or has reason to know of their presence in dangerous proximity to the condition, ***and***

(2) the condition is of such a nature that he has reason to believe that ***the trespasser will not discover it or realize the risk involved.***

b. **Note:** Holders of easements (e.g., power companies stringing wires over land) and licenses are subject to the same liability as possessors of land.

Example: John knows that Agatha likes to hike up Blueberry Hill to see the Mississippi. Although he has not given her permission to do so, he should warn her about hidden minefields on the land.

4. **"Attractive Nuisance" Doctrine**

a. A possessor of land is subject to liability for physical harm to ***children trespassing*** thereon caused by an artificial condition upon the land if

(1) the place where the condition exists is one upon which the possessor knows or has reason to know that children are likely to trespass; ***and***

(2) the condition is one of which the possessor knows or has reason to know and which he realizes or should realize will involve an unreasonable risk of death or serious bodily harm to such children; ***and***

(3) the children ***because of their youth do not discover the condition or realize the risk involved in intermeddling*** with it or in coming within the area made dangerous by it; ***and***

(4) the utility to the possessor of maintaining the condition and the burden of eliminating the danger are slight as compared with the risk to children involved; ***and***

(5) the possessor fails to exercise reasonable care to eliminate the danger or otherwise to protect the children.

b. This doctrine is based on foreseeability of harm to the child, not attraction onto the property. The artificial condition must pose an unreasonable risk of harm in light of the particular child's age.

Example: Tracy is a six-year-old girl who frequently trespasses on Cindy's land. Cindy knows that Tracy sometimes trespasses on her land. If there is a dangerous dump site on Cindy's land, Cindy must make it safe.

Example: Tracy is a six-year-old girl who frequently trespasses on Cindy's land. Cindy knows that Tracy sometimes trespasses on her land. If there is a cool abandoned car on Cindy's land that is rusty and dangerous, Cindy should remove it or cover it to prevent Tracy from injuring herself.

Example: Tracy is a six-year-old girl who frequently trespasses on Cindy's land. Cindy knows that Tracy sometimes trespasses on her land. Cindy will not have to build a fence around her pond, as natural bodies of water are generally not included within the rule.

C. GENERAL LIABILITY OF POSSESSORS OF LAND TO LICENSEES AND INVITEES

1. Activities Dangerous to Licensees

a. A possessor of land is subject to liability to his licensees for physical harm caused to them by his failure to carry on his activities with reasonable care for their safety if, but only if,

(1) he should expect that they will not discover or realize the danger, ***and***

(2) they do not know or have reason to know of the possessor's activities and of the risk involved.

Example: Adam has a license to enter onto Ingrid's land to swim in her lake. Unbeknownst to Adam, Ingrid has been sinking rocks in her lake to dispose of them. Ingrid must warn Adam of the presence of rocks in the lake.

2. Activities Dangerous to Invitees

a. A possessor of land is subject to liability to his invitees for physical harm caused to them by his failure to carry on his activities with reasonable care for their safety if, but only if, he should expect that they will not discover or realize the danger, or will fail to protect themselves against it.

b. The scope of ***duty owed an invitee is twofold:***

(1) ***a duty to inspect the premises, and***

(2) ***remedy any unsafe or dangerous conditions.***

Caveat: The duty of care owed to an invitee does not extend to areas outside the scope of invitation (e.g., behind the counter in a store, in the kitchen of a restaurant), and in such areas a person will be treated as a trespasser.

Example: Chris owns a general store in Boulder, Colorado. The shelves in one area are very wobbly and have the potential to collapse. This problem is not visible to the naked eye, however. If Chris does not fix the shelves and George, a customer, is injured when they collapse, Chris will be liable to George for his injuries.

3. Known or Obvious Dangers

a. A possessor of land is ***not liable to his invitees for physical harm caused to them by any activity or condition on the land whose danger is known or obvious to them,*** unless the possessor should anticipate the harm despite such knowledge or obviousness.

b. In determining whether the possessor should anticipate harm from a known or obvious danger, the fact that the invitee is entitled to make use of public land, or of the facilities of a public utility, is a factor of importance indicating that the harm should be anticipated.

Example: Polly owns a small wading pool on her property. She charges a $3 fee to use the pool. Many mothers and their babies come to the pool on a daily basis in the summertime. Because the pool is very shallow, Polly has posted a sign saying, "POOL ONLY 2 FEET DEEP!" Furthermore, it is fairly obvious that the pool is shallow because there are only 3 steps leading to the bottom. If Charlie, a father who brings his baby to the pool one day, dives into the pool and dies from a broken neck, Polly will not be liable.

4. **Public Employees**

   a. Where it can be found that the public employee comes for a purpose which has some connection with business transacted on the premises by the occupier, he is almost invariably treated as an invitee.

   Example: Examples of such invitees are garbage collectors, city meter readers, postmen and sanitary or building inspectors.

   Compare: On the other hand, courts have traditionally held ***firemen and policemen to be mere licensees.***

5. **Reasonable Under the Circumstances**

   A number of jurisdictions have eliminated the distinctions between the various classes of persons entering land, and simply hold the landowner to a "reasonable under the circumstances" test. In applying the tests, the nature of the entry is simply one factor in determining foreseeability and reasonability.

Torts Multistate Chart:

Duties Owed To Entrants Coming Onto The Land

Status	Duty Owed
Trespasser, undiscovered	No duty
Trespasser, known or anticipated	Ordinary care; ***duty to warn of dangerous*** conditions that ***are known to possessor*** (exception: no duty to warn of obvious natural conditions of the land (e.g., lake);
Licensee	Ordinary care; ***duty to warn of dangerous conditions which are known to possessor***;
Invitee	Ordinary care; ***duty to (1) inspect premises and/or land, and (2) make safe for protection of invitees who enter.***

D. LIABILITY OF LESSORS OF LAND TO PERSONS ON THE LAND

1. **General Rule**

   a. As a general rule, a lessor of land is not subject to liability to his lessee or others upon the land with the consent of the lessee or sublessee for physical harm caused by any dangerous condition which comes into existence ***after the lessee has taken possession.***

b. Where only ***a portion of the premises is leased,*** the lessor remains liable for physical harm caused by dangerous conditions in such common areas as hallways, elevators and stairways.

c. ***A lessor has a duty to warn of known existing defects*** that are not likely to be discovered by the lessee.

Example: Kate leases a farm from Leopold. After she begins her lease, a bridge across a stream falls into a dangerous state of disrepair. If Hope falls into the stream and drowns because the bridge fails, Kate, not Leopold, will be liable.

Example: Kate leases an apartment in Leopold's apartment house. After her lease begins, the door to the apartment building breaks and tends to slam on people. If Yolanda, a two-year-old, gets caught in the door and breaks her arm, Leopold, not Kate, will be liable.

2. **Where Lessor Contracts to Repair**

a. A lessor of land ***is subject to liability for physical harm*** caused to his lessee and others upon the land with the consent of the lessee or his sublessee ***by a condition of disrepair existing before or arising after the lessee has taken possession if***

(1) the lessor, as such, has contracted by a covenant in the lease or otherwise to keep the land in repair, ***and***

(2) the disrepair creates an unreasonable risk to persons upon the land which the performance of the lessor's agreement would have prevented, ***and***

(3) the lessor fails to exercise reasonable care to perform his contract.

b. Voluntary repair by the lessor, where there is no covenant to do so, subjects the lessor to liability for any negligent repair.

Example: Lenny promises Evan, his tenant, that he will repair the staircase in the house that Evan has rented. This promise is a provision in the lease. Lenny does not repair the stairway and never even tries to do so. If Evan falls two stories because the stairs break, Lenny will be liable.

Example: Lenny does not promise Evan that he will repair the stairs, but he takes it upon himself to do so. If he uses wormy boards that will not hold a person's weight and the stairs collapse, causing Evan to fall, Lenny will be liable in negligence.

3. **Land Leased for Purpose Involving Admission of Public**

a. A lessor who leases land for a purpose ***which involves the admission of the public is subject to liability*** for physical harm caused to persons who enter the land for that purpose by a condition of the land existing when the lessee takes possession, if the lessor

(1) knows or by the exercise of reasonable care could discover that the condition involves an unreasonable risk of harm to such persons, and

(2) has reason to expect that the lessee will admit them before the land is put in safe condition for, their reception, and

(3) fails to exercise reasonable care to discover or to remedy the condition, or otherwise to protect such persons against it.

Example: Nancy owns a historical building where Elvis once lived. She leases the building to Carrie, who plans to admit members of the public to see where Elvis slept. Carrie plans to begin the tours immediately upon inception of the lease. Nancy knows that the staircase in the building is weak. Nancy will be liable if any tourist falls through the stairs.

VI. NEGLIGENCE: DEFENSES

A. CONTRIBUTORY NEGLIGENCE

1. Defined

a. ***Contributory negligence is conduct on the part of the plaintiff which falls below the standard to which he should conform for his own protection,*** and which is a legally contributing cause cooperating with the negligence of the defendant in bringing about the plaintiff's harm.

b. Contributory negligence is a strict rule because a plaintiff who is 1% negligent ***is barred from recovering*** as a matter of law.

c. Contributory negligence ***is not a defense either to intentional torts, willful misconduct, or to a strict liability action.***

d. **Rescuers:** The ordinary negligence of a rescuer is not contributory negligence. Nor is assumption of the risk an available defense in a rescue situation.

2. When Bar to Action

a. Except where the defendant has the last clear chance (*see infra*), ***the plaintiff's contributory negligence bars recovery against a defendant whose negligent conduct would otherwise make him liable*** to the plaintiff for the harm sustained by him.

3. Violation of Legislation or Regulation

a. The plaintiff's unexcused violation of a legislative enactment or an administrative regulation that defines a standard of conduct for his own protection is contributory negligence in itself if it is a legally contributing cause of his harm.

b. The rules which determine whether such an enactment or regulation defines a standard of conduct for the protection of the plaintiff, and when the violation will be excused, are the same as those applicable to the defendant (*see, supra,* negligence *per se*).

4. **Conduct in Emergency**

   a. In determining whether the plaintiff's conduct is contributory negligence, the fact that he is confronted with a sudden emergency that requires rapid decision is a factor in determining whether his conduct is reasonable.

   b. The fact that the plaintiff is not negligent after the emergency has arisen does not preclude his prior contributory negligence from barring his recovery.

5. **Failure to Discover Condition of Highway**

   a. If the defendant negligently puts or maintains a highway in a condition dangerous for travel, a traveler who is injured by such condition is barred from recovery by his failure to exercise reasonable care to discover the condition of the highway.

B. LAST CLEAR CHANCE DOCTRINE

1. **Helpless Plaintiff**

   a. A plaintiff who has negligently subjected himself to a risk of harm from the defendant's subsequent negligence may recover for harm caused thereby if, immediately preceding the harm,

      (1) the plaintiff is unable to avoid it by the exercise of reasonable vigilance and care, and

      (2) the defendant is negligent in failing to utilize with reasonable care and competence his then existing opportunity to avoid the harm, when he

         (a) knows of the plaintiff's situation and realizes or has reason to realize the peril involved in it, ***or***

         (b) would discover the situation and thus have reason to realize the peril, if he were to exercise the vigilance that it is then his duty to the plaintiff to exercise.

   b. ***The "last clear chance doctrine" operates as a plaintiff's defense to mitigate the harshness of contributory negligence and to allow a negligent plaintiff full recovery where the last human wrongdoer failed to avoid the accident.***

   c. ***Where comparative negligence has been enacted, jurisdictions do not utilize the last clear chance doctrine.***

2. **Inattentive Plaintiff**

   a. A plaintiff who, by the exercise of reasonable vigilance, could discover the danger created by the defendant's negligence in time to avoid the harm to him, can recover if, but only if, the defendant

(1) knows of the plaintiff's situation, ***and***

(2) realizes or has reason to realize that the plaintiff is inattentive and therefore unlikely to discover his peril in time to avoid the harm, ***and***

(3) thereafter is negligent in failing to utilize with reasonable care and competence his then existing opportunity to avoid the harm.

C. COMPARATIVE NEGLIGENCE

1. General Rule

In several states general statutes applicable to all negligence actions, and in a great many others particular statutes applicable to certain types of cases, have abrogated the contributory negligence rule, and have substituted reduction of ***damages to be recovered by the negligent plaintiff in proportion to his fault.***

2. "Modified" v. "Pure" Comparative Negligence

a. Modified comparative negligence jurisdictions enable a negligent plaintiff to obtain a recovery, ***provided plaintiff's negligence is not equal to nor greater than that of defendant;*** otherwise, no recovery is permitted.

(1) Some jurisdictions allow recovery ***unless plaintiff's negligence is greater than that of defendant*** (i.e., a plaintiff 51% at fault could not recover in a modified comparative negligence jurisdiction).

(2) By contrast, some states apply the ***"unit rule"*** in dealing with multiple defendants under modified comparative negligence. ***Under the "unit rule", the plaintiff's negligence is compared with the aggregate negligence of all defendants,*** who may then through contribution adjust the loss among themselves.

b. Pure comparative negligence jurisdictions ***permit a negligent plaintiff to recover even where his negligence exceeds that of defendant.***

c. On the Multistate Bar Examination (MBE), students are instructed to follow ***pure comparative negligence*** unless the facts indicate otherwise.

Example: Peter Plaintiff suffers $50,000 damages and is 40% at fault. Donald Defendant is 10% at fault and Darren Defendant is 50% at fault. ***Analysis:*** Plaintiff can recover in a "pure" comparative negligence jurisdiction. However, in "modified" comparative negligence jurisdictions, there is a split of authority. In some states where multiple defendants are involved, the plaintiff's negligence is ***compared with that of each individual defendant.*** By applying this rule, in a suit by Peter Plaintiff against Donald Defendant, there would be ***no*** recovery since Peter's degree of fault exceeds Donald's. Conversely, in an action by Peter against Darren, there would be recovery since Plaintiff would be less at fault. In the latter case, Plaintiff would recover $30,000 (i.e., $50,000 reduced by 40% which represents Plaintiff's degree of fault). In a "unit rule" state, Plaintiff would be entitled to recover $30,000 from either Defendant or from Darren because her negligence would be less than the aggregate negligence of both defendants. In the event that Plaintiff did recover $30,000 from Donald, then Donald would be entitled to contribution from Darren.

D. ASSUMPTION OF RISK

1. General Principle

a. A plaintiff who voluntarily assumes a risk of harm arising from the negligent or reckless conduct of the defendant cannot recover for such harm.

b. Assumption of risk (i.e., *volenti non fit injuria*) may be done ***expressly*** (by agreement or by contract-exculpatory clauses or **impliedly**). The key elements of assumption of risk are:

(1) ***knowledge of the risk using a subjective standard of the particular plaintiff*** (Compare: objective, reasonable person standard for contributory negligence) ***and***

(2) ***voluntary assumption,*** involving some manifestation of consent sufficient to relieve the defendant of his duty of reasonable conduct (i.e., a jaywalker may be contributorily negligent, but he does not assume the risk, since he is not consenting to relieve oncoming drivers of their duty to use reasonable care toward him).

Example: Christy attends a Yankees game and is hit by a fly ball. She may not sue the Yankees because she is deemed to have assumed the risk that she will be hit by such a ball.

Example: Sara works at a toy factory. The factory uses dangerous chemicals in its manufacturing process. If Sara gets cancer from exposure to the chemicals, she will not be deemed to have assumed the risk of dangerous working conditions.

VII. MISCELLANEOUS CONSIDERATIONS IN NEGLIGENCE

A. VICARIOUS LIABILITY

1. Respondeat Superior Doctrine

An employer is liable for the tortious acts of his or her employees which are committed within the scope of employment and which cause injuries or property damage to a third person.

a. "Scope of employment" includes acts so closely connected and reasonably incidental to what the servant was employed to do, that they may be regarded as methods, however improper, to carry out the employer's objectives.

(1) The term ***"detour" is often used to denote permissible or slight deviations*** from an employee's scope of employment.

(2) A ***"frolic" characterizes an unauthorized and substantial deviation.***

(3) Intentional torts by servants are ***generally held not to be within the scope of employment unless the scope of employment includes the potential for use of force.***

Example: John operates a restaurant. One of his waiters is dissatisfied with his tip and hits customer. John is not liable.

Example: John operates a nightclub. He hires bouncers to control the crowd. One of his bouncers gets too rough, and strikes a customer. John will probably be liable.

b. Where a servant without authority hires an employee to perform or assist in his work, no liability can be imposed by ***respondeat superior***. (However, the master may be nonetheless liable by ***imputed negligence*** if the servant negligently entrusts performance of his work to a third person).

Example: Sam, a servant, lets his intoxicated friend Gina drive his delivery truck along the work route. Sam's employer may be liable under a theory of imputed negligence.

2. **Joint Enterprise.** When two or more individuals agree to enter into an undertaking in the performance of which they have a ***community of interest and mutual right of control,*** they are said to be engaging in a joint enterprise (also called a joint venture). Because such an arrangement is similar to a business partnership, each member is vicariously liable for the torts of the others committed within the scope of the enterprise.

a. A joint venture involves a more limited time period and a more limited purpose than a partnership. The common purpose of the venture is generally limited to a business or commercial (rather than social) purpose.

3. **Independent Contractors**

a. **General Principle.** ***The employer of an independent contractor is not (vicariously) liable for physical harm caused to another by an act or omission of the contractor or his servants.***

b. **Types of Persons Covered.** Any person to whom the construction, rebuilding, or repairing of a chattel is entrusted in such a way as to give him charge and control of the details of doing the work, irrespective of whether the work is done gratuitously or is to be paid for by his employer or is in any other way of financial or other benefit to the contractor.

c. **Exceptions:** An employer, however, is liable for:

(1) ***negligence in selecting, instructing or supervising the contractor,***

(2) ***non-delegable duties of the employer, arising out of some relation toward the public or the particular plaintiff; or***

(3) ***work which is specially, peculiarly or "inherently" dangerous.***

d. **Examples of Non-Delegable Duties.** Duty of city to keep streets in repair; duty to erect a wall around an excavation site; duty of lessor to maintain common passageways and reasonably make promised repairs; duty to keep premises safe for business invitees; duty to provide lateral support to adjoining land.

e. **Examples of "Inherently Dangerous" Activities.** Construction of dams and reservoirs; high tension electric wires; exhibition of fireworks; excavations near a public highway; construction or repair work on buildings.

4. **Ownership of a Vehicle**

a. **Negligent Entrustment.** Where it appears that the owner of a vehicle knows or should know of the negligent propensities of a driver to whom the vehicle is entrusted, the owner may be liable for the subsequent negligent act(s) of the driver.

b. **"Family Purpose" Doctrine.** An owner of an automobile ***is (vicariously) liable for the negligent acts of his agents or members of his family when using the auto for "family purposes".*** Under ***"Permissive Use" statutes, the owner's liability is further extended to include harm caused by anyone driving with consent.***

c. **Note:** In the absence of such statutes, an automobile owner is generally not vicariously liable for the torts of the driver (since negligence of the bailee is not imputed to the bailor).

B. IMPUTED CONTRIBUTORY NEGLIGENCE

1. **Driver-Passenger**

A driver's negligence ***will not be imputed*** to his (or her) passenger, whether the transportation be in a common carrier, a hired vehicle or a gratuitous conveyance, unless the relation between them is such that the passenger would be vicariously liable as a defendant.

2. **Domestic Relations**

a. **Husband - Wife.** Although common law imputed the contributory negligence of one spouse to another, this rule is no longer recognized today.

b. **Parent - Child.** Although ***a parent is generally not vicariously liable for the tortious conduct of his (or her) child***, most jurisdictions impose liability where:

(1) the parent entrusts the child with a dangerous instrumentality;

(2) the child engages in tortious conduct while acting as a servant or agent of the parent;

(3) the parent knows of the child's wrongdoing and consents to it; ***or***

(4) the parent fails to exercise proper control over his (or her) child.

3. **Bailments**

In the absence of statute, the bailment ***is not sufficient*** in itself to impute the contributory negligence of the bailee, and the bailor will be charged with such negligence only where there are additional factors which would make him liable to a third person as a defendant.

Example: Meg allows Lauren to drive her car. While driving Meg's car, Lauren is hit by a car. Lauren is struck both because the car ran a stop sign and because she failed to look both ways before entering an intersection. If Lauren is charged with contributory negligence, the charge will not be imputed to Meg.

Torts Multistate Chart:

VICARIOUS LIABILITY

RELATIONSHIP	CONTRIBUTORY NEGLIGENCE IMPUTED
Master - Servant	Yes
Joint Venture	Yes
Independent Contractor	No, unless inherently dangerous activity or non-delegable duty
Automobile Owner - Driver	No, unless imposed by statute
Driver - Passenger	No
Husband - Wife	No
Parent - Child	No, but liability in negligence may be imposed
Bailor - Bailee	No, but liability in negligence may be imposed
Tavern-Keeper/Patron	No, unless imposed by Dram Shop Act

C. WRONGFUL DEATH ACTIONS

1. **In General**

a. Common law tort actions became null upon the death of either party. ***Defamation and privacy actions still do not survive the victim's death***; however, property damage and personal injury may be recovered for most torts through statutory enactment.

b. A wrongful death action brought by a personal representative or spouse ***directly compensates the survivors*** for losses resulting from decedent's death. ***Pecuniary damages include loss of support, loss of services, loss of consortium, but not pain and suffering.*** Creditors have no claim. Contributory negligence of the deceased bars recovery.

c. Recovery for the negligent death of a viable fetus in utero is generally permitted by a wrongful death action.

Question:

Marla Marple was married to Donald Marple. For many years, the Marples tried to have a child but Marla was unable to get pregnant. Her family physician, Dr. Dork, had advised Marla that she was infertile and it was impossible for her to become pregnant. After missing her period for three months and experiencing other symptoms of pregnancy, Marla consulted with Dr. Dork. Without administering a pregnancy test, Dr. Dork examined Marla and concluded that she had the flu. He prescribed Tetracycline, an antibiotic drug, which Marla took for two weeks.

After discontinuing the Tetracycline, Marla continued to experience nausea, fatigue and other symptoms of pregnancy. She then consulted Dr. Blancard, another physician, who administered a pregnancy test which revealed that Marla was in fact four months pregnant. Thereafter, she gave birth to a child named Milton. When Milton developed teeth, they were black and discolored. At the age of twelve, Milton learned that the black discoloration of his teeth resulted from the Tetracycline that Marla took during her pregnancy.

If Milton asserts a claim against Dr. Dork based on malpractice in not administering a pregnancy test to Marla and prescribing Tetracycline, judgment for whom?

(A) Dr. Dork, because an unborn child does not have legal rights stemming from conduct that occurred before birth.
(B) Dr. Dork, because no duty of care is owed to an unborn child not in existence at the time medical treatment is rendered.
(C) Milton, because a child, if born alive, is permitted to maintain an action for the consequences of prenatal injuries.
(D) Milton, unless Marla was negligent in failing to seek proper prenatal care.

Answer:

(C) As a general rule, a surviving child has a right to recover for tortiously inflicted prenatal injuries. While foreseeability of future injury alone does not establish the existence of a duty owing to an unborn infant by its mother's physicians, it is now beyond dispute that in the case of negligence resulting in prenatal injuries, both the mother and the child in utero may be directly injured and are owed a duty. See *Albala v. City of New York* 429 N.E. 2d 786 (1981). Furthermore, the case of *Highson v. St. Frances Hospital* 459 N.Y. 2d 814 (1983) followed these principles in holding that a cognizable and independent cause of action exists on behalf of the infant in utero, who is born alive, against a physician for prenatal injuries. Since the discoloration of Milton's teeth was proximately caused by Dr. Dork's failure to administer a pregnancy test and prescription of Tetracycline to his pregnant mother, Marla, Milton may successfully maintain a cause of action for malpractice against Dr. Dork. Therefore, choice (C) is correct. Choice (D) is incorrect because even if Marla is contributorily negligent, Doctor Dork would nonetheless remain liable. Choices (A) and (B) are both incorrect as representing the former view before 1946, where recovery was denied on the basis of no duty of care owed to an unborn child.

2. **Survival Statutes**

   a. A survival statute ***preserves the claims of the decedent*** existing at death. Damages for pain and suffering, medical expenses, and lost wages until the time of decedent's death are paid to the estate (not to the beneficiaries) and are subject to claims of creditors.

VIII. STRICT LIABILITY

A. ABNORMALLY DANGEROUS ACTIVITIES

1. **General Principles**

   a. One who carries on an ***abnormally dangerous activity*** is subject to liability for harm to the person, land or chattels of another resulting from the activity, although he has exercised the utmost care to prevent the harm.

   b. This strict liability is limited to the kind of harm, the possibility of which makes the activity abnormally dangerous.

   c. ***An ultrahazardous activity is one which necessarily involves a risk of serious harm that cannot be eliminated no matter how much care is used*** and one which is not a matter of common usage.

   d. A strict liability action requires a prima facie showing that defendant breached an absolute duty to provide safety proximately causing harm to plaintiff's person or property.

B. ANIMALS

1. **Wild Animals**

   a. ***A possessor of a wild animal is subject to strict liability to another for harm done by the animal to the other person's body, land or chattels***, although the possessor has exercised the utmost care to confine the animal, or otherwise prevent it from doing harm.

   b. This liability is limited to harm that results from a dangerous propensity that is characteristic of wild animals of the particular class, or of which the possessor knows or has reason to know.

   c. Without knowledge of a domestic animal's dangerous propensities, an owner is not liable for injuries caused; however, after the first bite, such knowledge is presumed. The ***"one-bite" rule*** thus entitles every dog to one free bite.

2. **Domestic Animals.** One is not strictly liable for injuries caused by a domestic animal (e.g., dogs, cats, horses, mules, cows, and bees) ***unless the defendant has "scienter" or knowledge of the dangerous propensities of the animal.***

3. **Injury to Third Parties**

   a. Licensees and invitees injured by wild or abnormally dangerous domestic animals may recover in strict liability.

   b. ***Trespassers may not generally recover in strict liability for such animal-inflicted injuries.*** They may, however, recover in negligence where the landowner knows of their presence and fails to post warnings.

   Caveat: Strict liability recovery applies even to trespassers ***for injuries inflicted by vicious watchdogs.***

C. DEFENSES

1. **Assumption of Risk.** The ***plaintiff's assumption of risk of harm bars his (or her) recovery in a strict liability action.***

2. **Contributory Negligence.** The ***contributory negligence of the plaintiff is not a defense in a strict liability action.***

   a. **Exception:** The plaintiff's contributory negligence in knowingly and unreasonably subjecting himself to the risk of harm from the activity is a defense to strict liability. This kind of contributory negligence, which consists of voluntarily and unreasonably encountering a known risk, is called either contributory negligence or assumption of risk.

D. PRODUCTS LIABILITY

1. **Strict Liability of Seller of Defective Product**

   a. ***One who sells any product in a defective condition unreasonably dangerous to the user or consumer or to his property is subject to liability for physical harm thereby caused to the ultimate user or consumer, or to his property, if***

      (1) the seller is engaged in the business of selling such a product, and

      (2) it is expected to and does reach the user or consumer without substantial change in the condition in which it is sold.

   b. This rule applies even where

      (1) the seller has exercised all possible care in the preparation and sale of his product, and

(2) the user or consumer has not bought the product from or entered into any contractual relation with the seller.

2. **Application of Strict Liability Rule**

a. **Potential Defendants.**

(1) ***Commercial suppliers at all levels of the distribution chain (i.e., manufacturer, distributor, retailer) as well as commercial lessors, new home developers and sellers of used goods are potential defendants.***

(2) Occasional sellers and those supplying services (i.e., optometrist) cannot be strictly liable, but may be sued in negligence.

Question:

Edison was an inventor who developed many interesting creations. One of his most unique projects was an experimental methanol-powered automobile which took Edison three years to build. Edison proudly showed the auto to his friend, Foyt, who immediately fell in love with it. Foyt offered to buy the car for $25,000. Although Edison initially built the car for his own use, he couldn't resist Foyt's offer and sold him his invention.

Thereafter, Foyt was taking the car for a drive when the brakes suddenly failed. Foyt, who was driving 70 mph in a 40 mph zone, couldn't stop the car and it crashed into another vehicle. Foyt was seriously injured in the accident.

Assuming that the brakes were defective when the car was sold, will Foyt succeed in a strict products liability action against Edison?

(A) Yes, if Edison was in the business of selling his inventions.
(B) Yes, because the car was sold in a defective condition.
(C) No, because Foyt was operating the car at an excessive rate of speed at the time of the accident.
(D) No, because Edison was an inventor who built the car for his own use.

Answer:

(A) In order to be held strictly liable for the sale of defective products, ***the seller must be engaged in the business of selling products for use or consumption***. It therefore applies to any manufacturer, distributor, or retailer of such a product. This rule, however, ***does not apply to the occasional seller of a product***. In this regard, if Edison was in the business of selling his inventions, then he would be held strictly liable. On the other hand, he would not be held liable if on one occasion he sold an invention to a buyer or dealer.

(3) Manufacturers are also strictly liable for defective component parts which are already assembled into the products they sell (although indemnification is generally allowed).

b. **Potential Plaintiffs.**

(1) ***Direct privity between the plaintiff and the seller is not required*** in either strict liability or negligence actions.

(2) ***Users and consumers*** are clearly protected. Thus, the plaintiff need not be the purchaser of the product to recover.

(3) ***The majority trend allows suit by bystanders*** as well (See *MacPherson v. Buick Motors*, 1969).

(4) Strict liability also applies to protect rescuers where defective products threaten injury.

c. **Specific Areas.**

(1) ***Misuse of a product is no defense to strict liability where the misuse is foreseeable.***

(2) ***Failure to warn or give adequate directions involving an unreasonably dangerous product may provide grounds for strict liability*** even where the product is not defective. Use of warnings, however, does not prevent a product from still being unreasonably dangerous.

(3) Courts balance several factors to determine what makes a product unreasonably dangerous. Unavoidably unsafe products, such as knives and certain drugs, are not unreasonably dangerous.

(4) ***Use of disclaimers will not avert liability in strict liability or negligence actions.*** Disclaimers under warranty theory may be valid, but not as to personal injury.

(5) Damages for personal injury and property damage are recoverable.

(6) Defenses to strict products liability are similar to those discussed for strict liability.

Question:

Dantley purchased a new 1989 Comanche pickup from Aquirre Motors, an authorized Plymouth dealership. Two months after buying the vehicle, Plymouth, the manufacturer, notified Aquirre Motors in writing that all 1989 Comanche pickups were being recalled due to a defect in the steering mechanism. After receiving this notification, Aquirre Motors sent a letter to Dantley advising him of the problem and instructing him to bring the pickup to the dealership to have the defect repaired. Dantley read the recall letter but disregarded it. Three weeks later, Dantley loaned his pickup to his brother-in-law, Rodman, who wanted to transport some firewood to his house. When Dantley loaned Rodman the vehicle, he failed to inform him about the steering defect. As Rodman was driving the Comanche along a busy highway, the steering mechanism malfunctioned causing the truck to veer off the road and overturn into a ditch. Rodman was seriously injured in the accident. A subsequent investigation revealed that the accident was directly attributable to the defective steering mechanism that prompted the recall notice.

If Rodman asserts a strict liability action against Aquirre Motors to recover damages for his injuries, Rodman will

(A) recover, unless Rodman should have reasonably discovered the defect before the accident
(B) recover, because the accident was caused by the defective steering mechanism
(C) not recover, because Dantley was aware of the defect and failed to inform Rodman of the problem
(D) not recover, because there is no privity between Rodman and Aquirre Motors

Answer:

(B) Under Restatement of Torts 2d, Section 402A, a manufacturer or supplier of a product is strictly liable for any unreasonably dangerous defective condition existing at the time of sale. In this example, defendant Aquirre Motors, the supplier of the Comanche pickup truck, would generally be liable for the defective steering mechanism just as Plymouth, the manufacturer, would be. Yet a very difficult issue is presented by the fact that a recall letter was sent by defendant Aquirre to Dantley, and Dantley disregarded it. As a general rule, neither a warning notice nor a post-defect warning immunizes a manufacturer from liability. Nevertheless, when full responsibility for control of the situation is found to have shifted to a third party, that third party's failure to prevent harm may be viewed as a superseding cause, thereby cutting off a supplier's liability. While "it is apparently impossible to state any comprehensive rule as to when such a decision will be made," various factors such as degree of danger, magnitude of the risk of harm, the character and position of the third person who is to take the responsibility, his knowledge of the danger and the likelihood that he will or will not exercise proper care, his relation to the plaintiff or to the defendant, lapse of time, and perhaps other considerations are regarded by the court. In the present case, simply sending a recall notice would not, ipso facto, constitute a supervening cause relieving the manufacturer of liability.

3. **Negligence**

a. Commercial suppliers may be liable under a negligence theory for failing to exercise reasonable care in the inspection or sale of a product proximately causing harm to the plaintiff. For defective products, a plaintiff suing in negligence must show the existence of ***the defect and that the defect would have been discoverable upon reasonable inspection***.

b. Standard negligence defenses apply to products liability cases.

4. **Warranty Theories of Recovery Under the UCC**

a. **Express Warranty.** A seller making a representation of fact which is a basis of the bargain (i.e., more than mere "puffing") will be liable on the contract to the plaintiff upon breach of that warranty regardless of fault. Contributory negligence is no defense to an express warranty action. Privity requirements vary by jurisdiction in accordance with UCC 2-318, ranging from the purchaser's immediate family to all foreseeable plaintiffs.

b. **Implied Warranty**

(1) **Warranty of Fitness for a Particular Purpose.** Under this warranty the seller will be liable for goods found unfit for their intended purpose ***where the seller knows the particular purpose for which the goods are required*** and the buyer relies in fact on the seller's skill or judgment in supplying the goods.

(2) **Warranty of Merchantability.** Under this warranty the seller warrants that the goods ***are generally acceptable and generally fit for ordinary purposes***.

Question:

Olds restored old classic cars as a hobby. One such car was a 1955 Corvette Stingray that Olds purchased from a little old lady in Pasadena. Every weekend Olds would work on the Corvette which needed extensive restoration. For many years Olds purchased automobile parts and accessories from Augustine's Auto Supply store.

Olds went to Augustine's to purchase an engine gasket for the Corvette. Olds provided Augustine, the shop owner, with the necessary information and asked whether he had the part in stock. Augustine told Olds he wasn't sure but he would certainly check for him. Augustine went to the storage room and a few minutes later returned with a gasket in his hand. He sold the automotive part to Olds but never made any express warranties.

Olds installed the gasket and then took the Corvette for a test drive. Moments later, the engine "blew up" resulting in extensive damage to the car. A subsequent investigation revealed that Augustine sold Olds the wrong gasket that was suitable for Ford but not Corvette engines.

Olds brings suit against Augustine for breach of warranty. He will most likely

(A) win for breach of implied warranty of merchantability, because Augustine dealt in goods of that particular kind
(B) win for breach of implied warranty of fitness for particular purpose, because of the prior dealings of the parties

(C) lose, because Augustine did not make any express warranties regarding the sale of the gasket
(D) lose, because there is no evidence that the gasket that Augustine sold was flawed or defective

Answer:

(B) Once again, the Multistate tests very subtle fineline distinctions. ***The best way to prepare for the MBE is not by mindlessly reading general outlines but rather by practicing and familiarizing yourself with the 2,000 PMBR simulated Multistate questions!*** This question, for example, is testing ***the distinction between implied warranty of merchantability and implied warranty of fitness for particular practice***. If you think you're able to answer this question correctly simply because you read a Torts outline, good luck. Be advised that Olds' best theory of recovery is for breach of implied warranty of fitness for particular purpose because the seller knew that the engine gasket needed to be ***specifically suitable*** for a 1955 Corvette. Choice (A) is wrong because "merchantable" means that the goods are ***generally acceptable*** and generally fit for ordinary purposes. Here, we are not dealing with purchasing an auto part for a mass produced Toyota SUV but rather a classic 1955 Corvette Stingray.

(3) **In General.**

(a) Warranty liability ***does not apply to services*** (such as repairs, blood transfusions).

(b) Damages for personal injury, property damage, and ***intangible economic loss*** (such as loss of profits) are recoverable.

MBE Exam Tip: On the contrary, intangible economic loss is ***not recoverable*** in strict liability and negligence actions.

(c) Due to privity limitations, only the particular seller (or retailer) is liable, but not distributors or manufacturers.

(d) Disclaimers may serve as valid defenses, where not unconscionable. A warranty of merchantability may be disclaimed either orally or in writing, but only if the word "merchantability" is used.

IX. NUISANCE

A. TYPES OF NUISANCE

1. **Public Nuisance**

a. A public nuisance is ***an unreasonable interference with a right common to the general public.***

b. Circumstances that may sustain a holding that an interference with a public right is unreasonable include the following:

   (1) Whether the conduct ***involves a significant interference with the public health, the public safety, the public peace, the public comfort or the public convenience, or***

   (2) whether the conduct is proscribed by a statute, ordinance or administrative regulation, ***or***

   (3) whether the conduct is of a continuing nature or has produced a permanent or long-lasting effect, and, as the actor knows or has reason to know, has a significant effect upon the public right.

c. In order to recover damages in an individual action for a public nuisance, one must have suffered harm of a kind different from that suffered by other members of the public.

d. In order to maintain a proceeding to enjoin or abate a public nuisance, one must

   (1) have the right to recover damages (*see supra*), ***or***

   (2) have authority as a public official or public agency to represent the state or a political subdivision in the matter, ***or***

   (3) have standing to sue as a representative of the general public, as a citizen in a citizen's action or as a member of a class in a class action.

2. **Private Nuisance**

   a. **Definition.** A private nuisance is ***a thing or activity which substantially and unreasonably interferes with plaintiff's use and enjoyment of her land.***

      (1) **Substantial interference.** The interference with plaintiff's use and enjoyment must be substantial. This means that ***it must be offensive, inconvenient, or annoying to an average person in the community***. Plaintiff cannot by devoting her land to an unusually sensitive use make a nuisance out of conduct which would otherwise be relatively harmless.

      Example: Susan runs a facility for people who need peace and quiet. She strives to create a serene atmosphere for her clients. Karen, her next door neighbor, has five small children who run around and make a lot of noise. If Susan sues Karen for private nuisance, she will not be successful.

      (2) **Unreasonable interference.** The interference must be unreasonable, which means that either:

         (a) The gravity of plaintiff's harm outweighs the utility of defendant's conduct, or

(b) If intentional, the harm caused by defendant's conduct is substantial and the financial burden of compensating for this and other harms does not render unfeasible the continuation of the conduct.

b. **Relation to Trespass.** A trespass is an invasion of plaintiff's interest in the ***exclusive possession*** of land (e.g., an entry of something tangible onto the property). On the other hand, a nuisance is an interference with plaintiff's interest in the ***use and enjoyment of the land***, which does not necessarily require a physical intrusion.

Example: Amanda is a writer. Every day, she tries to get work done in the morning. If her neighbor, Callie, calls her every morning, this will not be a private nuisance. However, if Callie calls her fifteen times a morning after Amanda has asked her not to, this may be a private nuisance.

c. **Who Can Recover for Private Nuisance**

(1) For a private nuisance there is liability only to those who have property rights and alleges in respect to the use and enjoyment of the land affected, including private

(a) possessors of the land,

(b) owners of easements and profits in the land, and

(c) owners of non-possessory estates in the land that are detrimentally affected by interferences with its use and enjoyment.

d. **Elements of liability**

(1) One is subject to liability for a private nuisance if, but only if, his conduct is a legal cause of an invasion of another's interest in the private use and enjoyment of land, and the invasion is either

(a) intentional and unreasonable, ***or***

(b) unintentional and otherwise actionable under the rules controlling liability for ***negligent or reckless conduct.***

Examination Tip: Often the key determination on an examination question is to evaluate the reasonableness or unreasonableness of the defendant's conduct. This analysis involves weighing the gravity of the harm done to the plaintiff against the utility of the defendant's activity. Unlike in trespass, the court will balance several factors: compliance with applicable zoning ordinances; priority of occupation; the frequency and extent of the interference, applied objectively to normal persons; and the utility and social value of defendant's activity is important where injunctive relief or a damages award for permanent nuisance is being considered.

Multistate Nuance Chart:

TRESPASS ON LAND	NUISANCE
1. One who ***(1) intentionally, (2) negligently or (3) recklessly enters land in the possession of another*** or causes a thing or a third person to do so is subject to liability;	1. ***Substantial and unreasonable interference with one's use and enjoyment of the land;*** basis of nuisance may be intentional, negligent or absolute;
2. Consists of intrusions upon, beneath, and above the surface of the earth;	2. Consists of interference with (1) physical condition of the land (such as by vibrations or blasting which damages a house, the destruction of crops, flooding or the pollution of a stream); or it may consist of (2) a distrubance of the comfort or convenience of the occupant (such as by unpleasant odors, smoke, dust, loud noise, excessive light or even repeated telephone calls).
3. Incidental intrusions which cause no harm to the land as well as intrusions made under a mistaken belief of law or fact, nevertheless, subject the actor to liability.	

B. DEFENSES

1. Contributory Negligence

a. When a nuisance results from negligent conduct of the defendant, the contributory negligence of the plaintiff is a defense to the same extent as in other actions founded on negligence.

b. When the harm is intentional or the result of recklessness, contributory negligence is not a defense.

c. When the nuisance results from an abnormally dangerous condition or activity, contributory negligence is a defense only if the plaintiff has voluntarily and unreasonably subjected himself to the risk of harm.

2. Assumption of Risk

a. In an action for a nuisance, the plaintiff's assumption of risk is a defense to the same extent as in other tort actions.

3. Coming to the Nuisance

a. The fact that ***the plaintiff has acquired or improved his land after a nuisance will not by itself bar his action, but it is a factor to be considered in determining whether the nuisance is actionable.***

4. **Compliance With Statute**

   a. A relevant and persuasive, but not absolute, defense to nuisance arises upon evidence that defendant's conduct was consistent with applicable administrative regulations (i.e., zoning ordinance, pollution control regulation).

C. REMEDIES

1. **Damages.** For a private or a public nuisance, the usual remedy is damages.

2. **Injunctive Relief.** Where ***the legal remedy (i.e., money damages) is inadequate or unavailable, courts may grant injunctive relief***. The legal remedy may be deemed to be inadequate for a number of reasons (e.g., the nuisance is a continuing wrong or the nuisance is the kind that will cause irreparable harm). In determining whether an injunction will be granted, the court will undertake to ***balance the equities***, namely taking into account the (a) relative economic hardship to the parties from granting or denying the injunction, and (b) the public interest in continuing defendant's activity.

   Examination Tip: Keep in mind that a court may require the defendant to pay damages but deny injunctive relief.

3. **Abatement by Self-Help**

   a. **Abatement of Private Nuisance.** One has the privilege to enter upon defendant's land and personally abate the nuisance after notice to defendant and her refusal to act. The privilege extends to the use of all reasonable action which is necessary to terminate the nuisance, even to the destruction of valuable property, where the damage done is not greatly disproportionate to the threatened harm. But it does not extend to unnecessary or unreasonable damage, and there will be liability for any excess.

      Example: It may not be justifiable, for instance, to destroy a house merely because it is used for prostitution.

   b. **Abatement of Public Nuisance.** One who has suffered some unique damage has a similar privilege to abate a public nuisance by self-help. However, a public nuisance may be abated by a private individual only when it causes or threatens special damage to himself apart from that to the general public, and then only to the extent necessary to protect his own interests.

X. MISREPRESENTATION

A. INTENTIONAL MISREPRESENTATION (FRAUD, DECEIT)

1. **General Rule:** In order to establish ***a prima facie case of intentional misrepresentation, fraud or deceit, a plaintiff must prove six elements:***

   a. The defendant's ***false representation;***

   b. ***Scienter*** (knowledge that the representation is false);

c. An ***intent to induce plaintiff to act*** (or refrain from acting) in reliance upon the false representation;

d. ***Causation;***

e. ***Justifiable reliance*** by plaintiff upon the misrepresentation;

f. ***Damages*** (e.g. pecuniary loss).

2. ***Liability for Nondisclosure.*** As a general rule, there ***is no duty to disclose a material fact or opinion*** to another person. Consequently, a failure to disclose material facts or information will not generally satisfy the first element of this tort action. There are, however, ***four exceptions:***

a. **Fiduciary relationship.** Fiduciary or confidential relations carry with them the duty to make disclosure of all material facts.

(1) Examples:

(a) Executor-beneficiary

(b) Majority-minority stockholder

(c) Bank-depositor

(d) Principal-agent

(e) Family members or old friends

Question:

Agnes was employed as a bank teller at the Bowery Savings Bank. One morning Deke, a customer, entered the bank to make a deposit. As Deke handed the deposit to Agnes, she saw that he had a misprinted $5 bill in his possession. Agnes knew that the $5 bill, which had President Lincoln's picture upside down, was worth $500 to bill collectors. Agnes then asked Deke if he would like to exchange "that old $5 bill for a new bill." Deke accepted Agnes' offer and handed her the misprinted bill for a new one. One week later, Deke learned that the $5 bill which he gave Agnes was valued at $500.

If Deke asserts a claim against Agnes for deceit, will he prevail?

(A) Yes, because Deke was the true owner of the misprinted bill, and therefore he was entitled to the benefit of the bargain.
(B) Yes, because Agnes did not disclose the true value of the misprinted bill.
(C) No, because Agnes made no false representation of fact.
(D) No, because Deke was not justified in relying on Agnes' offer.

Answer:

(B) Since a bank or lending institution owes a fiduciary duty to its customers, Agnes will be liable for failing to disclose the true value of the misprinted bill. Choice (B) is therefore correct.

b. **Active Concealment Actionable.** Where a person actively conceals a material fact, he is under a duty to disclose this fact, and failure to do so constitutes an actionable basis for deceit.

Example: Sidney, a car salesman, turns back the mileage odometer on an automobile. He has concealed a material fact (the actual mileage of the automobile).

c. **Incomplete Statements.** If the defendant does speak, he must disclose enough information to prevent his words from being ***misleading***.

There is fraud in the following situations:

(1) A statement that discloses that property has been rented that does not disclose that such rental is illegal.

(2) Statement as to the income of a business that fails to disclose the pendency of a bankruptcy proceeding.

(3) Statement disclosing the existence of one graveyard on premises without disclosing another.

d. **New Information.** A person who has made a statement and subsequently acquires new information which makes it untrue or misleading, must disclose such information to anyone whom he knows to be still acting on the basis of the original statement. In other words, ***half of the truth may amount to a lie, if it is understood to be the whole.***

Example: Susan enters into a deal to sell her business to Rachel. After they have reached an agreement but before they have closed the deal, Susan's profits seriously decline. Susan has a duty to report the changed financial conditions to Rachel.

e. Many jurisdictions have modified the common law to create obligations to speak in certain contexts.

XI. DEFAMATION

A. FORMS OF DEFAMATORY COMMUNICATIONS

1. **Libel and Slander Distinguished**

a. **Libel definition.** Libel consists of the publication of defamatory matter by ***written or printed words***, by its embodiment in physical form or by any other form of communication that has the potentially harmful qualities characteristic of written or printed words.

b. **Slander definition.** Slander consists of the publication of defamatory matter by ***spoken words***, transitory gestures or by any form of communication other than those constituting libel.

(1) The area of dissemination, the deliberate and premeditated character of its publication and the persistence of the defamation are factors to be considered in determining whether a publication is a libel rather than a slander.

c. **Defamatory language injuring one's reputation.** ***A defamatory statement is "of or concerning" the plaintiff*** where it holds him up to scorn or ridicule in the eyes of a substantial number of respectable people in the community.

(1) The court determines what is defamatory.

(2) The jury determines if the material was so understood.

d. Where a statement is defamatory only upon a showing of ***extrinsic facts***, the plaintiff must plead and (1) prove ***inducement***; (2) establish defamatory meaning by innuendo; and (3) show that he himself was the intended plaintiff by ***colloquium***.

2. **Liability Without Proof of Special Harm - Libel**

a. **Special harm generally not required.** One who falsely publishes matter defamatory of another in such a manner as to make the publication a libel is subject to liability to the other although no special harm results from the publication. In such cases, ***damage to reputation is presumed.***

b. **Exception where special harm is required.** One exception exists to the general rule that libel is actionable without proof of special damages: ***where extrinsic facts are required to establish defamatory meaning (i.e., libel per quod)***, special damages are required, unless the libel falls within one of the four categories (see below) of slander *per se*.

3. **Liability Without Proof of Special Harm - Slander *per se***

a. ***Aside from the four categories of slander per se, proof of special damages is generally required in slander actions.***

b. One who publishes matter defamatory to another in such a manner as to make the publication a slander is subject to liability to the other although no special harm results if the publication imputes to the other

(1) ***a criminal offense,*** *or*

(2) ***a loathsome disease,*** *or*

(3) ***matter incompatible with his business, trade, profession, or office,*** *or*

(4) ***serious sexual misconduct***

4. **Publication**

   a. **Definition.** Defamatory matter is published where it is intentionally or negligently communicated to ***one other than the person defamed.***

   b. One who intentionally and unreasonably fails to remove defamatory matter that he knows to be exhibited (1) on land or (2) on chattels in his possession or (3) on chattels or land under his control is subject to liability for its continued publication.

   c. Publication to ***any third party who reasonably understands*** is sufficient.

   d. ***Each repetition of a defamatory statement constitutes a publication*** and may be actionable. Copies of the same commercial publication (i.e., newspaper) are viewed as a single publication.

   e. One who repeats, or republishes, a defamatory statement is liable to the same extent as the "primary" publisher. Furthermore, the liability of the "primary" publisher may increase where republication is either intended by him or is reasonably foreseeable. Those who disseminate material containing defamatory statements (i.e., "secondary" publishers such as newspaper and magazine vendors) are subject to liability only if they knew or should have known of defamatory material.

5. **Defamation of Private Person**

   a. One who publishes a false and defamatory communication concerning a private person, or concerning a public official or public figure in relation to a purely private matter not affecting his conduct, fitness or role in his public capacity, is subject to liability if, but only if, he

      (1) ***knows that the statement is false and that it defames the other, and***

      (2) ***acts in reckless disregard of these matters, or***

      (3) ***acts negligently in failing to ascertain them.***

   b. Note that ***private persons can prevail in defamation actions merely upon proof of negligence*** by the defendant; however, in this situation, the *Gertz v. Welch* case requires that damages may not be presumed and that the plaintiff must prove ***actual injury*** (loss of reputation, humiliation, mental anguish and suffering, as well as out-of-pocket loss). However, where private persons can establish malice (i.e., knowing falsity or reckless disregard of the truth) special damages - representing pecuniary loss - will be presumed.

6. **Defamation of Public Officials or Public Figures (Malice Standard)**

   a. One who publishes a false and defamatory communication concerning a public figure or public official (relating to his official conduct) ***is subject to liability if he has knowledge that the statement was false or acts in reckless disregard as to its truth or falsity.***

b. **Public figure – definition.** A public figure is one who voluntarily injects himself into the public eye or who has achieved such pervasive fame or notoriety that he is known to the general public.

c. *New York Times v. Sullivan* held that the First and Fourteenth Amendments apply to defamation actions regarding the official conduct of public official plaintiffs, and in these cases proof of "malice" is required.

d. The "malice" standard clearly provides media defendants with wide latitude in which to exercise First Amendment rights of free speech and press.

B. DEFENSES TO ACTIONS FOR DEFAMATION - ABSOLUTE PRIVILEGES

1. **True Statements.** One who publishes a statement of fact is not subject to liability for defamation ***if the statement is true.***

2. **Statements in the Course of Judicial Proceedings.** All participants in judicial proceedings (e.g., the judge, jurors, attorneys and witnesses) have an ***absolute privilege*** to publish defamatory matters concerning another, if it has some relation to the proceeding.

3. **Statements in the Course of Legislative Proceedings.** Legislators (including federal, state and local officers) and witnesses in legislative proceedings have ***an absolute privilege*** to publish defamatory matter concerning another.

   Note: To be absolutely privileged, statements made in judicial proceedings must bear some relation to the proceeding. No such requirement exists for ***legislative*** proceedings.

4. **Husband and Wife.** A husband or a wife is ***absolutely privileged*** to publish to the other spouse defamatory matter concerning a third person.

5. **"Equal Time" Broadcasts.** Material which is required to be published by radio or television stations, or newspapers (i.e., editorials and rebuttals, printed public notices) is absolutely privileged.

C. DEFENSES TO ACTIONS FOR DEFAMATION - CONDITIONAL PRIVILEGES

1. **Statements in the Defendant's Interest**

   a. An occasion makes a publication ***conditionally privileged if the circumstances induce a correct or reasonable belief that***

      (1) there is information that affects a sufficiently ***important interest of the publisher,*** and

      (2) the recipient's knowledge of the defamatory matter will be of service in the lawful protection of the interest.

   b. ***Examples:*** book reviews, movie critiques, statements by a parole board.

2. **Statements in the Interest of Third Persons**

   a. An occasion makes a publication ***conditionally privileged if the circumstances induce a correct or reasonable belief that***

      (1) there is information that affects a sufficiently ***important interest of the recipient or a third person,*** and

      (2) the recipient is one to whom the publisher is under a legal duty to publish the defamatory matter or is a person to whom its publication is otherwise within the generally accepted standards of decent conduct.

   b. In determining whether a publication is within generally accepted standards of decent conduct it is an important factor that

      (1) the publication is made in response to a request rather than volunteered by the publisher or

      (2) a family or other relationship exists between the parties.

   c. **Examples:** statement by former employer to prospective employer, reports made by credit bureaus as to a customer's credit rating.

   d. **Example:** Duncan was employed for seven years with ABC Company. After being terminated, he sought employment with XYZ Company. XYZ contacted ABC and asked for a job recommendation. The president of ABC stated, "If I were you, I wouldn't hire Duncan ... he's a thief." As long as the speaker reasonably believed the information to be true, there is a qualified privilege to act in the interest of others. Thus, ABC would not be liable for defamation.

3. **Statements in the Public Interest**

   a. An occasion makes a publication ***conditionally privileged if the circumstances induce a correct or reasonable belief that***

      (1) there is information that affects a sufficiently ***important public interest***, and

      (2) the public interest requires the communication of the defamatory matter to the public officer or a private citizen who is authorized or privileged to take action if the defamatory matter is true.

   b. **Examples:** reports of public hearings, statements made to police officers identifying suspected criminals.

D. ABUSE OF PRIVILEGE

1. **General Principle**

   a. One who publishes defamatory matter concerning another upon an occasion giving rise to a conditional privilege is ***subject to liability*** to the other if he abuses the privilege.

2. **Excessive Publication**

   a. One who, upon an occasion giving rise to a conditional privilege for the publication of defamatory matter to a particular person or persons, knowingly publishes the matter to a person to whom its publication is not otherwise privileged, abuses the privilege unless he reasonably believes that the publication is a proper means of communicating the defamatory matter to the person to whom its publication is privileged.

   b. Whereas the defendant has the burden of proving the existence of a privilege, the plaintiff has the burden to prove a qualified privilege has been lost through excessive publication or malice.

XII. INVASION OF THE RIGHT OF PRIVACY

A. FORMS OF INVASION

1. **Intrusion upon Seclusion**

   a. One who ***intentionally intrudes, physically or otherwise, upon the solitude or seclusion of another*** or his private affairs or concerns, is subject to liability to the other for invasion of his privacy, if the intrusion would be highly offensive to a reasonable person.

   b. Unlike all other forms of privacy, no publication is required in an intrusion upon seclusion action.

   Example: Surveillance of plaintiff in public as well as private places, photographs taken in private (not public) areas, examining plaintiff's personal effects or files, eavesdropping.

   Example: Sara, a movie star, is in her home getting dressed one morning when she spots a photographer outside her window. He has taken photos of Sara as she was getting dressed. Sara will have a cause of action against the photographer for intrusion upon seclusion and invasion of privacy in addition to any other torts that may have occurred.

   Example: Gregory stalks Cindy by following her everywhere. One night, while she sleeps, he goes through her bureau drawers. Cindy will have a cause of action against Gregory for invasion of privacy.

2. **Appropriation of Name or Likeness**

   a. One who ***appropriates to his own use or benefit the name or likeness of another*** is subject to liability to the other for invasion of his privacy.

   b. This tort requires the use of plaintiff's name or picture in connection with the promotion or advertisement of a product or service for ***commercial advantage***.

Example: Jonathan wishes to advertise a weight loss product. Without asking her permission, Jonathan puts Calista Flockhart's photo in an ad for the product. Flockhart will have a cause of action against Jonathan.

3. **Publicity Given to Private Life**

    a. One who gives publicity to a ***matter concerning the private life of another*** is subject to liability to the other for invasion of his privacy, if the matter publicized is of a kind that

    (1) ***would be highly offensive to a reasonable person, and***

    (2) ***is not of legitimate concern to the public.***

    b. Liability may attach ***even if the statement or publication is true.***

    c. Public disclosure of private facts ***is not actionable where the publication is newsworthy.*** This broad defense can apply to pictures published in newspapers as well as magazine articles on former celebrities and public figures. Private matters contained in public records are absolutely privileged.

    Example: John Carter, a highly respected Washington lawyer, is HIV-positive. Only a few family members know of his condition. In an effort to bring HIV-positive individuals to the public's attention, his brother sends an email to all of John's colleagues revealing his HIV-status. John will have a cause of action against his brother.

4. **Publicity Placing Person in False Light**

    a. One who gives publicity to a matter concerning another that ***places the other before the public in a false light*** is subject to liability to the other for invasion of his privacy, if

    (1) the false light in which the other was placed ***would be highly offensive to a reasonable person, and***

    (2) ***there is publicity.***

    b. False light privacy is akin to defamation in that the publicity, to be actionable, must be highly offensive and false. Where a plaintiff cannot sufficiently prove that material is sufficiently defamatory, false light privacy is the proper "fallback" tort.

    Example: Helen is angry with her former boyfriend, Craig. To get back at him, she posts signs all over Craig's neighborhood stating, "CRAIG is really a woman!" Helen has personal knowledge that Craig is a man. Craig will have a cause of action against Helen for invasion of privacy.

    c. *Time v. Hill* established that, where matter is published in the public interest, recovery for publicity placing plaintiff in a false light is only actionable upon proof of ***malice***. Thus, the *New York Times v. Sullivan* standard for malice was held to apply to the tort of invasion of privacy.

Example: Kendra does not want her state Senator, Carla, to be reelected. She publishes an article in her local paper stating that Carla has donated some of her campaign fund to terrorist causes. Kendra knows that this statement is a lie. Even if Kendra's motive in making the statement was to protect the public from Carla's poor leadership, Carla will have a cause of action against Kendra.

5. **Remedies**

   a. Proof of special damages is not required in privacy actions.

   b. Injunctions are generally available in cases of intrusion upon seclusion.

6. **Defenses**

   a. Defamation defenses of absolute and qualified privilege are applicable to privacy actions based on public disclosure of private facts and false light.

   b. Consent is a valid defense. Mistake as to consent is not a valid defense.

   c. ***Truth is no defense.***

XIII. MISUSE OF LEGAL PROCEDURE

A. MALICIOUS PROSECUTION

1. **Elements of a Cause of Action**

   a. A private person who initiates or procures the institution of criminal proceedings against another who is not guilty of the offense charged ***is subject to liability for malicious prosecution if***

      (1) ***he initiates or procures the proceedings without probable cause*** and primarily for a purpose other than that of bringing an offender to justice, ***and***

      (2) ***the proceedings have terminated in favor of the accused.***

      Example: Helen is still angry with her former boyfriend, Craig. Helen is a district attorney. She has Craig arrested on suspicion of being a terrorist. Craig is not a terrorist, and Helen knows this fact. A judge eventually dismisses the prosecution. Craig will have a cause of action against Helen for malicious prosecution.

2. **Damages**

   a. When a plaintiff establishes the essential elements of a cause of action for malicious prosecution, she is entitled to recover damages for

   (1) the ***harm to her reputation*** resulting from the accusation brought against her, and

   (2) the ***emotional distress*** resulting from the bringing of the proceedings.

B. WRONGFUL USE OF CIVIL PROCEEDINGS

1. General Principle

a. One who takes an active part in the initiation, continuation or procurement of civil proceedings against another ***is subject to liability to the other for wrongful civil proceedings if***

(1) ***he acts without basis and primarily for a purpose other than that of securing the proper adjudication of the claim*** on which the proceedings are based, ***and***

(2) except when they are ex parte, the proceedings have terminated in favor of the person against whom they are brought.

Example: Amy dislikes her new neighbor, Jason. To try to get him to move out of the neighborhood, Amy sues Jason for private nuisance, alleging that his music is too loud. Amy knows that Jason rarely plays his music so that it can be heard outside of his home and always turns it down if asked. When the court hears the evidence against Jason, it dismisses the case. Jason has a cause of action against Amy for wrongful use of civil proceedings.

C. ABUSE OF PROCESS

1. General Principle

a. One who uses a legal process, whether criminal or civil, against another ***primarily to accomplish a purpose for which it is not designed***, is subject to liability to the other for harm caused by the abuse of process.

XIV. ECONOMIC RELATIONS

A. INJURIOUS FALSEHOOD (TRADE LIBEL)

1. **In General.** Injurious falsehood or "trade libel" applies to statements that are injurious to plaintiff's business or products (hence the term "slander of goods"). It does not, however, apply to pecuniary loss inflicted by interference with the plaintiff's personal reputation already covered in defamation.

a. **Distinguishing between disparagement and defamation.** If the statement made charges the plaintiff with personal misconduct, or imputes to him reprehensible characteristics, it is regarded as libel or slander. On the other hand, if the aspersions reflect only upon the quality of what he has to sell, or the character of his business as such, it is disparagement.

Example: On CBS This Morning, Bryant Gumbel insults Monica Lewinsky's new line of handbags, calling them "made of pigskin." Sales of the bags (which are not made of pigskin) noticeably diminish, and Monica is forced to declare bankruptcy. Monica may have a cause of action against Bryant for trade libel if they are not made of pigskin.

b. **Proof of special damages.** The plaintiff must always plead and prove as an essential part of his cause of action means ***special damages*** (i.e., a ***pecuniary loss***).

c. **Damages.** Plaintiffs may not recover for personal elements of damage such as mental suffering.

d. **Elements:**

(1) Publication

(2) Derogatory statement

(3) Relating to plaintiff's title to his property, or its quality, or to his business

(4) Causing interference with his relations with others to his disadvantage

B. INTERFERENCE WITH CONTRACTUAL RELATIONS

1. **In General.** The main type of interference with economic relations that has been marked out by the courts, and regarded as a separate tort, is referred to as ***inducing breach*** of ***contract*** or ***interference with contract***.

2. **Nature of Original Contract.** Virtually any type of contract may be the basis for this type of tort action. The contract must (1) be in force and effect; (2) be legal; and (3) not be opposed to public policy.

   a. **Exception:** For reasons that have not been very clearly stated, ***contracts to marry*** have received special treatment, and almost without exception the courts have refused to hold that it is a tort to induce the parties to break them.

3. **Manner of Interference.** In order to be held liable for interference with a contract, the defendant must be shown to have ***caused the interference***. It is not enough that he merely has reaped the advantages of the broken contract after the contracting party has withdrawn from it.

   Example: Kristen calls Jeffrey, who she knows to be involved in a contract with Jameson. Kristen promises Jeffrey that she will go on a date with him if he breaks the contract with Jameson. Unbeknownst to Jeffrey, Kristen plans to have her company take over Jeffrey's business with Jameson once Jameson breaks the contract. If Jeffrey does breach as a result of Kristen's bribe, Kristen will be liable for interference with a contract.

   a. **Preventing performance.** There have also been many decisions in which the action has been allowed where the defendant has merely ***prevented the performance*** of a contract, or has made the performance more difficult and onerous.

   Example: Donald Defendant prevents Peter Promisor from supplying Paul Plaintiff with goods by calling an illegal strike among his workmen. Donald will be liable for interference with contract.

4. **Intent.** Interference with contract is almost entirely an ***intentional tort***. Liability has not been extended to the various forms of negligence by which performance of a contract may be prevented or rendered more burdensome.

5. **Damages**

    a. **At law.** Where the damages suffered can be compensated with money, then an action at law is appropriate.

        (1) If substantial loss has occurred, one line of cases tends to adopt the contract measure of damages, limiting recovery to those damages that were within the contemplation of the parties when the original contract was made.

        (2) Another line of cases, however, apply a tort measure but limit the damages to those which are sufficiently "proximate," with some analogy to the rules of negligence.

    b. **Equity.** Since the remedy at law is often inadequate because the damages suffered cannot be compensated with money (or cannot be estimated with any accuracy), interference with contract is commonly a ground for the jurisdiction of equity. Plaintiffs have frequently sought ***injunctive relief*** in such situations.

C. INTERFERENCE WITH PROSPECTIVE ADVANTAGE

1. **Basis.** This tort protects the probable "expectancy" interests (of ***future*** contractual relations) of a party, such as (1) the prospect of obtaining employment or (2) the opportunity of obtaining customers.

    Example: Nancy really wants to get a job as an associate at a large Washington law firm. From a friend of hers at the firm, Nancy learns that her main competition for the job is Mark. Concerned that Mark will beat her out for the job, Nancy starts a rumor that Mark is unreliable and lied about being admitted to the Maryland bar. If her lies prevent Mark from getting the job, he will have a cause of action against her for interference with prospective advantage.

    a. **Non-commercial transactions.** Although earlier cases held that recovery would be denied for interference with an expected gift or legacy under a will, modern decisions have expanded this tort action to protect such non-commercial expectancies.

        (1) **Equitable relief.** In such cases, courts of equity have granted relief by imposing a ***constructive trust***.

        (2) **Tortious conduct requirement.** It should be noted, however, that all such cases (e.g., suppression of a will or fraudulently inducing testator to make a will or prospective gift) whether in a tort action or under a constructive trust have involved conduct tortious in itself, such as ***fraud, duress*** or ***defamation***.

2. **Motive or purpose.** As with intent to interfere, with the usual basis of this action turns upon the defendant's ***motive*** or ***purpose***. Although earlier decisions required

so-called "malice," modern decisions hold a defendant liable where his conduct is unlawful in itself (e.g., involves violence, intimidation, defamation, injurious falsehood, fraud, etc.) or is malevolent, such as evincing a desire to do harm to the plaintiff for its own sake.

a. **Prima facie.** Proof of the intentional interference and resulting damage establishes what the courts have called a "prima facie tort," and casting upon the defendant the burden of avoiding liability by showing that his conduct was privileged.

   (1) **Competition.** The most common defense centers around the privilege of competition. In sum, it is no tort to beat a business rival to prospective customers. Thus, in the absence of prohibition by statute, illegitimate means or other unlawful conduct, a defendant seeking to increase his own business may cut rates or prices, allow discounts or enter into secret negotiations behind the plaintiff's back, refuse to deal with him or threaten to discharge employees who do.

1. Strict Liability — Defective Products
2. Liability Limited to Suppliers
3. Ultrahazardous Activities
4. Distinction between Battery and Infliction of Mental Distress
5. Battery
6. Battery
7. Battery — Transferred Intent
8. Battery — Offensive Conduct
9. Battery — Intent
10. Battery — Harmful or Offensive Contact
11. Trespassing Animals — Strict Liability
12. Battery — Offensive Contact
13. Battery
14. Trespass — Physical Invasion of Property
15. Battery — Intent/Assault — Intent
16. Battery — Intent/Assault — Intent
17. Negligence — Unforeseeable Plaintiff
18. Negligence per se — Violation of Statute
19. Intentional Infliction of Emotional Distress
20. False Imprisonment — Intent to Confine
21. Private Nuisance — Trespass Distinguished
22. Invasion of the Right of Privacy
23. Defamation/Infliction of Mental Distress
24. Proximate Cause– “Unforeseeable Plaintiff”
25. Self–Defense
26. Negligence — “Attractive Nuisance” Doctrine
27. “Emotional Distress” — Liability to Family Members

28. Battery/Trespass
29. Deceit
30. Trespass
31. Intentional Infliction of Mental Distress
32. Rescue Doctrine — Attempted Suicide Situation
33. Assault — Arrest Without a Warrant
34. False Arrest/False Imprisonment
35. Trespass — Privilege of Private Necessity
36. Trespass — Liability for Damages
37. Defense of Consent — Excessive Use of Force
38. Battery — Consent Defense
39. Negligence — Strict Liability
40. Defamation
41. Products Liability — Restatement 2d, §402A
42. Products Liability — Strict (Assumption of Risk)
43. Trespass — Reckless Entry
44. Trespass — Intentional Entry
45. Products Liability — Implied Warranty of Fitness
46. Products Liability — Normal Use
47. Negligent Manufacturing/Emotional Distress
48. Products Liability
49. Negligence — Breach of Duty of Care
50. Products Liability — Restatement 2d, §402A
51. Negligence — Retailer's Duty in Sale of Auto
52. Products Liability — Defenses
53. Strict Liability for Trespassing Animals
54. Strict Liability for Dangerous Animals

55. Negligence — Duty of Care of Common Carrier
56. Airline's Responsibility for Intentional Torts of Passenger(s)
57. Joint Tortfeasors Acting in Concert
58. Defective Products — Strict Liability
59. Modified Comparative Negligence
60. Duty of Care Owed to Invitees
61. Strict Liability — Acts of God
62. Intentional or Reckless Infliction of Emotional Distress
63. Strict Liability — Defenses
64. Strict Liability — Breach of Implied Warranty
65. Apportionment of Damages
66. Last Clear Chance Doctrine — Inapplicable in Comparative Negligence Jurisdictions
67. Negligence — Foreseeable Intervening Force
68. Negligence — Actual Loss or Damage Required
69. Public Invitee
70. Licensee
71. Contribution Among Joint Tortfeasors
72. Strict Liability — Defective Products
73. Negligence — Failure to Warn of Dangerous Conditions
74. Rescue Doctrine
75. Airplanes — Basis of Liability Under Modern View
76. Superseding Cause — Unforeseeable Intervening Cause
77. Parent Not Vicariously Liable for Tortious Conduct of Child
78. Strict Liability — Defective Products
79. Strict (Products) Liability — Extends to Sellers Only
80. Negligence — Failure to Inspect
81. Breach of Express Warranty

82. Intentional Torts — Emergency Defense
83. Negligence — Basis of Liability
84. Negligence — Basis of Liability
85. Parents — Contributory Negligence
86. Comparative Negligence — Apportionment Statute
87. Comparative Negligence — Apportionment Statute
88. Last Clear Chance Doctrine
89. Duty of Care Owed to Licensees/Invitees
90. Licensee — Duty to Warn of Dangerous Conditions
91. Intentional Infliction of Mental Distress
92. False Imprisonment
93. Negligence — Captain of the Ship Doctrine
94. Invitees — Duty of Possessor of Land
95. Negligence — Burden of Proof
96. Negligence/Strict Liability Distinction
97. Proximate Cause/Cause in Fact
98. "Unforeseeable Plaintiff" — J. Andrews' View
99. Negligence/Duty of Care of Innkeeper
100. Invasion of Right to Privacy
101. Infliction of Emotional Distress
102. Misrepresentation
103. Nuisance
104. Invasion of Right to Privacy
105. Unforeseeable Intervening Force
106. Cause in Fact/Legal Cause
107. Proximate Cause — Foreseeable Intervening Force
108. Negligence — "Attractive Nuisance" Doctrine

109. Negligence — “Attractive Nuisance” Doctrine
110. Negligence — “Attractive Nuisance” Doctrine
111. Nuisance — Remedies Available
112. Directed Verdicts — Negligence Action
113. Pre-Natal Injuries
114. Battery — Substantial Certainty Test
115. Res Ipsa Loquitur
116. Conversion/Negligence
117. Rescue Doctrine
118. Trespass — Elements
119. Trespasser — Liability of Possessor of Land
120. Invitee — Duty of Occupier to Inspect
121. Products Liability — Strict Liability for Misrepresentation
122. Vicarious Liability — *Respondeat Superior* Doctrine
123. *Respondeat Superior* Doctrine
124. Indemnification
125. Trespass — Liability for Property Damage in Emergency
126. Products Liability
127. Assault — Apprehension of Fear
128. Infliction of Mental Distress — Liability to Third Persons
129. Common Carrier — Special Duty of Care
130. Battery — Transferred Intent
131. Assault — Intent to Frighten
132. Battery — Offensive Conduct
133. Defamation — Private Figure
134. Infliction of Mental Distress
135. False Imprisonment

136. Causation Substantial Factor Test
137. Negligence — Superseding Cause
138. False Imprisonment — Intentional Act Requirement
139. Duty of Independent Contractor
140. False Imprisonment — Shopkeeper's Privilege
141. Joint Venture — Elements
142. Vicarious Liability
143. False Imprisonment/Assault
144. Trespasser — Duty of Care Owed
145. Trespasser — Duty of Landowner
146. Sovereign Immunity — "Proprietary" Functions
147. Negligence — Burden of Proof
148. "Rescue Doctrine"
149. Negligence — Joint Venture
150. Conversion — Bailee Exceeding Authorized Use of Chattel Property
151. *Res Ipsa Loquitur*
152. Negligence — Apportionment of Damages
153. Private Nuisance — Definition
154. Invasion of Right of Privacy — Explanation
155. Libel or Slander — Requirement of Communication/Publication
156. Strict Liability — Wild Animals
157. Nuisance — Requirement of Possession
158. Libel or Slander — Damages
159. Slander — Requirement of Actual Damage
160. Libel — Qualified Privilege
161. Contributory Negligence
162. Fire — Basis of Liability

163. Nuisance — Resulting from Defendant's Negligent Conduct

164. Qualified Privilege — Warning Employee of Employee's Past Misconduct

165. Defendant Negligent While Acting in an Emergency

166. Gratuitous Bailment — Duty of Care Owed to Bailee

167. Slander — "Public Interest" Privilege

168. Special Standard of Care — Tradesmen

169. False Imprisonment

170. Causation — Substantial Factor Test

171. Deceit — Nondisclosure

172. Duty of Care — Lessor of Land

173. Invasion of Privacy — Requirement of Malice

174. Defamation — Requirement of Malice

175. Libel *per se* — Damages Presumed

Questions 1–2 are based on the following fact situation.

Tresh purchased a new Buick Riviera convertible from Cummings Motors. After driving the car 2,000 miles, Tresh sold it to Boyer. Boyer loaned the auto to his friend, Ford. As Ford was operating the vehicle within the posted speed limit, the brakes suddenly failed. Unable to stop the car, Ford struck a taxi which was being driven by York. The colliding cars ended up on the sidewalk, injuring Cerv, a pedestrian. The collision was due solely to the defective brakes on Boyer's car.

1. If Cerv asserts a strict liability action against Cummings Motors, the car dealer will most likely be

   (A) liable, if the car was defective when it was sold to Tresh
   (B) liable, if Cummings failed to make a reasonable inspection of the car before selling it to Tresh
   (C) not liable, because Cerv was not the purchaser of the car
   (D) not liable, if Cerv had been exercising reasonable care, he could have avoided the accident

2. If Cerv asserts a strict liability action against Tresh, the plaintiff will most likely

   (A) prevail, if Tresh failed to make a reasonable inspection of the car before selling it to Boyer
   (B) prevail, if the brakes were defective when Tresh sold the car to Boyer
   (C) not prevail, because Tresh was not engaged in the business of selling automobiles
   (D) not prevail, because Ford's operation of the vehicle was an independent, intervening cause of Cerv's injuries

Question 3 is based on the following fact situation.

Zeke was employed as a night security guard by Hercules Chemical Company (hereinafter referred to as Hercules) at its Wilmington warehouse. In the warehouse Hercules stored a multitude of flammable chemicals and explosives that were used to supply various industrial and national defense firms. Hercules used the most modern methods available in the storing and packaging of its materials.

One humid evening in late August a powerful electrical storm was illuminating the skies around Wilmington. A bolt of lightning hit the warehouse setting off an explosion which seriously injured Zeke. Assume worker's compensation laws do not apply.

3. If Zeke asserts a claim against Hercules, he will most likely

   (A) prevail, because the accident occurred while Zeke was acting within the scope of employment
   (B) prevail, because Hercules would be strictly liable
   (C) not prevail, because the explosion occurred in an unforeseeable manner
   (D) not prevail, because Zeke assumed the risk by working at the warehouse

Question 4 is based on the following fact situation.

Juan Marichal, an outstanding pitcher for the San Francisco Giants and Boston Red Sox, had just been voted into Baseball's Hall of Fame. At his induction in Cooperstown, New York (the site of the Hall of Fame), Marichal was presented a plaque and received various other awards during the ceremony. Following the awards presentation, Marichal then gave a speech thanking everyone for his induction. The ceremony was attended by hundreds of baseball fans, officials of both the National and American Leagues, all of the major news media and various other former baseball players. After making his speech, Marichal left the podium and walked back to his chair a few feet away. As he was about to sit down, Johnny Rosebud, a former Los Angeles Dodger player who was seated behind Marichal, pulled Juan's chair from under him. Marichal fell to the floor. Although he was not injured, Marichal was deeply humiliated by the incident.

4. If Marichal asserts a claim against Rosebud, his best theory of recovery is for

   (A) assault
   (B) battery
   (C) intentional infliction of mental distress
   (D) invasion of right to privacy

Question 5 is based on the following fact situation.

Juan and Carlos were students at Culver Junior High School. In Latin class one morning, Carlos decided to play a practical joke on Juan. As Juan was about to sit down at his desk, Carlos pulled Juan's chair from behind. As a result, Juan fell on his rump. Although he was not injured, Juan was embarrassed by the incident.

5. If Juan asserts a claim against Carlos, Juan will most likely

   (A) recover for assault
   (B) recover for battery
   (C) recover for intentional infliction of mental distress
   (D) recover for trespass to chattels

Questions 6–7 are based on the following fact situation.

Ernie "Happy" Johnson and Jerry "Boss Man" Money were sanitation workers who were employed by the Ingelmarsh City Sanitation Department. They were old friends who also played baseball together in the Ingelmarsh City Recreational League. Both were members of "The Dumpsters," which was a team sponsored by the Ingelmarsh Sanitation Department.

One night after a tough loss to "The Bullets," a team composed of Ingelmarsh police officers, Ernie and Jerry decided to stop at Pat's Steakhouse for a late snack. As they drove up the "drive-thru" line, Rita Ritz, one of Pat's waitresses, informed them through the intercom system that the restaurant was closing and no further orders would be accepted. She told Ernie and Jerry that the last car to be served was the one directly in front of theirs. Ernie, who was driving the car, became angry and yelled into the intercom machine, "Listen, babe, 'Boss Man' and me is hungry. We want two cheese-steak sandwiches, a large fries and two cokes." Rita retorted, "I'm terribly sorry, but we cannot accept your order."

Shortly thereafter, Rita handed the food order to the passengers in the car (immediately in front of Ernie's). When the latter saw Rita servicing them, he turned to Jerry and said, "Man, I thought it would be fun having a cheese-steak tonight. Now I'm feeling sad and no one makes 'Happy' sad." Ernie then drove his automobile up to the service window and shouted at Rita, "You can't do this to us." When Rita laughed, Johnson suddenly reached into the car's glove compartment and pulled out a gun. He aimed at Rita and fired the weapon intending to hit her. The bullet missed Rita but hit Paul West, a customer, wounding him in the head.

6. In an action by West against Johnson for battery, plaintiff will be

   (A) successful, since Johnson intended to shoot Rita
   (B) successful, because the shooting created a "clear and present danger" that someone else could suffer serious bodily injury
   (C) successful, because there was a "substantial certainty" that West would be hit by the bullet
   (D) unsuccessful, because Johnson did not intend to shoot West

7. In an action by West against Ritz to recover for his personal injuries, plaintiff will most likely

   (A) recover, because Ritz's conduct was the proximate cause of West's injuries
   (B) recover, because it was foreseeable that Ritz's conduct would result in West being shot
   (C) not recover, because Johnson's shooting was not a foreseeable act of Ritz's conduct
   (D) not recover, because Johnson intended to shoot Ritz, not West

Questions 8–9 are based on the following fact situation.

Granny Goodridge, aged 72, was riding in an elevator at the World Trade Center in New York City. When the elevator stopped on the fifth floor, Smokey Robinson entered the elevator smoking a "Panama Red" cigar. Smokey was standing in front of Granny on the elevator when Granny tapped him on the shoulder. When Smokey turned around, Granny pointed to the "No Smoking" sign and said, "Excuse me, sir, would you mind putting that cigar out?" Smokey indignantly responded by inhaling heavily on his cigar, and then blowing a big puff of smoke into Granny's face. When the elevator stopped on the next floor, Smokey then departed.

8. If Smokey institutes a civil action against Granny, Smokey will most likely:

   (A) recover for battery
   (B) recover for negligence
   (C) not recover, since Smokey's prohibited conduct would preclude recovery as a matter of law
   (D) not recover, since Granny's conduct was customary and reasonably necessary under the circumstances

9. In a civil suit brought by Granny against Smokey, the plaintiff will have actions for:

   (A) Assault since no actual body contact occurred.
   (B) Battery even though no actual physical harm occurred.
   (C) Intentional infliction of emotional distress because of the extreme and outrageous nature of Smokey's conduct.
   (D) No cause of action.

Question 10 is based on the following fact situation.

Under a contract between Ball Sports Company and the Chris Evers Manufacturing Company, the latter manufactured a tennis ball practice machine with the name "Ball Sports" engraved on each machine. Ball Sports distributed the machines through wholesalers and retailers of sporting goods. In its sales brochure and advertising materials, Ball Sports referred to the machines as "Ball Sports Co. Tennis Machines."

Thomas Jefferson High School purchased one of the machines from Ball Sports Co. Members of the "Tee Jay" Tennis Team regularly utilized the Ball Sports tennis machine during the course of their daily practice sessions.

One afternoon, Patsy, first substitute on the varsity tennis squad, was playing a practice match with her teammate Ellen, who had recently "nosed out" Patsy for a starting position on the team. After their match, while Ellen was bending over to retrieve her stray balls, Patsy turned on the tennis machine, aimed its "stroke" arm at Ellen, and it began releasing tennis balls at her. Patsy then tried to turn the machine off. However, the machine starter mechanism became stuck in the "on" position and continued to release tennis balls. When Ellen turned around, the next ball struck her on the side of her face.

10. In a civil suit brought by Ellen against Patsy, the plaintiff is likely to recover for

    (A) assault only
    (B) battery only
    (C) assault and battery
    (D) false imprisonment

Question 11 is based on the following fact situation.

Joseph and Herb were brothers. This summer nothing very exciting was happening in their lives because they were stuck inside their rented house studying for the bar exam. One day during their thirty-minute lunch break, however, they heard on the radio that the circus was in town and that an elephant had escaped. Since their house was located in the hills less than a mile north of the more densely populated circus grounds they decided to look out the back window. Only a few minutes later, to their sheer delight and surprise, there was the elephant walking right through the yard. Unfortunately the elephant trampled their landlord's flower garden before its exit from the property. Herb called the circus and his quick action led to the eventual capture of the animal. Carol, the landlord, was upset at the prospect of having to replace the fine flower bed for which she had paid gardeners so much money to maintain. Joseph, remembering what he'd just learned in torts about wild animals, reassured Carol that she could recover if she sued the circus.

11. If Carol brings suit against the circus to recover damages to her flower garden caused by the elephant, she will most likely

    (A) recover, because the circus is strictly liable for the elephant's trespass
    (B) recover, but the circus is subject to liability for trespass only
    (C) recover, but the circus is subject to liability for nuisance only
    (D) recover, only if the circus failed to exercise the utmost care to confine the elephant or otherwise prevent it from escaping

Question 12 is based on the following fact situation.

Rider entered a subway car at the 42nd Street station. Since all of the seats were occupied, Rider stood in the subway car and grabbed a pole to secure his balance. As the subway car was proceeding crosstown, Rider glanced at a voluptuous blonde girl standing next to him. Suddenly, the subway car made an unexpected stop. Rider momentarily lost his balance, and grabbed the blonde girl around the waist (to avoid falling). Once Rider regained his balance, he removed his hands from the girl's waist and grasped the pole again.

12. In a civil action instituted by the blonde girl against Rider, he will most likely be found

    (A) liable for battery
    (B) liable, if Rider mistakenly believed that the girl consented to the contact
    (C) not liable, since Rider's conduct was socially acceptable under the circumstances
    (D) not liable, since the girl was not harmed by the contact

Question 13 is based on the following fact situation.

Dugan, a heroin addict, needed money to support his drug habit. Armed with a pistol, Dugan decided to rob Conroy's Convenience Store. Dugan entered the store, pointed the pistol at a cashier and demanded money. The cashier reached into the cash register and nervously handed Dugan $500. He then fled and ran down the street.

When he left the store, Dugan was pursued by Silver, a security guard employed by Conroy's, who witnessed the latter stages of the robbery. As he chased Dugan, Silver pulled out his own service revolver and shouted, "I've got a gun ... stop or you're dead meat." Dugan paid no heed to this warning and continued running. Silver then fired his revolver at Dugan. The bullet missed Dugan but shattered the living room window in Howser's home. Howser, who heard the gunshot sound and saw her window break, became extremely frightened. Believing that someone was trying to kill her, Howser went into shock from fear, and, as a result, required hospitalization. Silver had been instructed by Conroy's never to fire his gun at a fleeing suspect.

13. If Howser asserts a claim against Conroy's, will the plaintiff prevail?

    (A) No, because Silver acted contrary to Conroy's instructions.
    (B) No, unless Silver was negligent in shooting at Dugan.
    (C) Yes, if any of the shattered glass touched Howser.
    (D) Yes, because a firearm is an inherently dangerous instrumentality.

Questions 14–16 are based on the following fact situation.

While relaxing at poolside one Sunday afternoon, Dickie was struck by a golf ball driven by Marty, a 14-year-old boy, who was playing the 9th hole at the Pike Creek Golf Club. The fairway for the 9th hole was 65 feet wide and 437 yards long, with a dogleg in an easternly direction. Between the fairway and Dickie's property was a "rough" containing brush and low lying trees.

As Marty was approaching the green, he hit a towering shot which deflected off a tree, struck Dickie, bounced off his head and knocked a straw hat off of his girlfriend Patty's head. Although the ball did not strike Patty herself, she became startled and fell from her beach chair, thus breaking her arm.

At trial plaintiff offered uncontested evidence that golf balls from the Club's links regularly traversed onto his property two to three times a day.

14. Which of the following statements is most accurate regarding the liability of the Pike Creek Golf Club/Marty for trespass?

    (A) Defendants are not liable, since they did not intentionally cause the golf ball(s) to traverse onto the plaintiff's property.
    (B) Defendants would remain liable for the unpermitted intrusion of the golf ball(s) onto the plaintiff's property.
    (C) Since the plaintiff should have reasonably anticipated that living next to a golf course would result in stray golf balls landing on his property, defendants would not be held liable.
    (D) Since the golf balls did not substantially interfere with the plaintiff's use and enjoyment of his land, defendants would not be held liable.

15. Which of the following would be Dickie's proper cause of action against Marty as a result of the golf ball hitting his head?

    (A) assault but not battery
    (B) battery but not assault
    (C) assault and battery
    (D) neither assault nor battery, since Marty did not intentionally cause Dickie to be struck

16. If Patty initiates a suit against Marty to recover damages for her broken arm, Patty will

    (A) recover for assault only
    (B) recover for battery only
    (C) recover for assault and battery
    (D) not recover

Questions 17–18 are based on the following fact situation.

Laurie was the owner of Twilight Park, an old dilapidated stadium, that was located on the outskirts of San Francisco. Twilight Park, which was built in 1932, had been the home stadium for the San Francisco Baby Bulls, a professional baseball team for thirty years. However, in 1962 the Baby Bulls franchise moved to Denver and was re-named the Horned Frogs. Since 1962, Twilight Park was left unattended and had deteriorated to such an extent that the walls were in danger of collapsing.

On Friday January 13, 1987, an earthquake struck San Francisco and the outlying Bay area. The earthquake, which registered a 6.9 on the Richter scale, effectuated considerable damage in the city of San Francisco and caused Twilight Stadium to collapse. As the stadium crumbled to the ground, a large section of the press box fell on top of a car that was parked nearby. The auto was crushed, causing its gas tank to rupture. As a result, a large quantity of gasoline spilled along the street and flowed downhill. The gasoline collected in front of Cepeda's home, which was located about a mile from the stadium.

Two hours after the earthquake struck, Kirkland was walking in front of Cepeda's home smoking a cigarette. When he discarded his lighted cigarette butt in the street, the gasoline exploded. The explosion blew the windows out of Cepeda's home. Cepeda, who was sitting in the living room watching television, was struck by the flying glass and injured.

The damaged automobile was owned by Wagner. At the time Twilight Park collapsed, Wagner's vehicle had been illegally parked in front of a fire hydrant. This was in violation of a local ordinance which prohibited parking within 50 feet of a fire hydrant.

17. If Cepeda asserts a claim for his injuries against Laurie, which of the following is Laurie's best defense?

    (A) The earthquake was an act of God.
    (B) Laurie's negligence, if any, merely created a passive condition and was not the active cause of Cepeda's injury.
    (C) Laurie could not reasonably have been expected to foresee injury to a person in Cepeda's position.
    (D) Kirkland's act of discarding the lighted cigarette in the street, which sparked the explosion, was the proximate cause of Cepeda's injury.

18. If Cepeda asserts a claim for his injuries against Wagner, which of the following, if true, is Wagner's best defense?

    (A) The earthquake was an act of God.
    (B) Wagner parked in front of the fire hydrant after hearing a radio broadcast warning motorists of the earthquake.
    (C) The purpose of the parking ordinance was to facilitate access to the hydrant by fire trucks, not to protect against such accidents.
    (D) Cepeda would not have been injured if Laurie had properly maintained Twilight Park.

Questions 19–22 are based on the following fact situation.

Tillie Taylor was a member of the Children of the Earth, a quasireligious communal organization dedicated to the spiritual rebirth of its members, who devote their lives to the preservation of the natural environment. During one of the organization's group encounter sessions, Raj Reel, the group's leader, who knew that Tillie was a paranoid schizophrenic, accused Tillie of being disloyal to her fellow "brothers and sisters." Tillie's "disloyalty" stemmed from the fact that she had telephoned her parents in disobedience of the group's Code of Conduct. Ostracized from the group, Tillie fled the commune and returned to her parents' home that evening.

After unsuccessfully trying to lure Tillie back to the group's movement, Raj decided to employ a "last ditch" effort to secure her return. Raj leased a billboard located across the street from Tillie's house. Raj had the billboard printed to read:

"TILLIE, THE CHILDREN OF THE EARTH
COMMAND YOUR RETURN"

As a result of the billboard, Tillie suffered severe nervous shock and refused to leave her house, fearful that she would be abducted by her former "brothers and sisters."

19. As a result of the billboard, Tillie brings suit against Raj and the Children of the Earth for intentional infliction of emotional distress. Tillie will most likely

    (A) succeed, since the billboard was the cause in fact of Tillie's mental suffering
    (B) succeed, since Raj was aware of Tillie's mental instability
    (C) not succeed, since the billboard itself would not be outrageous in character
    (D) not succeed, since the group only intended to secure Tillie's return

20. In an action for false imprisonment against Raj and the Children of the Earth, Tillie will most probably

    (A) recover, since Tillie's confinement resulted from the implicit threat on the billboard
    (B) not recover, since Tillie's confinement was self-imposed
    (C) not recover, since the defendants did not intend for her to be confined in her home
    (D) not recover, since Tillie was under no constraint to remain in her house

21. In determining whether the billboard would constitute a private nuisance, the court will consider which of the following factor(s) to be relevant in evaluating its decision?

    I. To determine whether the billboard is an invasion of the plaintiffs interest in the exclusive possession of his land.
    II. The right of defendants to make reasonable use of the billboard as weighed against plaintiff's personal discomfort.
    III. The interference of the billboard with the property interests of the individual in the community.

    (A) I
    (B) II and III
    (C) I and II
    (D) I, II and III

22. If Tillie asserts a claim based on invasion of privacy against Raj and the Children of the Earth for the billboard, the most likely outcome is that Tillie will

    (A) prevail, since the billboard intruded upon her seclusion and solitude
    (B) prevail, if Tillie were able to prove malice on the defendants' part
    (C) not prevail, since the billboard was not objectionable as defamatory
    (D) not prevail, since Tillie's own membership in the group privileged them to seek her return

Question 23 is based on the following fact situation.

Sidney and Sofie Schlept are husband and wife. They live in Milwaukee, Wisconsin where Sidney works as a shipping clerk at the Schlitz Brewery. One afternoon Sidney and Sofie were shopping at K-Mart when Sofie saw a dress featured from the Jacqueline Smith clothing line that she especially liked. Sofie, who weighed over 300 pounds, was unable to find a size large enough to fit her. She then saw Regina Rude, a store clerk, and asked if the store carried the dress in her size. Rude looked at Sofie and said, "You look like a hippopotamus and I'm sorry but we don't carry this dress in the hippo size." Sofie became very upset and hurried out of the store.

23. If Sofie asserts a tort action against K-Mart based upon Regina's actions, Sofie will

    (A) win, if the statement was overheard by another customer
    (B) win, because Regina's conduct was extreme and outrageous
    (C) lose, if Regina was merely stating an opinion
    (D) lose, if Sofie only suffered hurt feelings

Questions 24–25 are based on the following fact situation.

Lloyd and Benson were old friends who enjoyed hunting together. One weekend Lloyd and Benson went on a quail hunting expedition in a remote wilderness area deep in the Wasatch Mountains of northeastern Utah. They were hunting in a very desolate area surrounded by mountainous terrain which was located at least fifty miles from any habitation. With hunting rifles in hand, they were ambling around but no game was visible. After a rather uneventful morning with nothing to shoot at, Lloyd suddenly spotted a Utah condor, a large nearly extinct vulture. The condor was of an endangered species; and to shoot one in Utah was a criminal offense.

Unable to resist the temptation, Lloyd took a shot at the condor. The bullet missed the vulture but struck Bush, a state forest ranger, who was hiding in a secluded area, watching a trail frequented by drug smugglers. The bullet hit Bush in the eye and permanently blinded him. Neither Lloyd nor Benson were aware of Bush's presence.

24. If Bush asserts a claim against Lloyd to recover damages for his injury, Bush will

    (A) prevail, because his injury was caused by Lloyd's unlawful act
    (B) prevail, because firearms are dangerous instrumentalities imposing strict liability on the user
    (C) not prevail, because Lloyd had no reason to anticipate the presence of another person in such a remote area
    (D) not prevail, because Lloyd did not intend to shoot Bush

25. Assume for the purposes of this question only that when Lloyd fired his rifle at the condor, Bush heard the gunshot and thought that he was being attacked by drug smugglers. Bush fired his gun towards Lloyd's muzzle flash. The bullet from Bush's gun struck Lloyd and seriously wounded him. If Lloyd asserts a claim against Bush to recover damages for his injury, Lloyd will

    (A) prevail, because Lloyd had no intent to harm Bush, and therefore Bush was not entitled to fire back
    (B) prevail, because Bush was not entitled to use force likely to cause death or serious bodily injury to enforce gaming laws
    (C) not prevail, because Bush reasonably believed that he was under attack
    (D) not prevail, because Bush was not the original aggressor

Questions 26–27 are based on the following fact situation.

Alice is sitting on her front porch watching her husband Bruce, who is mowing the lawn. Carl, who hates Bruce but is a friend of Alice's, whose presence is known to him, draws a pistol and threatens to kill Bruce. Alice, who is pregnant, suffers severe emotional distress as a result of the trauma and soon afterwards has a miscarriage.

26. In an action by Alice against Carl for mental anguish resulting in her miscarriage, Alice will

    (A) lose, because Carl did not know that Alice was pregnant
    (B) win, because it is highly probable that Carl's extreme and outrageous conduct would cause emotional distress to Alice
    (C) lose, because Carl's actions were directed against Bruce, so only Bruce may recover for emotional distress
    (D) win, because she is Bruce's wife

27. Same facts as in question 26, except that Alice is in the living room and does not see the confrontation between her husband and Carl. After Carl threatens Bruce, Bruce runs into the house and tells Alice what occurred. As a result, Alice suffers a miscarriage. In an action by Alice against Carl for mental anguish resulting in miscarriage, Alice will

    (A) recover, even though she was not present when the threat was made
    (B) recover, because she would not have suffered the miscarriage had it not been for Carl's threat on her husband's life
    (C) not recover, since she was not present when the threat was made
    (D) not recover, because "transferred intent" is non-applicable in mental distress cases

Question 28 is based on the following fact situation.

Clyde Cooch, a prominent judge, lived next door to Lester Biggs. Recently Judge Cooch had sentenced Lester Biggs' son, Dopey, to six months in prison on a narcotics charge. One afternoon while judge Cooch was mowing his lawn, Lester decided to avenge his son's conviction. Lester set up his water sprinkler behind some shrubbery separating their adjoining properties. As the judge was mowing his lawn and came within reach of the water sprinkler, Lester turned on the sprinkling device, and doused the judge with water.

28. Judge Cooch would be able to recover against Lester for which of the following tort(s):

    (A) negligence
    (B) battery
    (C) assault and battery
    (D) battery and trespass

Question 29 is based on the following fact situation.

Each year the Avondale Boy's Club sponsors a "Baseball Card Bonanza". During the three-day event, collectors of baseball cards gather, exchanging and swapping old cards. Marcus and Allen, twelve-year-old youngsters at the bonanza, were looking at each other's cards when they were approached by Cliff, a thirty-two year old collector. Cliff asked the boys if he could look through their baseball cards. The boys nodded affirmatively.

As Cliff was flipping through Marcus' cards, he found a 1948 Tops picture card of Branch Rickey, the former owner of the Brooklyn Dodgers. Cliff, who knew the card was worth over $500, offered Marcus 50 cents for the card. Marcus thought the card had very little value because he knew that Rickey was not a major league baseball player. So Marcus accepted the 50 cents and gave Cliff Rickey's baseball card. The next day Marcus found out that the baseball card was worth $600.

29. If Marcus asserts a claim against Cliff for deceit, will Marcus prevail?

    (A) Yes, because Cliff did not disclose the true value of the card.
    (B) Yes, because Marcus was the true owner of the card and was entitled to the benefit of the bargain.
    (C) No, because Cliff made no false representations of fact.
    (D) No, because Marcus was not justified in relying on Cliff's offer.

Question 30 is based on the following fact situation.

On Tuesday, Ruben purchased a new riding lawn mower from Sears. The next day, Ruben was cutting the grass in his backyard with the mower when it started to rain. Ruben stopped the mower and turned off the motor switch. He went inside his house and decided to wait until the rain stopped before mowing the rest of the lawn. A few minutes later while Ruben was inside his house, the lawn mower suddenly lurched forward, rolled down a hill and entered onto his neighbor, Gomez's property. The mower cut Gomez's prize rose bushes, destroying them.

It was later determined that the lawn mower's motor switch was defective. Even though Ruben turned the starter switch to the off position, the mower's engine did not shut off. Since the mower was built with a new silent rotary engine, Ruben had no reason to know that it was still running when he went into the house. Ruben would not have been able to discover the defect by any feasible means of inspection.

30. If Gomez asserts a claim against Ruben for trespass, will Gomez prevail?

    (A) Yes, because the lawn mower entered onto Gomez's property.
    (B) Yes, because Ruben is strictly liable for the damage caused by the defective mower.
    (C) No, because Ruben was using the mower for its intended purpose.
    (D) No, because the defective motor switch was not discoverable by reasonable inspection.

Questions 31–32 are based on the following fact situation.

Dickie "Mulehorse" Nixon was the star fullback for Whittier College football team. After missing two practices, Nixon was "dropped" from the team by Archie Cox, the head football coach. Following his dismissal, Nixon met with Cox and asked if he could rejoin the team. Cox told Nixon that he was despised by the other players and under no circumstances could he return to the team. As Nixon was leaving Cox's office very dejected, the coach then said to him, "Hope you decide to transfer, Mulehorse, everybody hates your guts around here".

Later that same evening, Nixon wrote a suicide note in which he stated, "Coach Cox is responsible for my despondency. If I can't play football for Whittier, I don't want to live." After swallowing a bottle of Quaalude barbiturates, Nixon fell unconscious in his dormitory room. Moments later, Pat Checkers, Nixon's roommate, entered the room and saw his limp body on the floor. Checkers read the suicide note and then attempted to administer aid. Failing to revive him, Checkers picked up Nixon and carried him to the college's first aid center. Nixon received prompt medical attention and soon recovered from his drug overdose. Checkers, however, was less fortunate. He suffered a hernia caused by carrying Nixon's 210 pound body across the campus grounds.

31. If Nixon asserts a claim against Cox to recover damages for his injuries, Nixon will most likely

    (A) prevail, if Cox intended to cause him to suffer emotional distress
    (B) prevail, because Cox's remark did in fact cause Nixon to suffer emotional distress
    (C) not prevail, because Nixon's drug overdose resulted from his own voluntary act
    (D) not prevail, unless Cox knew that Nixon was an extremely sensitive person

32. If Checkers asserts a claim against Nixon to recover damages for his injuries, will he prevail?

    (A) No, because Nixon did not intend to harm anyone other than himself.
    (B) No, unless attempted suicide was a criminal offense in the jurisdiction.
    (C) Yes, because Nixon intentionally put himself in a position of peril.
    (D) Yes, because he succeeded in saving Nixon's life.

Questions 33–34 are based on the following fact situation.

On Thursday morning May 14 two plain clothes Riverdale police officers were shot to death while trying to arrest a paraplegic bank robber who had failed to surrender to begin a 20-year prison term.

Following the killings, the Riverside police issued an "all-points-bulletin" for the arrest of Jack Franklin, a 40-year-old Caucasian, height: 6 feet, weight: 150-155 lbs., and who had been paralyzed below the waist from a Riverdale bank robbery (that occurred 16 months earlier).

On Friday May 15 Bill Nelson, a security guard at a local department store, was walking down Main Street in Riverdale when he noticed a tall black man who fit Franklin's description walking with a slight limp. Nelson approached the person (and believing him to be Franklin), pulled a gun and arrested him. Nelson held the man in custody until the police arrived a short time later. The police officer informed Nelson that he had arrested the wrong person. The man had told Nelson that his name was Jones, not Franklin. Jones was humiliated by the false arrest.

33. If Jones asserts a claim for assault against Nelson, he will

(A) succeed, if Jones saw Nelson pointing the gun at him
(B) succeed, if Nelson's mistaken belief was unreasonable
(C) not succeed, because Nelson didn't intend to injure Jones
(D) not succeed, because Jones didn't suffer any injury from Nelson's act

34. If Jones asserts a claim for false imprisonment against Nelson, Jones will

(A) prevail, because he was intentionally detained against his will
(B) prevail, because Nelson unreasonably believed that Jones committed the crime
(C) not prevail, because Jones did not suffer any harm
(D) not prevail, since the period of detention was necessary to establish the detainee's identity

Questions 35–36 are based on the following fact situation.

Al Allen, a retired cattle rancher, was flying his private plane, a Rover 170, from Orlando to Jacksonville in the state of Florida to visit with his daughter and grandchildren. While carefully and skillfully operating his airplane, he suddenly realized that one of his engines was gone. He then was forced to make an emergency landing under the reasonable belief that it was necessary to do so for the protection of himself and his airplane. He landed in Mr. Blossom's orange grove. The landing was rough and caused considerable damage to the orange trees as well as to the airplane.

35. A necessary element in determining if Al is liable for trespass is whether

(A) Al knew that the property belonged to a private person
(B) Al had reasonable grounds to believe that the orange grove belonged to a private person
(C) Al was privileged to enter the land of another under the circumstances
(D) Al knew or should have known that he would have damaged the property

36. If Mr. Blossom brings suit against Al to recover for the damage done to his orange grove, the most likely result is that Blossom will

(A) recover, because Al was a trespasser
(B) recover, even though Al may not be liable for trespass
(C) recover, only if Al was negligent in his entry onto the property
(D) not recover, since Al was privileged to be on the land

Question 37 is based on the following fact situation.

Mohammed is a twenty-six-year-old Iranian graduate student at Culver City College. Byrne, a fellow classmate, knew that Mohammed was a staunch supporter of Ayatollah Khomeini. As they were leaving class one afternoon, Byrne walked beside Mohammed and chanted, "Long live the Shah! Long live the Shah!" Mohammed angrily confronted Byrne and said, "Let's settle this outside in a fist fight." Byrne replied. "You're on."

The two students went outside and "squared off". Byrne threw the first punch and hit Mohammed in the face with his bare fist. Unknown to Byrne, Mohammed placed a set of brass knuckles on his fist and hit Byrne in the face with brass knuckles. The force of the blow broke Byrne's nose. It was later determined that the use of the brass knuckles inflicted exactly the same damage as if Mohammed had hit Byrne with his bare fist.

37. The best argument for rejecting the defense of consent in an action by Byrne for either assault or battery is that

    (A) Mohammed's use of the brass knuckles exceeded consent under the circumstances
    (B) Mohammed was only acting in self defense
    (C) Byrne's insults provoked Mohammed's use of excessive force
    (D) Mohammed's punch would have inflicted the same harm with or without the use of the brass knuckles

Question 38 is based on the following fact situation.

Carlos and Hymie were fourteen year-old eighth graders at Paul Revere Junior High School. They were both members of the school's junior varsity football team. Carlos, who weighed 170 pounds, was stockily built and played center on the football team. Hymie was lanky, weighed about 145 pounds and was the team's quarterback. Carlos and Hymie often engaged in friendly tests of strength, such as arm wrestling and weight lifting contests, to see who was stronger.

One afternoon both youngsters were in the school gymnasium getting ready for football practice. As they were putting on their football uniforms, Carlos turned to Hymie and said, "Hey, weakling, why don't you punch me in the chest with your best shot?" Hymie replied, "No, I'm afraid I might hurt you." Carlos then said, "Are you kidding ... you can't hurt me. C'mon give me your best shot." Carlos stood up, stuck out his muscular chest, and prepared to have Hymie hit him. Hymie proceeded to cock his fist and then punched Carlos in the chest as hard as he could. Immediately thereafter, Carlos slumped to the floor, gasping for air. Realizing that Carlos was seriously hurt, Hymie tried to render assistance but to no avail.

Seconds later Carlos stopped breathing and died. Unknown to either Carlos or Hymie, Carlos had a defective heart and suffered a heart attack resulting from the blow to the chest.

38. In a wrongful death action, Hymie will likely

    (A) be held responsible, because he committed a battery by hitting Carlos in the chest
    (B) be held responsible, because Carlos' consent was ineffective
    (C) not be held responsible, because Carlos' consent was effective
    (D) not be held responsible, unless Hymie delivered the punch with greater strength than Carlos anticipated

Question 39 is based on the following situation.

On October 14, 2004, Dix purchased a new Toyota van from Sheridan Toyota Imports. Two weeks later, Dix was driving to work when the brakes suddenly failed. Dix tried to stop the van for a red light but the brakes failed to operate. As a consequence, Dix drove through the red light and collided with a car driven by lorg.

Subsequently, Iorg asserted a claim against Dix to recover for the injuries she suffered in the accident. At the trial, the only evidence offered by the plaintiff concerning the cause of the accident was the testimony of Polk, an engineering expert. He testified that a manufacturing defect had caused the brakes to suddenly fail.

39. Based on the facts stated above, a motion by Dix to dismiss at the end of Iorg's case should be

    (A) granted, because Iorg presented no evidence that Dix was negligent
    (B) granted, because Iorg was neither the user or consumer of the defective product
    (C) denied, because Dix had a non-delegable duty to maintain the brakes in a safe condition
    (D) denied, because Dix is strictly liable for injuries caused by a manufacturing defect in an auto which he had purchased

Question 40 is based on the following situation.

Woodstock owned Mar Vista, a thirty acre tract, located just outside White Plains in Newton County. After prosperity burst upon White Plains in the late 1990s, Woodstock sub-divided the property into thirty lots and built townhouses on each of the lots. After selling all thirty of the lots, the various homeowners formed the Mar Vista Homeowner's Association (hereinafter referred to as MHA). Thereafter, MHA adopted a Declaration of Covenants which provided, inter alia, that each homeowner was required to pay an annual assessment charge to be used "for the promotion of the health, safety and welfare of residents within the subdivision and for the enhancement of education, social life and community welfare."

In January, 2000, MHA properly and legally assessed each home owner an assessment charge of $750. Charlotte Craig, who owned a townhouse in the subdivision, refused to pay the assessment. Charlotte, a recent widow, was experiencing financial problems and claimed she couldn't afford to pay the $750. As a result, Alfred E. Newman, president of MHA, sent Charlotte the following letter:

> "Article 1 of the Declaration of Covenants requires all homeowners to pay their annual assessment charge on the first day of January for the said year. By failing to make this payment, the MHA shall have the right to collect the amount due by action of law. Your prompt attention to this matter is greatly appreciated."

Three weeks elapsed and Alfred did not receive any response from Charlotte. He then wrote her a second letter which stated:

> "Before instituting legal action, this is MHA's final demand for your $750 assessment charge. It is unfortunate that deadbeats like you ruin our community."

A copy of this letter was mailed to the twenty-eight other residents of Mar Vista. Newman even sent a copy of the letter to the editor of *The Plains Press*, the county newspaper, that had a circulation of 20,000 subscribers. In its next edition, the *Press* published Newman's letter on its editorial page.

40. If Charlotte sues Newman for defamation, she will probably

    (A) not prevail, because Newman was acting to protect a legitimate public interest
    (B) not prevail, unless reasonable persons would regard the statement as a factual assertion and not an expression of opinion
    (C) prevail, because Newman obviously acted with malice by sending the letter to the newspaper
    (D) prevail, because the language of Newman's letter would be highly offensive to reasonable persons

Questions 41–42 are based on the following fact situation.

Aspen, Inc. was the exclusive manufacturer of a very popular snowmobile named "Snow King". On each of the "Snow King" models Aspen installed a speed regulating device which prevented the snowmobiles from exceeding 50 m.p.h. Aspen distributed the snowmobile through wholesalers and retailers across the country. In its sale brochures and advertising materials, Aspen advises all of its distributors against making any modifications on snowmobiles without first conferring with Aspen's staff of engineers.

In the town of Killington, Jean-Claude operated "The Ski and Snow Shop" which was the exclusive retailer of "Snow Kings" in the area. Amid complaints from previous buyers regarding Snow King's speed limitations, Jean-Claude removed the speed regulators from all the Snow King models in stock.

Daredevil purchased one of the Snow Kings from Jean-Claude which had the speed regulator removed. One day Daredevil and his friend, Spacey, were driving the Snow King through a snow covered field, at speeds in excess of 70 m.p.h. As Spacey stood up from his seat to get a better view of a family of reindeer, their snowmobile hit a snowcovered rock. The force of the impact threw Spacey from the Snowmobile, and caused Daredevil to lose control of the Snow King, crashing into a tree. Both Daredevil and Spacey were seriously injured.

41. If Daredevil institutes a strict liability action he will most likely recover against

    (A) Aspen if they were aware of the removal of the speed regulator
    (B) Aspen even though they were unaware of the removal of the speed regulator
    (C) The Ski and Snow Shop only
    (D) Both Aspen and The Ski and Snow Shop

42. In a personal injury action by Spacey, he will most likely

    (A) recover against Aspen and The Ski and Snow Shop for strict liability
    (B) recover against Aspen and The Ski and Snow Shop in negligence
    (C) recover against the Ski and Snow Shop in strict liability unless he assumed the risk by standing up
    (D) not recover against Aspen or The Ski and Snow Shop in strict liability because he was contributorily negligent

Question 43 is based on the following fact situation.

Vic Vicory was an attorney who had an office in Greensboro. After winning a big antitrust case, Vic and a few associates decided to celebrate and have a few drinks at The Rainbow Room, a popular downtown watering hole. After having two gimlets (a cocktail containing vodka and Rose's lime juice), Vic left his friends and drove home.

Vic, who was a bit tipsy, began driving in an erratic and reckless manner. He was traveling at an excessive speed along a residential section of town when he approached a sharp curve in the roadway. Trying to negotiate the turn, Vic lost control of his vehicle and it veered off the road and landed on the front lawn of Edna Edsell's property.

43. If Edna asserts a claim against Vic for trespass, she will most likely

    (A) prevail, because Vic was operating his car recklessly
    (B) prevail, because Vic entered onto her property
    (C) not prevail, unless Vic damaged her land
    (D) not prevail, because he did not intentionally enter onto her property

Question 44 is based on the following fact situation.

Carr owned a beautiful tract of land in the Big Bear mountain range. The property was purchased by Carr and used as a family vacation retreat. About 200 yards of Carr's property bordered along the Big Bear Lake shoreline. Ott lived on a stream that flowed along one boundary of Carr's land and ran into the lake. When Carr acquired ownership of Big Bear tract, he had a channel dredged across his land from the stream to the lake at a point some distance from the mouth of the stream. Ott erroneously believed that the channel was a public waterway. Since the channel served as a convenient shortcut to the lake, Ott made frequent trips across the channel in his fishing boat. In no way did Ott's use of the channel cause any harm or damage to Carr's property.

44. After Carr learned about Ott's use of the channel, he requested that Ott desist further entry onto the waterway. Ott, who until that time was unaware of Carr's ownership claim, agreed. Nonetheless, Carr brought suit against Ott to recover damages for trespass. Judgment for whom?

    (A) Ott, because when he used the channel he believed that it was a public waterway.
    (B) Ott, if he discontinued using the channel after learning of Carr's ownership claim.
    (C) Carr, but recovery is limited to nominal damages for Ott's intentional use of the channel.
    (D) Carr, unless Ott had no other navigable access to the lake.

Questions 45–46 are based on the following fact situation.

Paul Pharmy was a salaried registered pharmacist employed by The Drug Outlet, a drug store. James Hendricks owned and operated the business. Kathy Klepach, a long-time customer of The Drug Outlet, presented a prescription to Paul for the medication Clinoril, which was prescribed by her physician to treat her arthritic condition. Paul was in a rush that day because of a backlog of prescriptions to fill, and he misread Kathy's prescription. He filled her prescription with Clinitest, a caustic substance not for internal use. He labeled the container with the instructions for Clinoril: "Take one tablet twice a day."

Kathy followed the instructions, consumed the Clinitest and suffered severe injuries to her stomach and esophagus.

45. In a strict liability action against Pharmy, his best defense is:

    (A) It was the cashier and not he who personally received the money for the medication.
    (B) He was not a seller of the product upon whom liability may be imposed.
    (C) He exercised reasonable care under the circumstances.
    (D) Neither The Drug Outlet nor Hendricks was the manufacturer upon whom ultimate liability falls.

46. In a negligence action against Pharmy, which of the following facts, if true, would support Pharmy's defense?

    (A) The doctor's handwriting was practically illegible.
    (B) Kathy had taken Clinoril regularly in the past.
    (C) There was poor lighting at the drug counter.
    (D) Clinitest was blue in color, but Clinoril was red.

Question 47 is based on the following situation.

Trent Trover purchased a gallon of non-fat milk from Fireside Market. The milk, which was sold in a plastic container, had been processed and packaged by Guernsey Farms. That evening Trent was preparing dinner and poured himself a glass of milk from the container purchased at Fireside. He then sat down to eat his meal and proceeded to take a mouthful of milk. As he did so, Trent felt something furry lodge in his mouth. He immediately spit out the furry object and saw that it was a dead mouse. Trent suffered severe emotional distress but was not accompanied by any physical illness or injury.

47. If Trent asserts a claim against Guernsey based on negligent manufacturing, he will most likely

    (A) recover, because he suffered severe emotional distress
    (B) recover, under the doctrine of res ipsa loquitur
    (C) not recover, because Guernsey's negligence only caused mental disturbance
    (D) not recover, because Trent's proper cause of action is for intentional infliction of mental distress

Questions 48–49 are based on the following fact situation.

On Friday night, Chase was injured in an automobile accident after his Chevy was sideswiped by an unidentified motorist. Following the accident, Chase was admitted to the Jerri Ford Medical Center where he was treated for his injuries. While at the hospital, Chase was diagnosed as having suffered a broken back and placed in traction. Dr. Demeral, Chase's physician, assembled the traction apparatus and positioned Chase's left leg in an overhead stirrup at a 40 degree angle. Chase, who was in a body cast, was instructed to lie supine in a vertical position on the bed.

On Saturday morning after breakfast, Chase was experiencing a bad case of diarrhea and requested a bed pan from Nurse Needy. She was placing the bed pan under Chase's body when the stirrup, holding his leg, broke. This caused Chase's leg to fall against the metal framing along the side of the bed, fracturing his tibia. The traction apparatus was manufactured by Laid Back. There was no safety latch on the stirrup device to prevent its failing off if not securely fastened in place.

48. If Chase asserts a claim against Laid Back, he will most likely

    (A) prevail, because the stirrup broke while the traction apparatus was in normal use
    (B) prevail, if Laid Back's failure to include a safety latch made the traction apparatus defective
    (C) not prevail, because the traction apparatus was no longer within the control of Laid Back
    (D) not prevail, if Dr. Demeral did not properly attach the stirrup when assembling the traction apparatus

49. If Chase asserts a claim against the Jerri Ford Hospital and Dr. Demeral, he will most likely

    (A) prevail, if the stirrup was not securely fastened
    (B) prevail, unless Chase's injury was caused by a defect in the traction apparatus
    (C) not prevail, if Chase has a valid claim against Laid Back
    (D) not prevail, unless Chase produces evidence that Nurse Needy was negligent when placing the bed pan under his body

Questions 50–52 are based on the following fact situation.

Garp had purchased a new Peugeot station wagon from Santa Monica Import Motors. One evening, Garp, who was an independent research chemist, was transporting in his car a load of foam rubber from his home to his laboratory. On his way, he stopped by the Xenon Corp. to pick up a quantity of highly inflammable petroleum derivatives that he needed in his work. These were sold in ordinary glass gallon jugs.

Shortly after putting the jugs in the back of his car, Garp was driving along a city street when he saw the traffic light facing him turn from green to amber. He sped up, hoping to cross the intersection before the light turned red. However, he quickly realized that he could not do so and applied the brakes, which failed. Garp then swerved to avoid hitting a bus that was crossing the intersection at a right angle to him.

As a result of the swerve, Garp's car rode up on the sidewalk and overturned, pinning Pedro, a pedestrian. Both Garp and Pedro were severely injured. Also, the jugs in the back of the car were broken by the impact and the chemicals spilt out onto the sidewalk. Moments later, Dr. Jay, a physician who saw the accident, ran over to render medical assistance. As he approached Garp's car, however, Dr. Jay slipped on the petroleum and fractured his ankle.

50. If Garp asserts a claim against Santa Monica Import Motors based on strict liability in tort, will the plaintiff prevail?

    (A) Yes, because the brakes failed while Garp was driving his car.
    (B) Yes, if the brakes failed because of a defect present when Garp purchased the car.
    (C) No, if Garp contributed to his own injury by speeding up.
    (D) No, if Santa Monica Import Motors carefully inspected the car before selling it.

51. If Pedro asserts a claim based on negligence against Santa Monica Import Motors and if it is conclusively proven that the brake failure resulted from a manufacturing defect in the car, will Pedro prevail?

    (A) No, because Pedro was not a purchaser or user of the car.
    (B) No, if Garp was negligent in driving onto the sidewalk.
    (C) Yes, because Santa Monica Import Motors placed a defective car into the stream of commerce.
    (D) Yes, if the defect could have been discovered through the exercise of reasonable care by Santa Monica Import Motors.

52. If Dr. Jay asserts a claim against Garp based on strict liability, will the plaintiff prevail?

    (A) Yes, because Garp was engaged in an abnormally dangerous activity by transporting highly inflammable petroleum in his car.
    (B) Yes, because the transportation of inflammable petroleum in glass jugs necessarily involves a high degree of risk of serious harm.
    (C) No, because Dr. Jay assumed the risk by voluntarily acting as a Good Samaritan.
    (D) No, because it was unforeseeable that Dr. Jay's injury would result from the type of harm threatened.

Questions 53–54 are based on the following fact situation.

Spring Lakeshore Associates operated a resort community in the Finger Lake region of New York State. Bob and Barbara Benson purchased one acre of land bordering on Lake Twana from Spring Lakeshore as a cabin site. Shortly thereafter, they erected a two bedroom cabin and also built a fence on their property line. The only access to the Benson's property was over a small bridge which led to an entrance gate.

The property adjacent to the Bensons was owned by Tom and Alice Winslow. The Winslows were the owners of several horses which they allowed to roam about within their fenced enclosure.

When the Bensons arrived at their cabin for a short vacation, they left the entrance gate open and immediately began cleaning up the property. Later, Bob Benson was outside working in the shed, when he noticed one of the Winslows' horses. Bob told his son Billy to get the horse off the property. As Billy neared the horse, he shouted to it, whereupon the horse wheeled and lashed out with his rear hoof, striking the boy in the face. It was later discovered that the horse had apparently broken through the Winslows' fence and had wandered onto the Bensons' property.

53. In a trespass action against the Winslows, the Bensons will most likely

(A) recover, because of the Winslows' negligence in failing to maintain control or supervision over the horse
(B) recover, only if the Winslows knew of the horse's propensity to roam
(C) recover, on the theory of strict liability
(D) not recover, since the owners of domesticated animals are not strictly liable for their trespasses

54. In a personal injury action initiated by the Bensons on behalf of their son Billy, the Winslows will most likely

(A) be held liable, under the theory of strict liability
(B) be held liable, if they knew or had reason to know of the horse's dangerous propensities
(C) not be held liable, since the horse was not within the custody and control of the owners
(D) not be held liable, since the Winslows took adequate precautions in fencing the area where the horses roamed

Questions 55–56 are based on the following situation.

Tippi Tate was a first-class passenger on Repulsive Airlines flight #1273 from Atlanta to Chicago. Tippi, an attractive model, was traveling to Chicago on a modeling assignment. Seated next to Tippi was Billy Martin, a middle age marshmallow salesman, who was returning home after attending a business convention in Atlanta. Tippi, who was extremely exhausted after a long and hectic day, tried to sleep during the flight but was constantly being annoyed by Martin. Once the flight departed, Martin started ordering drinks of scotch and water from Dottie Downer, the stewardess. As he became inebriated, Martin made advances to Tippi who tried to ignore him. When Tippi refused to talk to him, Martin became very abusive and continued to harass Tippi. Although there were many empty seats available in the first-class section, Tippi decided to remain seated next to Martin. Finally, after Dottie had served Martin his tenth drink of scotch, he became belligerent and punched Tippi in the mouth. Tippi's two top teeth were knocked loose and she suffered a cut lip.

55. If Tippi asserts a claim against Repulsive Airlines based on negligence, she will most likely

(A) prevail, because as a first-class passenger the airline owed her a special duty of care
(B) prevail, because the stewardess should have been aware that her conduct caused an unjustifiable risk of harm
(C) not prevail, because the airline is not vicariously liable for the tortious conduct of its passengers
(D) not prevail, because Tippi assumed the risk by not moving to another seat away from Martin

56. If Tippi asserts a claim against Repulsive Airlines based on battery, she will most likely

    (A) prevail, because the stewardess's conduct was reckless
    (B) prevail, because it was foreseeable that Martin would act in such a belligerent manner after becoming intoxicated
    (C) not prevail, unless Martin was an employee or agent of the airline
    (D) not prevail, because an airline is not vicariously liable for the intentional torts of its passengers

Question 57 is based on the following situation.

One Sunday afternoon the Los Angeles Raiders and Denver Broncos were playing a professional football game at Mile High Stadium in Denver. During the game, Flores, a Raiders' fan, went to the men's room to take a leak. There were four other men, including Tripuka, in the restroom when Flores entered. Flores, who was wearing a Raiders cap, was standing at the urinal when Tripuka approached from behind and said, "The Raiders really stink, man." Flores turned around and remarked, "Listen slimeball, you smell worse than the stench from this urinal." Tripuka then punched Flores in the mouth. A fight ensued. During the fracas someone hit Flores over the head with a bottle which caused him to suffer a serious concussion. Flores does not know for certain who struck him with the bottle.

57. If Flores asserts a claim against Tripuka and the other three men (who were in the restroom during the fight) to recover for the head injury, will Flores prevail against Tripuka?

    (A) Yes, because Tripuka was the instigator who struck the first blow that started the fracas.
    (B) Yes, if Tripuka and the other men were acting in concert.
    (C) No, if it is proved that Tripuka did not actually strike Flores with the bottle.
    (D) No, unless there is evidence that Tripuka struck Flores over the head with the bottle.

Question 58 is based on the following fact situation.

Monica purchased a new dishwasher from Sears Appliance Store. This dishwasher had been manufactured by the Electron Company. After the dishwasher had been installed in Monica's home, it functioned properly for the first month. Then it began to make a loud, rattling noise whenever it was in use. Monica called the Sears agent who assured her that it was not uncommon for the dishwasher to make such a noise. Moreover, he indicated that the machine's clamoring sound would eventually disappear with continued use.

One week later after a dinner party, placed her most expensive china set in the dishwasher and turned on the machine. After the dishwasher had been in operation for a few minutes, Monica heard the rattling noise followed by the sound of breaking china. She immediately stopped the machine. Upon looking inside, she saw that a blade from the dishwasher had broken, destroying her entire china set.

58. If Monica asserts a claim for strict liability against Electron Company, will she prevail?

    (A) Yes, because the dishwasher was defective.
    (B) Yes, because she was the purchaser of the dishwasher.
    (C) No, because Monica was not personally injured.
    (D) No, because a reasonably prudent person would have discontinued using the dishwasher after becoming aware of the rattling noise.

Question 59 is based on the following fact situation.

At approximately 3:00 p.m. on December 3, Motorist was speeding down Main Street at the same time that Pedestrian was crossing the street. When Pedestrian started to cross the street, she saw the traffic light was red. She momentarily stopped, thought about waiting until the light turned green, but then decided to cross anyway. As Pedestrian was halfway across the street, Motorist, who was driving 50 m.p.h. in a 25 m.p.h. zone, struck her with his vehicle. Pedestrian suffered a broken pelvis and internal injuries in the accident. While in the hospital, Pedestrian's insurance company paid $10,000 of her medical expenses. Six months later, Pedestrian brought suit against Motorist to recover damages for all her medical expenses. This jurisdiction has a "modified" comparative negligence statute in effect.

59. Suppose a jury returned a special verdict with the following findings: (1) Motorist was 60% negligent in speeding; (2) Pedestrian was 40% at fault in crossing the street against the red light; and (3) Pedestrian suffered damages from the accident totaling $50,000. After the verdict, the court was advised that Pedestrian's insurance company had already paid Pedestrian $10,000. As a result, the court should enter a judgment for Pedestrian in the amount of

    (A) $50,000, because Motorist's negligence was greater than Pedestrian's
    (B) $30,000, the proportion of Pedestrian's damages caused by Motorist's negligence, but the payment of $10,000 in hospital expenses will be disregarded under the collateral source rule
    (C) $20,000, the proportion of Pedestrian's damages caused by her own negligence, but the payment of $10,000 in hospital expenses will be disregarded under the collateral source rule
    (D) $10,000, the proportion of Pedestrian's damages caused by her own negligence, less the $10,000 in hospital expenses already paid by the insurance company

Question 60 is based on the following fact situation.

Liz and her boyfriend, Lucus, were having dinner at the Golden Dragon Chinese restaurant in Chinatown when she excused herself to go to the bathroom. The restaurant was owned and operated by Wong. As Liz was walking past a table where Elliot, another customer, was seated, she slipped and fell on an egg roll that was lying on the floor. When she fell, her head struck a serving tray which was located in the aisle. The fall caused Liz to suffer a severe concussion. Elliot knew that the egg roll was on the floor and, although he could have done so, he did not warn Liz.

60. If Liz asserts a claim against Wong for the injuries she suffered from the fall, she will most likely

(A) recover, because the egg roll on the floor constituted an unsafe condition of the premises
(B) recover, if the egg roll was on the floor for a substantial period of time before the accident
(C) not recover, unless Wong knew that the egg roll was on the floor
(D) not recover, if Elliot was responsible for knocking the egg roll off his table

Question 61 is based on the following fact situation.

Linden Laboratories manufactures nitroglycerin (a heavy oily explosive poisonous liquid used chiefly in making dynamite) at its Union City plant. Late one evening there was an explosion at Linden's plant facility. The force of the explosion caused the ceiling on Youngman's house to collapse, seriously injuring Youngman. The Youngman home was located two blocks away from Linden's plant.

61. Youngman now asserts a tort action against Linden to recover damages caused by the explosion. Which of the following, if established, would furnish Linden with a valid defense?

I. Linden uses extraordinary care in the manufacture and storage of nitroglycerin and was not guilty of any negligence that was causally connected with the explosion.
II. Linden has a contract with the federal government whereby all the nitrogylcerin manufactured at its Union City plant is used in U.S. military weapon systems.
III. The explosion was caused when lightning (an act of God) struck the plant during an electrical storm.

(A) III only
(B) I and II only
(C) II and III only
(D) Neither I, II nor III

Question 62 is based on the following fact situation.

Connie Chung was seven months pregnant and expecting her first child. One afternoon, Connie was in the kitchen of her home preparing a snack when she suddenly heard the loud screeching noise of automobile tires. She immediately looked out her window and saw a car driven by Andy Anderson strike Benny Bing, a nine year-old youngster, who was walking home from school. Anderson was traveling eighty miles per hour when his vehicle went out of control. The car jumped the curb and hit Benny as he was walking along the sidewalk in front of Connie's home. Connie witnessed the incident and saw Bennie hurled 50 feet in the air and land unconscious on her neighbor's front lawn. As a result of her shock from this horrible accident, Connie suffered a miscarriage.

62. If Connie asserts a claim against Anderson, the most relevant issue regarding her right of recovery is

(A) whether a person can recover damages caused by shock unaccompanied by bodily impact
(B) whether a person can recover damages for harm resulting from shock caused solely by another's peril or injury
(C) whether a person can recover damages based on the defendant's breach of a duty owed to another individual
(D) whether it is foreseeable that a person may suffer physical harm caused solely by an injury inflicted on another individual

Questions 63–64 are based on the following fact situation.

Under a contract between Ball Sports Company and the Chris Evers Manufacturing Company, the latter manufactured a tennis ball practice machine with the name "Ball Sports" engraved on each machine. Ball Sports distributed the machines through wholesalers and retailers of sporting goods. In its sales brochure and advertising materials, Ball Sports referred to the machines as "Ball Sports Co. Tennis Machines."

Thomas Jefferson High School purchased one of the machines from Ball Sports Co. Members of the "Tee Jay" Tennis Team regularly utilized the Ball Sports tennis machine during the course of their daily practice sessions.

One afternoon, Patsy, first substitute on the varsity tennis squad, was playing a practice match with her teammate Ellen, who had recently "nosed out" Patsy for a starting position on the team. After their match, while Ellen was bending over to retrieve her stray balls, Patsy turned on the tennis machine, aimed its "stroke" arm at Ellen, and it began releasing tennis balls at her. Patsy then tried to turn the machine off. However, the machine starter mechanism became stuck in the "on" position and continued to release tennis balls. When Ellen turned around, the next ball struck her in the face, breaking her nose.

63. Which of the following parties would be held liable in a strict liability action initiated by Ellen?

    I. Thomas Jefferson High School
    II. Chris Evers Manufacturing Company
    III. Ball Sports Company
    IV. Patsy

    (A) I and IV
    (B) I and III
    (C) II and III
    (D) I, II and III

64. In a strict liability action by Ellen against Ball Sports Company, which of the following defenses, if any, should prevail?

    (A) Patsy's operation of the tennis machine was the legal cause of Ellen's injuries.
    (B) Chris Evers Manufacturing Co., as the manufacturer of the tennis machine, has the sole responsibility for any defects therein.
    (C) Ball Sports Co. would be relieved of liability because of Ellen's unforeseeable misuse.
    (D) No defense.

Question 65 is based on the following fact situation.

While on vacation in Hawaii, John and Andy went scuba diving in the ocean off the island coast of Maui. Each of them was equipped with a spear gun which they planned to use to kill dolphins. As they were swimming both men saw what appeared to be a large fin entangled in a nearby coral reef. Simultaneously, they shot their spear guns at the projecting winglike figure. Unknown to either John or Andy, it was not a fish but another scuba diver whom they shot at. The victim, Randy, was struck and slightly wounded by one of the spears.

65. Randy asserts a claim for damages against John and Andy. At trial, the judge should instruct the jury to rule

    (A) in favor of both defendants if no evidence is presented showing who actually shot the spear that injured Randy
    (B) against both defendants jointly unless one of them proves that he did not shoot the spear that struck Randy
    (C) against each defendant for one-half of the amount of damages because they both acted independently and not jointly
    (D) against each defendant for one-half of the amount of damages because they both shot their spear guns simultaneously

Question 66 is based on the following fact situation.

Driver and Passenger were driving to work in the former's automobile one morning. As they were traveling at a speed of 20 mph (which was within the posted speed limit), Passenger suddenly pointed to an overturned vehicle along the side of the highway and said, "Look at that car upside down." Driver turned to look at the overturned vehicle. As he was looking toward the side of the road, Driver failed to see an abandoned vehicle with a flat tire in the highway about 200 feet in front of his oncoming auto. Seconds later Driver crashed into the rear of the abandoned auto and was injured. The jurisdiction has a relevant comparative negligence statute in effect.

66. If Driver asserts a claim against the owner of the abandoned auto, the most likely result is that Driver will

(A) recover all of his damages, because the defendant created a dangerous condition
(B) recover only a portion of damages, because the abandoned auto was in plain view
(C) recover nothing, because he had the last clear chance to avoid the collision
(D) recover nothing, because Passenger's act was a supervening cause

Questions 67–70 are based on the following fact situation,

O'Keefe owned a two story building in Society Hill which he leased to Brooks. Brooks established a hardware store on the first floor, and equipped the second floor as an apartment in which he lived with his wife and children. The two floors were connected by an outside wooden staircase with a handrail. The staircase was in a dilapidated condition at the time Brooks entered into the leasehold agreement with the realty company. When Brooks took possession of the building on October 1st, he notified O'Keefe about the condition of the staircase and insisted that it be repaired. Although O'Keefe orally promised Brooks that he would remedy the condition, he failed to do so.

Believing that it would help to attract customers, Brooks had a public pay telephone attached to the outside wall of the building. The telephone, which was manufactured by Eastern Electric, is owned and operated by the Diamond Telephone Company.

On Thursday, November 25th, the store was closed for Thanksgiving. Norton, who lived two doors away, walked to the hardware store to use the telephone. He wanted to call his son and daughter-in-law to wish them a Happy Thanksgiving, but his home phone was out of order. Norton picked up the receiver, inserted twenty cents and then, he received an electrical shock. Although Norton was momentarily stunned, he did not suffer any injuries. Unknown to Norton, a telephone repairman, an employee of Diamond, had incorrectly re-wired the telephone the previous day, causing a short circuit in the telephone mechanism.

Later that evening, Brooks and his wife were receiving some friends for a small dinner party. Trixie, one of the guests, arrived at 7:00 P.M. and mounted the stairs to the second floor apartment. When she was half way up the stairway, which had not been repaired, it collapsed, seriously injuring Trixie.

67. If Norton institutes a personal injury action for negligence against the Diamond Telephone Co., he will most likely

    (A) recover, since the telephone repairman's error would constitute the proximate cause of Norton's injuries
    (B) recover, since the telephone repairman's error was a substantial factor in causing Norton's injuries
    (C) recover, under the doctrine of *respondeat superior*
    (D) not recover, since Norton did not sustain any injuries

68. Which of the following would best describe Norton's legal status in his utilization of the telephone?

    (A) licensee
    (B) gratuitous licensee
    (C) public invitee
    (D) business visitor

69. Which of the following would best describe the duty of care owed by Brooks to Trixie?

    (A) no duty of care
    (B) a duty to inspect the premises for unknown dangers and disclose their existence to others
    (C) a duty to warn of any known dangerous condition on the premises
    (D) an absolute duty of care

70. In a negligence action initiated by Trixie to recover for injuries sustained as a result of her fall, she will most likely

    (A) recover against Brooks only, since as a general rule, a lessor of land is not liable to his lessee or to others on the land for physical harm caused by any dangerous condition which existed when the lessee took possession
    (B) recover against O'Keefe only, since a lessor of land is subject to liability for physical harm caused to, his lessee and others upon the land by a condition of disrepair existing before the lessee has taken possession
    (C) recover against O'Keefe only, since under the public use exception a lessor who leases land for a purpose which involves the admission of the public is subject to liability for physical harm caused to such persons by a hazardous condition existing when the lessee takes possession
    (D) recover against Brooks and O'Keefe, since both the lessor and the lessee would be liable to others for their failure to remedy the defective staircase

Question 71 is based on the following fact situation.

Surgeon operated on Patient in an operating room in the Marina General Hospital. Surgeon was assisted by Intern, who was assigned to the operation by the hospital, and Nurse, who was on the staff of the hospital. During Patient's convalescence, he complained of pain not explicable as an ordinary post-operative symptom. On investigation, it turned out that Intern and Nurse, who had worked together in bandaging him, had done so in such a way as to constrict certain blood vessels. The faulty bandaging had caused acute pain and retarded Patient's recovery.

After Patient's eventual recovery, he sued Intern, claiming $20,000 in damages. Before the case went to trial, Patient and Intern agreed to a settlement in which Intern paid Patient $12,000 and Patient released Intern from all further claims for liability arising out of the incident.

71. If Intern brings suit against Nurse for contribution, the most likely result is that intern will

    (A) prevail, because one who settles without judgment can recover contribution
    (B) prevail, because Nurse's liability is established under res *ipsa loquitur*
    (C) not prevail, because one who settles without judgment cannot recover contribution
    (D) not prevail, because Intern's proper remedy is indemnification not contribution

Questions 72–74 are based on the following fact situation.

Bendix, a manufacturer of appliances, put a washing machine of a new and advanced design on the market. Two years of experimental use prior to commercial marketing had demonstrated that the machine laundered clothes more cleanly, more rapidly, and at a lower cost than any previous model.

After nine months of commercial sales on a nation-wide basis, Bendix discovered that an electrical unit in the machine tended to overheat greatly when the machine was heavily loaded or used continuously for more than one hour. Bendix promptly notified all dealers that it was recalling machines still in dealers' stock for corrective adjustment. It also provided all dealers with forms of notice to previous purchasers, warning the purchasers of the hazard, urging the purchasers to arrange with the dealers to pick up the machines, with full reimbursement to the purchasers (at the manufacturer's expense); and advising the purchasers who wished to use the machines pending pick-up by the dealer to do so only with a clothes load of not more than 1/2 the machine's capacity and for no longer than 3/4 of an hour.

Doris, a purchaser, having been notified, arranged on Thursday to have a dealer pick up her machine on the following Monday. Over the weekend, Doris was visited by Peggy, her married daughter and two grandchildren aged 5 and 3. On Saturday, Doris left the house to go shopping. She forgot to warn Peggy about the washing machine. Peggy undertook to do a heavy load of accumulated laundry including children's clothing and bedding. She loaded the machine fully and repeatedly for an hour and a quarter. Leaving the laundry room with the children in it, she retired for a brief nap. The machine overheated; its paint caught fire and the fire spread to the window curtains and generally into the room. The children were felled by the smoke. Awakened by the smoke, Peggy rushed down to the laundry, screaming for help. Nellie, a neighbor, rushed into the house after phoning the fire station. Together they entered the laundry room and lifted and carried out the children. Peggy and Nellie both suffered injuries from the fire and smoke in rescuing the children. Firemen arrived soon thereafter and extinguished the fire.

72. If Peggy asserts a claim based on strict liability against Bendix for damages, the probable result is that Bendix will

    (A) win, because she was not the purchaser of the washing machine
    (B) win, because Bendix issued warnings to dealers and purchasers regarding the defect
    (C) lose, because Bendix negligently designed the washing machine
    (D) lose, because the washing machine was defective and unreasonably dangerous

73. If Peggy asserts a claim against Doris, the most likely result is that Peggy will

    (A) recover, because Doris failed to warn her about the hazardous condition of the washing machine
    (B) recover, because Doris was aware that the washing machine was defective
    (C) not recover, because Doris did not create the risk of harm
    (D) not recover, under the family purpose doctrine

74. If Nellie brings suit against Doris to recover for her personal injuries, judgment for whom?

    (A) Doris, because she owed no duty of care to Nellie.
    (B) Doris, because Nellie voluntarily assumed the risk by acting as a Good Samaritan.
    (C) Nellie, because she was injured while acting in an emergency situation.
    (D) Nellie, but her proper remedy is against Bendix not Doris.

Questions 75–76 are based on the following fact situation.

The Anderson Family had been traveling across country on a camping trip when they decided to pull into Yellowstone National Park. During their stay at Yellowstone, the Anderson Family camped out in a recluse area of the campgrounds surrounded by tall pine trees. Numerous signs had been posted throughout the campgrounds warning campers of the extremely dry conditions prevailing in the forest area due to a summer long drought. On the morning of their departure, the Andersons cooked breakfast over an open campfire. After breakfast the Andersons began to pack their gear into the van when Mr. Anderson instructed his fourteen-year old son, Homer, to put the campfire out. Homer fetched two pails of water from a nearby pond and tossed the water over the campfire. Believing that he had extinguished the fire, Homer joined his family in the van and the Andersons drove away. Unknown to Homer and his family, the campfire was still smoldering when they left.

Shortly thereafter, a wind gust blew the flames from the fire to some nearby brush. Due to the extremely dry conditions the brush quickly ignited, starting a raging forest fire. The Forest Rangers dispatched a firefighting team which included two helicopters equipped to fight the fire. While these helicopters were fighting the blaze from above, the smoke surrounding one of the helicopters became so intense that the pilot lost all visibility. At the same time Reggie, who was operating a small private plane, saw the blaze and recklessly descended into the smoke. In the Pilot's attempt to veer out of the intense smoke, his helicopter collided with Reggie's low flying plane, causing the aircrafts to crash to earth. Both Pilot and Reggie were killed in the resulting explosion.

75. In a wrongful death action by the estate of Reggie against the estate of Pilot the defense LEAST likely to succeed would be:

    (A) Reggie assumed the risk by unreasonably exposing himself to a known danger.
    (B) Reggie was contributorily negligent in failing to exercise reasonable care in the operation of his airplane.
    (C) Under the circumstances Reggie had the last clear chance to avoid the collision.
    (D) Reggie would be strictly liable for engaging in an abnormally dangerous activity.

76. In a wrongful death action brought by Pilot's estate against Homer and Mr. Anderson, the judgment should be for

    (A) Pilot's estate, since Homer was negligent in failing to properly extinguish the campfire
    (B) Pilot's estate, since Mr. Anderson is vicariously liable for the tortious conduct of his child
    (C) The Andersons, since Reggie's reckless operation of his aircraft would be viewed as a superseding cause terminating the defendant's liability
    (D) The Andersons, since Homer's conduct would be judged as that of a child of like age, intelligence and experience, and therefore, reasonable under the circumstances

Question 77 is based on the following fact situation.

The state of Drycreek has the following statutes regarding liquor sales in effect:

> "Section 1212. Whoever sells intoxicating liquor to any person who is intoxicated or inebriated is guilty of a misdemeanor. This section shall not apply in the case of sales of intoxicating liquor by a hotel, motel, or inn to any person registered and resident as a guest in such hotel, motel, or inn, for consumption upon the premises thereof."
>
> "Section 1213. It shall be unlawful for any vendor with a valid state liquor license to sell intoxicating beverages during the Sunday Sabbath. Anyone in violation of this section shall be guilty of a misdemeanor and fined not less than $100 nor more than $1000."

Drycreek state authorities have regularly enforced the aforementioned dramshop statute and "blue law" prohibiting Sunday liquor sales. At 12:30 a.m. on Sunday morning, Wino entered Sonoma's Liquor Store and purchased a bottle of wine. Gallo, the clerk who made the sale, thought the time was 11:30 p.m. Saturday night because that was the time shown on the store's wall clock. Unknown to Gallo, the clock was malfunctioning and was running an hour slow. Thus, the clock displayed the wrong time when Gallo sold the wine to Wino. When Gallo made the sale, Wino did not appear to be visibly inebriated. After making the purchase, Wino drank the entire bottle of wine. He then drove off in his car, and struck Pedestrian, injuring him. At the time of the accident, Wino was intoxicated from drinking the wine.

77. If Pedestrian asserts a claim against Sonoma's Liquor Store, will the plaintiff prevail?

   (A) Yes, because Sonoma's was negligent per se by selling the wine in violation of the "blue law" prohibiting Sunday liquor sales.
   (B) Yes, if the accident would not have occurred but for the sale of the wine to Wino.
   (C) No, if the purpose of the "blue law" prohibiting Sunday liquor sales was to aid in the observance of the Sabbath.
   (D) No, because Gallo did not violate the dramshop statute and his violation of the "blue law" resulted from the clock's malfunctioning.

Questions 78–81 are based on the following fact situation.

Lee owns and operates a drug store. In 1997 he modernized his store and, among other things, installed a new front door. The door was made entirely of transparent glass framed by a very narrow metal strip. The handle is a flat, 3 inch by 4 inch pedal, which one pushes by hand to enter the store and which is mounted below chest height, on a small metal device set in the glass next to the latch. There are no signs, markings, or warnings on the glass itself.

Ariste, the architect in charge of the modernization, specified that the door be constructed of tempered glass. However, before beginning the construction, Lee talked to Glass, the president of Glass Service Company, a manufacturer and supplier of all types of glass, who told Lee that 1/2 inch thick plate glass is half the price of tempered glass and that the great majority of residential and small business establishments use plate glass for such doors. Furthermore, Mr. Glass told Lee that plate glass was "super safe" and could withstand considerable pressure.

Thereafter, Lee instructed Ariste to install the front door using plate glass rather than tempered glass. Ariste agreed but warned Lee that tempered glass is five times stronger than plate glass; is more difficult to scratch; can withstand a blow from a hammer; and even breaks into pieces with rounded edges rather than the sharp and jagged edges of broken glass.

Nonetheless, Ariste followed Lee's instructions and purchased the plate glass from Glass Service Company. Ariste then went ahead and hired Culver, an independent contractor, who renovated Lee's Drug Store and installed the new front door. The renovation work was completed in October and the store re-opened for business later that same month.

On January 8, 1998, Mrs. Shopper and her nine-year-old son, Victor, went to Lee's Drug Store to purchase some merchandise. As they approached the store, Victor was skipping ahead of his mother. Until he was within a few steps of the door he thought it was open; when he realized it was in fact closed, he slowed down and, while still "going faster than walking," pushed his hand against the pedal-handle to push open the door. His hand slipped off the pedal and at the same time there was a "kind of exploding noise." The plate glass shattered and broke, cutting Victor's hand and wrist.

78. If Mrs. Shopper, on behalf of her son, asserts a claim against Glass Service Company based on strict liability, the plaintiff will

    (A) prevail, if the plate glass was defective
    (B) prevail, because Mr. Glass represented the plate glass as being "super safe"
    (C) not prevail, if Culver negligently installed the plate glass door
    (D) not prevail, if Victor negligently pushed open the glass door

79. If Mrs. Shopper, on behalf of her son, asserts a claim against Culver based on strict liability in tort, the plaintiff will

    (A) prevail, if the plate glass was defective when installed
    (B) prevail, unless Victor was negligent when he pushed open the door and his negligence caused the glass to explode
    (C) not prevail, because Culver was not engaged in the sale of the plate glass
    (D) not prevail, because Culver had no relationship of privity with the plaintiff(s)

80. If Mrs. Shopper, on behalf of her son, asserts a claim against Lee based on negligence and establishes negligent manufacture of the plate glass by the Glass Service Company, the plaintiff will

    (A) prevail, because Lee is liable for its supplier's negligence
    (B) prevail, because Lee instructed its architect to install plate glass rather than the more durable tempered glass
    (C) not prevail, unless Lee could reasonably have been expected to discover the defect prior to installation
    (D) not prevail, if Lee introduces undisputed evidence that the door in question had never broken before and was used by hundreds of customers prior to the accident

81. If Lee asserts a claim against the Glass Service Company, Lee will most likely

    (A) prevail, because Mr. Glass represented the plate glass as being "super safe"
    (B) prevail, only If the plate glass was negligently manufactured
    (C) prevail, only if the plate glass was defective
    (D) not prevail, if Victor was negligent and his negligence caused the glass to break

Questions 82–85 are based on the following fact situation.

Lucinda, who was ten years old, decided to go sleigh riding during a heavy snow and ice storm. She planned to go sledding down Hill Street, a steep and winding thoroughfare. Hill Street, which was located around the corner from Lucinda's home, was a popular sledding site because of its precipitous incline. Lucinda's parents had given her permission to sled down Hill Street.

On the way to Hill Street, Lucinda met Veronica, a classmate who was twelve, and asked if she wanted to join her. Veronica agreed and the two girls walked to the top of Hill Street together. There the youngsters mounted the sled. Lucinda was sitting in front and controlling the steering mechanism while Veronica was behind her. They started their descent at a relatively good speed.

As they were about halfway down the road, they approached the intersection of Hill Street and Maple Drive. Jenner, who was driving his car along Maple Drive, entered the intersection at the same time as the girls on the sled. When Veronica saw Jenner's auto cross into their path, she shouted to Lucinda to fall off the sled. Lucinda became frightened and refused to jump off. Just before the sled collided with the car, Veronica pushed Lucinda off the sled. Her push caused Lucinda to fall and break her leg. Veronica couldn't get off the sled in time and was struck and injured by Jenner's car.

82. If Lucinda's parents, on behalf of their daughter, assert a claim against Veronica to recover damages for Lucinda's broken leg, will they prevail?

(A) No, if Veronica believed that Lucinda was in imminent peril when she pushed her off the sled.
(B) No, unless Veronica acted unreasonably when she pushed Lucinda off the sled.
(C) No, if Jenner was driving negligently.
(D) No, because Veronica had Lucinda's implied consent to act in an emergency.

83. If Lucinda's parents, on behalf of their daughter, assert a claim against Jenner to recover damages for her broken leg, they will most likely

(A) prevail, if Jenner's car would have hit Lucinda had Veronica not pushed her off the sled
(B) prevail, because Veronica's intervening act was foreseeable
(C) not prevail, because Jenner did not cause Lucinda's broken leg
(D) not prevail, unless Jenner negligently created an apparent risk of harm to Lucinda

84. If Veronica's parents, on behalf of Veronica, assert a claim against Jenner to recover damages for her injuries, they will most likely

(A) prevail, unless Jenner was driving his vehicle within the posted speed limit
(B) prevail, unless Lucinda was negligent in steering the sled
(C) not prevail, unless Jenner was driving negligently when the accident occurred
(D) not prevail, unless Jenner had the last clear chance to avoid the accident

85. Assume the following facts for this question only. Veronica did not push Lucinda off the sled. Instead Jenner's car struck the sled killing Lucinda. Lucinda's parents have asserted a wrongful death action against Jenner. In defense, Jenner has pleaded the defense that both Lucinda and her parents were guilty of contributory negligence. If it is found that Jenner was negligent, will Lucinda's parents recover?

(A) Yes, unless both Lucinda and her parents were negligent.
(B) Yes, because Jenner's negligence was subsequent to any negligence of Lucinda's parents.
(C) No, if either Lucinda or her parents were negligent.
(D) No, because the snowstorm prevented Jenner from seeing Lucinda in time to avoid striking her.

Questions 86–88 are based on the following diagram and fact situation.

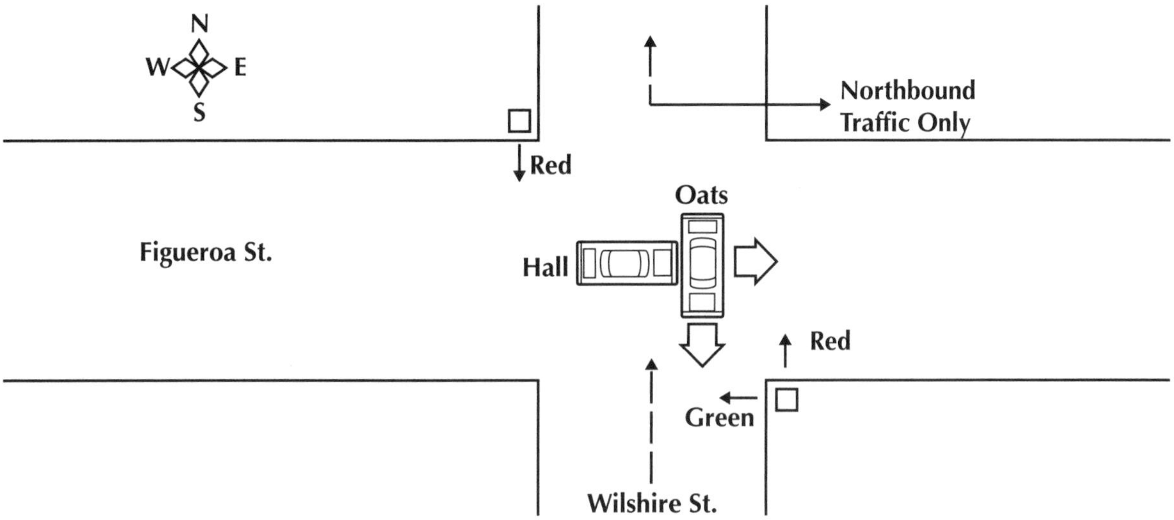

Wilshire Street is a public thoroughfare, designated as a one-way street for northbound traffic. Wilshire and Figueroa Streets intersect at right angles. The intersection is controlled by traffic lights. Hall was driving his car east on Figueroa Street and did not see the traffic light. He entered the intersection at a time when the light was red for eastbound traffic and green for northbound traffic. Oats, in violation of statute, was proceeding south on Wilshire Street and he entered the intersection without looking for any cross traffic and struck Hall's car.

Hall suffered damages in the amount of $5,000. Oats, on the other hand, suffered damages in the amount of $1,000. Hall brought suit against Oats to recover his damages. Oats denied liability and filed a counterclaim against Hall for his damages. Both drivers were negligent with 30% of the negligence attributable to Oats and 70% of the negligence attributable to Hall.

86. Assume for the purposes of this question only that a statute in the jurisdiction provides: "The amount actionable for personal injury or injury to property attributable to a person injured in not exercising ordinary care shall not bar recovery for damages but shall be diminished in proportion to the amount of negligence attributable to the person injured. There shall be no set-off of damages between the respective parties." Which of the following is the appropriate judgment in the case?

(A) Hall recovers $5,000 from Oats and Oats recovers $1,000 from Hall.
(B) Hall recovers $3,500 from Oats and Oats recovers $300 from Hall.
(C) Hall recovers $1,500 from Oats and Oats recovers $700 from Hall.
(D) Hall recovers nothing from Oats and Oats recovers $700 from Hall.

87. Assume for the purposes of this question only that the jurisdiction has a statute in effect which provides: "Contributory negligence shall not bar recovery in an action to recover damages for negligence resulting in injury to person or property if such negligence was not as great as the negligence of the person from whom recovery is sought. Any damages allowed shall be diminished in proportion to the amount of negligence attributable to the person who is seeking recovery." Which of the following is the appropriate judgment in the case?

    (A) Hall recovers $3,500 from Oats and Oats recovers nothing from Hall.
    (B) Hall recovers $1,500 from Oats and Oats recovers nothing from Hall.
    (C) Hall recovers nothing from Oats and Oats recovers $700 from Hall.
    (D) Neither party recovers anything from the other.

88. Assume for the purposes of this question only that the jurisdiction does not follow the comparative negligence principle and that Oats had the last clear chance to avoid the collision. How much, if anything, could Hall recover?

    (A) $5,000, or the full amount of his damages.
    (B) $4,000, or the full amount of his damages minus Oats damages.
    (C) $3,500, or 70% of his damages.
    (D) Nothing, because Hall was negligent per se by driving through the red light.

Questions 89–90 are based on the following fact situation.

Felix, a high school English teacher, lived in a large apartment building. In his spare time, he did artistic painting. Not infrequently, Felix would even sell some of his paintings to his friends and neighbors. One Sunday morning, Felix was cleaning clothes in the laundry room which was located in the basement of the apartment building. Also in the laundry room was Floyd, a neighbor, who lived down the hall from Felix. Floyd, who had purchased a couple of Felix's paintings in the past, asked him if he had any new paintings for sale. Felix indicated that he had just completed a new work of art and invited Floyd to come to his apartment to look at it. Floyd accepted Felix's invitation and told him that he would see him in about an hour. As Floyd was walking out the laundry room, Felix told him, "By the way, bring along your son, Scott, so he can play with Junior (Felix's son) while we talk business." Floyd agreed and later that same day both he and Scott arrived at Felix's apartment.

After they entered, Scott and junior went into the den to play together. Felix and Floyd were in the living room looking at the new painting when Floyd walked toward it in order to inspect it more carefully. As he approached the painting, he suddenly slipped on a rubber ball which junior had left on the living room floor. Floyd fell and fractured his left arm. In excruciating pain, Floyd began yelling, "Help, please help me!" Responding to his father's screams Scott ran from the den to the living room. Unknown to Scott, there was a glass door separating the two rooms. In his haste, Scott crashed into the glass door, seriously injuring himself.

89. Which of the following best describes the legal status of Floyd and Scott after they entered Felix's apartment?

    (A) Floyd and Scott were both invitees
    (B) Floyd and Scott were both licensees
    (C) Floyd was an invitee and Scott was a licensee
    (D) Floyd was a licensee and Scott was an invitee

90. If Floyd, on behalf of Scott, asserts a claim based on negligence against Felix, the plaintiff will

    (A) succeed, because an independent duty of care was owed to Scott
    (B) succeed, because Felix failed to warn Scott about the glass door
    (C) not succeed, because Felix's duty was only to warn Scott of any known dangerous conditions on the premises
    (D) not succeed, because Scott assumed the risk by running into the glass door

Questions 91–92 are based on the following fact situation.

Missy Meese was a recent graduate of Columbia Law School in New York. After graduation, Missy moved to Los Angeles where she had been offered a position in the entertainment law firm of Smack, Downer and Weed. When she moved to Los Angeles, Missy was told that her job was contingent on passing the California bar examination which was being offered in July. In preparing for the bar examination, Missy enrolled in BRA (Bar Review of America). During her bar review preparation, she had heard about PMBR's supplemental Multistate workshop. Although she had not pre-enrolled in PMBR, Missy planned to attend the weekend workshop and pay for the course at registration. The PMBR seminar was scheduled for the weekend of July 18, 19 and 20 at the Bonaventure Hotel. Students were advised that registration on the first day of the seminar was to be held between 8:00 a.m. and 9:00 a.m.

On the morning of July 18, Missy arrived late at the PMBR seminar after getting stuck in freeway traffic. By the time Missy got to the hotel, registration for the course had already been completed. When Missy looked into the room where the seminar was being conducted, she saw the PMBR lecture had begun and everyone was inside busily taking notes. Panicky, Missy picked up a set of course materials that were lying on the registration table and entered the seminar without paying. Although Missy intended to pay the $295 enrollment fee, no one was at the registration table to take her money. After attending the weekend seminar, Missy sent PMBR a cashier's check for $295 on Monday morning.

Unknown to Missy, PMBR's regional director, Dean Chance, noticed that she had entered the seminar without paying. After ascertaining her identity from a fellow student who knew Missy, PMBR filed a complaint with the local prosecutor, and a warrant was issued for her arrest. The complaint charged Missy with the crime of larceny by trick, for deliberately failing to pay for services rendered. After the complaint was issued, Missy's check arrived at PMBR's office on Wednesday morning. PMBR deposited the check but failed to inform the prosecutor that payment had been received. On Friday, Missy was arrested and held in custody overnight before the matter was resolved.

Missy suffered severe emotional distress at the publicity she received in the local newspapers and the humiliation she sustained for being arrested and held in police custody. Terribly upset, Missy was unable to take the bar exam and, thus, lost her job at Smack, Downer and Weed.

91. If Missy asserts a claim against PMBR based on infliction of emotional distress, will Missy prevail?

    (A) Yes, because Missy did not intend to defraud PMBR.
    (B) Yes, if PMBR made no effort to inform the prosecutor that the registration fee had been paid in full.
    (C) No, because PMBR did not intend to cause Missy to suffer severe emotional distress.
    (D) No, because filing the complaint with the prosecutor was not outrageous conduct.

92. If Missy asserts a claim for false imprisonment against the arresting officers, will Missy prevail?

    (A) Yes, because Missy had not committed a crime at the time she was arrested.
    (B) Yes, because Missy was arrested and held in custody overnight.
    (C) No, because Missy was arrested and held in custody under an arrest warrant.
    (D) No, because PMBR honestly believed that Missy had defrauded it when it filed its complaint.

Questions 93–95 are based on the following fact situation.

Safeway Supermarket (hereinafter referred to as SS) had just reopened after a six month renovation period. The renovations included the repair, replastering and repainting of the entire ceiling and walls by the AAA Painting Co.

The day following the reopening of SS, Mike, the store's manager, noticed small fragments of plaster on the floor which appeared to have fallen from a part of the ceiling about 10 square feet in area. Mike immediately posted signs in that area which read: "Caution Falling Plaster". In addition, Mike promptly called the AAA and requested a repairman to attend to the problem.

That afternoon, Becky was shopping in the supermarket and wanted to purchase some canned goods in the posted area. Moving quickly, Becky reached for the desired items. Suddenly at that moment, a section of the ceiling fell and struck Becky, injuring her very seriously.

93. If Becky asserts a claim based on negligence against SS, she probably will

    (A) prevail, because SS is strictly liable under the circumstances
    (B) prevail, because SS failed to take adequate precaution to insure the safety of its patrons against such an unreasonable risk of harm
    (C) prevail, because SS is vicariously liable for the negligence of its independent contractor in the performance of a nondelegable duty
    (D) not prevail, since SS took adequate precautions in having signs posted warning customers of the risk of harm

94. In an action by Becky against AAA Painting Co. based on the theory of negligence, which of the following is the most accurate statement regarding the burden of proof?

    (A) Becky must prove beyond all reasonable doubt that AAA negligently repaired the ceiling.
    (B) Becky must prove by a preponderance of the evidence that AAA negligently repaired the ceiling.
    (C) AAA must prove by a preponderance of the evidence that they were not negligent in repairing the ceiling.
    (D) There is an irrebutable presumption of negligence on the part of AAA under the doctrine of *res ipsa loquitur*.

95. Assume for the purposes of this question only, that shortly before Becky entered SS, Driver had just parked his automobile in front of the supermarket. Realizing that he did not have any change for the parking meter, Driver entered SS to "break" a ten dollar bill (even though he didn't intend to purchase any items at the supermarket). After Driver obtained change from one of the grocery clerks, a section of the ceiling fell on him as he was about to leave the store. Driver suffered serious head injuries from the falling plaster. In an action by Driver against SS for negligence, plaintiff will most likely

    (A) recover, since SS was negligent in failing to protect its business invitees against known dangerous conditions
    (B) not recover, because SS only had an obligation to disclose to its licensees any known dangerous conditions on the premises
    (C) recover, only if Driver had intended to purchase merchandise when he entered the store
    (D) not recover, because SS was not the insurer of the safety of its business invitees and its only duty was to warn them of known dangerous conditions

Question 96 is based on the following fact situation.

Cycle company manufactured a bicycle that it sold to Bike Shop, a retail bicycle dealer, which in turn sold it to Roth. Shortly thereafter, while Roth was riding the bicycle along a city street, he saw a traffic light facing him turn from green to amber. He sped up, hoping to cross the intersection before the light turned red. However, Roth quickly realized that he could not do so and applied the brake, which failed. To avoid the traffic that was then crossing in front of him, Roth turned sharply to his right and onto the sidewalk, where he struck Perez, a pedestrian. Both Perez and Roth sustained injuries.

96. If Perez asserts a claim based on negligence against Cycle Company and if it is found that the brake failure re-sulted from a manufacturing defect in the bicycle, will Perez prevail?

    (A) Yes, because Cycle Company placed a defective bicycle into the stream of commerce.
    (B) Yes, if the defect could have been discovered through the exercise of reasonable care by Cycle Company.
    (C) No, because Perez was not a purchaser of the bicycle.
    (D) No, if Roth was negligent in turning onto the sidewalk.

Questions 97–98 are based on the following fact situation.

Rancher owns a 2,000 acre cattle ranch in the remote hills of western Wyoming. For some time Rancher's cattle had been seized upon by roaming packs of wolves. In order to protect his livestock from these attacks Rancher erected a fence around his property. In addition, Rancher installed electrical wiring on the fence. The wiring transmitted an electric current which would emit a shock upon contact with the fence. Although the voltage was calculated to frighten animals away from the fence, it was of such low intensity that it posed no risk of injury to a human being, even a small child. Consequently, Rancher did not post any notice of the electrical wiring device.

One day Cowboy was riding his horse along the outskirts of Rancher's property, when a gust of wind blew his Stetson hat onto the fence. Cowboy, who had undergone major heart surgery, wore a pacemaker. When Cowboy touched the top of the fence to retrieve his hat, the electrical current short-circuited his pacemaker, resulting in Cowboy's death by electrocution.

97. In a wrongful death action by Cowboy's estate against Rancher, the installation of the electrical wiring device would most likely constitute:

 (A) the legal cause of Cowboy's death
 (B) the cause-in-fact of Cowboy's death
 (C) the legal cause and the cause-in-fact of Cowboy's death
 (D) neither the legal cause nor the cause-in-fact of Cowboy's death

98. Assume for the purposes of this question that Rancher is held to be liable in the above wrongful death action of Cowboy. The rationale supporting that decision would be:

 (A) This jurisdiction adheres to Judge Andrews' view regarding negligence.
 (B) This jurisdiction adheres to Judge Cardozo's view regarding negligence.
 (C) Rancher breached his duty of due care by failing to post any warnings regarding the electrical wiring.
 (D) "But for" the installation of the electrical wiring device, Cowboy, as a foreseeable plaintiff, would not have died of electrocution.

Questions 99–100 are based on the following fact situation.

The Alameda Aces and the Schenectady Spikers were playing for the National Volleyball Tournament Championship in Las Vegas on June 15. The Alameda team was staying at the Golden Nugget Hotel where it was practicing in preparation for the title match. Rip Repulski, the Schenectady assistant coach, learned that Rocky Colavito, the Alameda team captain, was staying in room 1212. On June 10, Repulski checked into the Golden Nugget Hotel and rented room 1213, which he knew adjoined Colavito's room. In order to obtain information about the Alameda team's strategy for the championship game, Repulski used electronic devices to listen to and record conversations between Colavito and his teammates. While Repulski was listening to one such conversation, a thief picked the lock on Repulski's hotel room door, entered, hit Repulski over the head, and stole his wallet. Repulski, who suffered a concussion, was hospitalized for three days. The lock on Repulski's hotel room door fully complied with a local ordinance that prescribed minimum security standards for hotel locks.

99. If Repulski asserts a claim against the Golden Nugget Hotel for damages for his injury and loss of his wallet, Repulski will

 (A) prevail, if the lock was defectively designed
 (B) prevail, because he was a business visitor on Golden Nugget's property
 (C) not prevail, because the thief's act was an intervening cause
 (D) not prevail, if the Golden Nugget used reasonable care in selecting the lock

100. If Rocky Colavito asserts a claim against Repulski based on invasion of privacy, will Colavito prevail?

 (A) Yes, because Repulski was recording the conversation for the use and advantage of the Schenectady team.
 (B) Yes, because Colavito had a reasonable expectation of privacy in his hotel room.
 (C) No, if Repulski's electronic devices did not physically intrude into Colavito's room.
 (D) No, unless there was publication of the recorded conversations.

Questions 101–102 are based on the following situation.

Circus Vargas operates a county fair in a rural part of Monroe County in the state of Georgia. For purposes of entertainment, the circus has retained the Wawa Family to perform an acrobatic act; and it has engaged the Sparklettes Company to present a fireworks display three times a week. It is Circus Vargas' practice to finish each day's entertainment by discharging a so called "aerial bomb" into the sky. After exploding, the "aerial bomb" emits a spectacular rainbow fireworks display that is seen for miles around.

Sammy Snodgrass is a ten-year-old son of Sally and Seymour Snodgrass. One afternoon, Sammy and a few friends went to the fairgrounds to see the circus. After paying their admission, they were about to enter the "big top" when Sammy came upon an "aerial bomb" lying on the ground. Ignorant of what the object really was, but in an exploratory mood, young Sammy applied a match to the fuse of the fireworks device. It exploded and seriously injured Sammy.

After the accident and before Mr. and Mrs. Snodgrass had retained a lawyer, Purvis Pearlman, the adjuster for Circus Vargas' insurance carrier, contacted the Snodgrasses several times trying to negotiate a settlement of their claim against the circus. On each occasion, Pearlman told the Snodgrasses there was no need for them to hire an attorney because the Georgia Civil Code did not provide for recovery in such a situation. Pearlman was aware that this information was blatantly false. He also warned the Snodgrasses that unless they accepted his offered settlement of $5,000, they would receive nothing.

For over a month, Pearlman continued to harass the Snodgrass family. Outraged by Pearlman's actions, Mr. and Mrs. Snodgrass sought the advice of a neighbor who recommended that they consult with an attorney. They went ahead and retained a lawyer who subsequently negotiated a $250,000 settlement with Pearlman's insurance company.

101. If the Snodgrasses assert a claim against Pearlman to recover damages for infliction of emotional distress, they will

(A) recover, because Pearlman's actions exceeded the bounds of common decency
(B) recover, because Pearlman was trying to take unfair advantage of the Snodgrasses
(C) not recover, if the Snodgrasses did not suffer emotional distress that was severe
(D) not recover, because the Snodgrasses eventually received a $250,000 settlement from Pearlman's insurance company

102. If the Snodgrasses assert a claim against Pearlman for misrepresentation, will they prevail?

(A) Yes, because Pearlman's settlement offer of $5,000 was grossly inadequate.
(B) Yes, because Pearlman knew that laws of the state provided for recovery in such a case.
(C) No, because Pearlman's statements did not cause the Snodgrasses any monetary loss.
(D) No, because Pearlman's statements concerned unresolved issues of legal opinion.

Question 103 is based on the following situation.

Peter Petsky is the owner of Pet Products Company which is engaged in the manufacture and sale of a variety of pet supplies. Peter's company manufactures such products as pet furniture, toys, beds, collars, leashes, cages, vitamins etc. These items are distributed to pet stores throughout the United States and Europe. Since 1999, Pet Products has conducted its operations from a large factory located in the town of Bismark. One of Peter's biggest selling products is specially manufactured high frequency dog-calling whistles. These whistles are sold to dog training schools and kennel divisions of many police departments. Although these whistles are not audible to people, they are audible to dogs over considerable distances.

In 2004, Rula Lenska purchased an undeveloped lot in Bismark. On her property Rula constructed a Pet Hotel which was used as a boarding kennel for dogs and cats. This boarding facility was situated about 100 yards from Peter's factory. Unknown to Rula, high frequency sound waves often emitted from Peter's factory when dog-calling whistles were being tested. These sound waves caused Rula's dogs to howl uncontrollably for many hours during the day and seriously interfered with the operation of her business.

103. Rula now brings an action against Peter and the Pet Products Company to recover damages for the interference with her business caused by the high frequency sound that reaches her kennel. The court should rule in favor of

(A) Peter, because Rula came to the nuisance after his factory had already been in operation for a number of years.
(B) Peter, because Rula's business is abnormally sensitive to harm caused by the high frequency sound waves.
(C) Rula, because the high frequency sound waves constitute a trespass to Rula's premises.
(D) Rula, because the high frequency sound waves have seriously interfered with the operation of her business.

Question 104 is based on the following fact situation.

Horace Anderson, a well-known Washington newspaper columnist, was researching the background of Edgar Moose, the presidential nominee for Attorney-General, then awaiting Senate confirmation. Larry Liddy, one of Anderson's eager young apprentices, concocted a plan which he hoped would enable him to gain Anderson's favor.

Late one evening, without telling anyone, Liddy broke into Moose's private office and copied several letters pertaining to "dirty tricks" involving Moose during the presidential campaign. When Liddy presented Anderson with the fruits of his diligent research, Anderson was quite impressed and immediately printed excerpts from the material.

104. If Moose asserts a claim against Anderson for invasion of right to privacy, the plaintiff will most likely

(A) prevail, because Liddy's action was an unlawful invasion of private facts
(B) prevail, only if the publication was not newsworthy
(C) not prevail, if the Senate confirms the findings which Anderson printed, thus establishing no "false light"
(D) not prevail, if Anderson did not conspire with Liddy

Questions 105–108 are based on the following fact situation.

Late one evening, Rudy Rum entered Pete's Pub, a bar owned by Pete Brandywine. Even though Rudy was already visibly intoxicated, Bob the bartender, served him five bourbons. Bob's actions were contrary to Pete's explicit directions to his bartenders, as well as in violation of a state statute making it a Class B misdemeanor to serve alcoholic beverages to any person who is visibly intoxicated. When Rudy left the Pub, he staggered to his auto, barely sober enough to get into the car and started driving home.

Rudy had driven only three blocks from the bar, weaving back and forth across the highway, when he collided with another car driven by Butch. As a result of the accident, Rudy suffered a broken nose and Butch received severe facial lacerations and bruises. Seeing the men lying on the edge of the highway bleeding profusely, a bystander summoned an ambulance which rushed Rudy and Butch to Holmdale Hospital.

After Rudy's nose was reset, he was transferred to a room in the west wing of the hospital. In extreme pain, Rudy asked Nurse Nancy for a pain killer. Without seeking the doctor's approval, Nancy administered an injection of morphine which she should have known to be an excessive dosage. Rudy died an hour after the injection; cause of Rudy's death was morphine poisoning.

After Butch was treated for his facial wounds, an examination indicated that he was suffering from a hernia. Taking advantage of his hospitalization, Butch decided to undergo a hernia operation. As a result of a surgical error, Steve, the surgeon, performed the routine hernia operation unsuccessfully. Thus, following the surgery, Butch suffered an aggravation of the hernia condition.

105. In a wrongful death action by the executors of Rudy's estate against Bob the bartender, the strongest argument in Bob's behalf would be that

(A) under the doctrine of respondeat superior, Pete would be vicariously liable for Rudy's death
(B) Nurse Nancy's injection of the morphine constituted a superseding cause which relieved Bob of liability
(C) it was unforeseeable that Rudy would die as result of his automobile injuries
(D) Bob's liability for Rudy's injuries terminated after Rudy's operation to reset his broken nose

106. In a personal injury action by Butch, which of the following defendants would be liable for the unsuccessful hernia operation/complications?

(A) Bob the bartender and Pete Brandywine
(B) Executors of Rudy's estate
(C) Holmdale Hospital and Steve the surgeon
(D) All of the above

107. Nurse Nancy's injection of morphine to Rudy would most likely constitute

(A) a cause in fact, but not a legal cause of Rudy's death
(B) a legal cause, but not a cause in fact of Rudy's death
(C) a cause in fact and a legal cause of Rudy's death
(D) neither a legal cause nor a cause in fact of Rudy's death

108. Bob the bartender's act of serving Rudy would most likely be viewed as the

(A) proximate cause of Butch's facial injuries
(B) superseding cause of Butch's facial injuries
(C) direct cause of Butch's facial injuries
(D) intervening cause of Butch's facial injuries

Questions 109–110 are based on the following fact situation.

Bob Patterson, a 151/2-year-old, was sledding down a pathway through a wooded area of land owned by Charles and Carol Kane. Bob had frequently used the pathway for sledding in the previous months. The path, made of concrete, led through the woods from a public highway to a pond in the rear of the Kane property. The pathway was used for sledding and the pond for skating by the residents of the neighboring areas without the consent of the owners. Furthermore, the Kanes failed to post any signs forbidding trespassing.

After Bob had been sledding down the pathway for approximately three hours one morning, he was joined by his six-year-old cousin Brian. On their first downhill run together, Bob lost control of the sled, and steered it into a tree, thus causing serious bodily injuries to both Bob and his cousin Brian.

109. If Bob's parents, in his behalf, bring suit against the Kanes for his personal injuries, they will:

(A) recover, under the "attractive nuisance" doctrine
(B) recover, if the Kanes knew or should have known of the frequent trespasses
(C) not recover, since Bob was a trespasser
(D) not recover, since a 15½-year-old boy should have realized the risk

110. A possessor of land is subject to liability for physical harm to trespassing children caused by an artificial condition on the land if

(A) a possessor fails to exercise reasonable care to eliminate the danger
(B) the children because of their youth fail to realize the danger
(C) a possessor knows or should know of the trespasses
(D) all of the above

Questions 111–112 are based on the following fact situation.

Strawbridge and Merryweather are adjoining landowners in an area of large estates located in the "chateau" region of southeastern Louisiana. In 1955, Strawbridge inherited his estate from his father whose family had owned the property continuously since 1812. Merryweather purchased his estate In 1960. Two years later, Merryweather moved a giant magnolia tree from another section of his property and had it replanted within ten feet of the border between their respective estates. At that time, Merryweather ignored Strawbridge's protest that, by locating the tree so close to his land, Merryweather was increasing the risk of injury to Strawbridge's stable, which housed many valuable racing horses. The stable, built in 1957, stood on a portion of Strawbridge's land located only ten feet from the border and twenty feet from the place where Merryweather now has replanted the magnolia. Merryweather had often complained to Strawbridge of the noises and odors emanating from the stable. Not infrequently, putrid stenches emitted from Strawbridge's property caused by large accumulations of horse manure that were left unattended.

Hurricanes are quite common in the area. In 1980, in the midst of a hurricane, the magnolia fell on Strawbridge's stable, killing horses valued at $250,000.

111. Suppose that in 1962 Merryweather brought an appropriate action to enjoin Strawbridge's use of the stables. Judgment for whom?

(A) Strawbridge, because Merryweather moved onto his property after the stable had been built.
(B) Strawbridge, because a homeowner is entitled to make reasonable use of his property.
(C) Merryweather, because the noise coupled with the odors substantially interfered with the use and enjoyment of his land.
(D) Merryweather, because Strawbridge was negligent in permitting the manure to be left unattended.

112. Assume for the purposes of this question only that Strawbridge asserts a claim against Merryweather to recover damages caused by the tree falling on the stable and killing his horses. During trial, the only evidence Strawbridge presented was that the hurricane uprooted the tree causing it to fall onto his property, and thereby resulting in the damage as claimed. At the end of Strawbridge's case, Merryweather moved for a directed verdict. Merryweather's motion will most likely be

(A) granted, because Strawbridge did not produce any evidence to show that Merryweather was negligent
(B) granted, because Strawbridge's damages resulted from an act of God
(C) denied, because hurricanes were common in the area
(D) denied, because the trier of fact may still infer liability for trespass

Question 113 is based on the following fact situation.

Marla Marple was married to Donald Marple. For many years, the Marples tried to have a child but Marla was unable to get pregnant. Her family physician, Dr. Dork, had advised Marla that she was infertile and it was impossible for her to become pregnant. After missing her period for three months and experiencing other symptoms of pregnancy, Marla consulted with Dr. Dork. Without administering a pregnancy test, Dr. Dork examined Marla and concluded that she had the flu. He prescribed Tetracycline, an antibiotic drug, which Marla took for two weeks.

After discontinuing the Tetracycline, Marla continued to experience nausea, fatigue and other symptoms of pregnancy. She then consulted Dr. Blancard, another physician, who administered a pregnancy test which revealed that Marla was in fact four months pregnant. Thereafter, she gave birth to a child named Milton. When Milton developed teeth, they were black and discolored. At the age of twelve, Milton learned that the black discoloration of his teeth resulted from the Tetracycline that Marla took during her pregnancy.

113. If Milton asserts a claim against Dr. Dork based on malpractice in not administering a pregnancy test to Marla and prescribing Tetracycline, judgment for whom?

(A) Dr. Dork, because an unborn child does not have legal rights stemming from conduct that occurred before birth.
(B) Dr. Dork, because no duty of care is owed to an unborn child not in existence at the time medical treatment is rendered.
(C) Milton, because a child, if born alive, is permitted to maintain an action for the consequences of prenatal injuries.
(D) Milton, unless Marla was negligent in failing to seek proper prenatal care.

Question 114 is based on the following fact situation.

Keiki, a graduate of University of Hawaii Law School, received notice that she had successfully passed the Hawaii bar exam. To celebrate passing, Keiki went out with a few friends to the Aloha Hut, a popular campus bar. While sitting at the bar, Malihini, Keiki's friend, ordered a round of "Hula Girls" for everyone. A "Hula Girl" is an extremely potent alcoholic drink consisting of 2 oz. of dry gin, 1 oz. French vermouth with 1 tsp. grenadine. After the drink is mixed, it is then served in a glass with an inverted lemon peel which is cut at the ends to represent a grass skirt.

Although Keiki had never heard of a "Hula Girl" before, she was in a festive mood and drank it anyway. A few minutes later, Keiki became very dizzy and attempted to stand up from the bar stool. As she tried to walk to the restroom, she got nauseous and then vomited over Haole, a customer, sitting at a nearby table. Haole was embarrassed and greatly humiliated by the incident.

114. If Haole asserts a claim against Keiki, the plaintiff will most likely

(A) prevail, because Keiki's conduct was extreme and outrageous
(B) prevail, because an offensive touching resulted
(C) not prevail, because Keiki's actions were involuntary
(D) not prevail, because Keiki was unaware what she was drinking

Question 115 is based on the following fact situation.

Cassie and her four-year-old son, Noah, were Christmas shopping at F.A.O. Schwartz Toy Store in midtown Manhattan. F.A.O. Schwartz, which operates one of New York's largest retail toy stores, sells a complete array of toys, games, dolls, hobbies and crafts. The items were displayed on a variety of tables and shelves which were easily accessible to the customers. While Cassie was walking down one of the aisles, her attention became focused on a "Howdy Doody" doll that was prominently exhibited on an overhead display shelf. When Cassie approached the doll display, she reached up to grab the "Howdy Doody" doll. As she did so, Cassie failed to see a "Buffalo Bob" doll lying on the floor. She tripped over the doll and fell down, fracturing her hip.

115. If Cassie asserts a claim against F.A.O. Schwartz for her injuries, will the doctrine of *res ipsa loquitur* be applicable on the issue of the toy store's liability?

(A) Yes, because Cassie was a business invitee on the premises of the toy store.
(B) Yes, because F.A.O. Schwartz was in control of the premises at the time of the accident.
(C) No, because the "Buffalo Bob" doll may have been dislodged by another customer.
(D) No, unless the "Buffalo Bob" doll had been displayed on the edge of the shelf in a negligent manner by one of F.A.O. Schwartz's employees.

Question 116 is based on the following fact situation.

Blackman and Dykstra were law school roommates. One evening, Blackman lent Dykstra his car to attend a Moody Blues concert at the Pantages theatre. Before going to the theatre, Dykstra drove to Hernandez's home to buy some marijuana. Hernandez lived approximately two miles from the Pantages. After picking up the marijuana, Dykstra then drove to the concert. As he was driving to the concert, Dykstra smoked two marijuana cigarettes so that he could be "high" for the show. While the car was parked outside the theatre, it was struck by another car and damaged. Repairs will cost $750. The driver of the vehicle that struck Blackman's car fled the scene and cannot be identified.

116. If Blackman asserts a claim against Dykstra for the damage to Blackman's car, the plaintiff will recover

(A) the value of the car before it was damaged because the car was damaged while under Dykstra's dominion and control
(B) the value of the car before it was damaged because Dykstra used the car for a purpose other than that for which it was lent
(C) the cost of repairing the car because the car was damaged while under Dykstra's dominion and control
(D) nothing, unless Dykstra was negligent and his negligence was the cause of the car's being damaged

Question 117 is based on the following fact situation.

Felipe was employed as a repairman for Electro, a municipal electrical company. He repaired damaged electrical power lines and replaced old, worn-out equipment whenever necessary. After a violent tornado had ripped through the city, Electro was busily trying to restore electrical power to its customers.

The morning after the storm Felipe was perched on a ladder trying to repair a high voltage power line. As he was removing the cover of the transformer box, the ladder suddenly slipped on the wet ground. Felipe struggled to maintain his balance and luckily the ladder came to rest against the transformer box. Matty, who was walking on the street below, saw Felipe's precarious predicament and began to climb the ladder to aid him. As Matty was ascending the ladder, his foot slipped and he fell to the ground. His fall caused the ladder to jar loose the transformer box, which in turn sent Felipe falling to the pavement. Felipe and Matty both sustained serious injuries.

117. If Matty asserts a claim against Electro for his injuries, he will most likely

(A) prevail, because he was attempting to rescue Felipe
(B) prevail, because a public utility company is strictly liable in tort
(C) not prevail, if he were negligent in climbing the ladder
(D) not prevail, unless Felipe was negligent in not affixing the ladder properly

Questions 118–121 are based on the following fact situation.

Pedestrian, walking along Chestnut Street at 10:20 P.M. on December 3, 2004, urgently needed to find a restroom. just ahead Pedestrian noticed the Secaucus Supper Club, a private dinner Club. As Pedestrian approached the Club, he noticed a sign over the front door which read: "ADMITTANCE TO MEMBERS ONLY". Although Pedestrian was not a member of the exclusive Club, he entered the dimly lit Club and was directed to a door marked "Gentlemen." After making use of the restroom facilities, Pedestrian washed his hands and proceeded to turn on the electric blowdryer. The dryer, because of a malfunctioning heating coil, emitted intense heat which caused severe burns to Pedestrian's hands. Pedestrian was unaware of the fact the fifteen minutes earlier Patron, having received similar injuries from the malfunctioning dryer, notified Owner who immediately taped a "DO NOT USE" sign on the dryer. However, the sign had fallen to the floor and it was lying face down under the bathroom sink when Pedestrian was making use of the restroom.

Later that evening in the Supper Club, Glutton ordered the Club's famous "homemade" Manhattan clam chowder. While eating the chowder, Glutton broke a tooth on a pebble in the soup, which a reasonable inspection would not have discovered. When Glutton complained to the Club's management, Owner admitted that the chowder was not, in fact, homemade but that it had been poured from a can of chowder manufactured by Seashore Soups, Inc. and supplied to the Club by General Wholesalers.

118. Which of the following would best describe Pedestrian's legal status?

    (A) trespasser
    (B) guest
    (C) licensee
    (D) invitee

119. Which of the following would best describe the duty of care owed by the Secaucus Supper Club to Pedestrian?

    (A) No duty of care.
    (B) A duty to inspect the premises for unknown dangers and disclose their existence to others.
    (C) A duty to warn of any known dangerous conditions on the premises.
    (D) An absolute duty of care.

120. In a personal injury action by Patron against the Secaucus Supper Club, Patron will most likely

    (A) recover, since the Club was under an absolute duty of care to make the premises safe for the protection of its patrons
    (B) recover, only if the Club had prior knowledge of the dangerous condition of the dryer
    (C) not recover, since the Club was under no obligation to inspect the premises to discover unknown dangers
    (D) not recover, unless the Club failed to make a reasonable inspection of the dryer for the safety of its patrons

121. In a strict liability action by Glutton against the Secaucus Supper Club, he will most likely

    (A) recover, since the Club misrepresented the soup as their own "homemade" chowder
    (B) recover, only if the Club had received prior notice of the defective condition of the soup
    (C) not recover, since a reasonable inspection of the soup would not have disclosed the existence of the pebble
    (D) not recover, since the soup would not constitute an unreasonably dangerous product when it was served to Glutton

Question 122 is based on the following fact situation.

Edgar Beaver was a law clerk with the law firm of Yu, Work, Hardt & Latter. He normally worked from 9:00 a.m. to 5:00 p.m. each day or an average of 40 hours per week. One morning, Edgar came to the office at 9:00 a.m., and started preparing a brief for an upcoming trial. After completing his work at 5:00 p.m. that afternoon, he was about to leave the office when Mr. Hardt, the senior partner of the law firm, summoned him. Mr. Hardt told Edgar that the law firm was representing an important client on an urgent matter which needed immediate research. Edgar was advised that he would be required to stay at the law office that night and prepare a memorandum. When Edgar hemmed and hawed, Mr. Hardt handed him the file and said, "I don't care if you stay all night, you better have this memo on my desk by 8:00 a.m. tomorrow morning."

Following Mr. Hardt's instructions, Edgar stayed at the office until 2:00 a.m. preparing the memorandum. By the time he finished, Edgar was totally exhausted after having worked a total of 17 hours that day. Afterwards, Edgar left the office and started to drive himself home. Because of his fatigue, he didn't see Nora Nightingale crossing the street. His car struck Nora seriously injuring her.

122. Nora has asserted a tort action against the law firm of Yu, Work, Hardt & Latter to recover damages for her injuries. Which of the following, if offered by the law firm in defense, are legally persuasive arguments?

I. By requiring Edgar to stay at the law office and finish the memorandum, the law firm did not breach any duty owed to Nora.
II. The law firm is not legally responsible for its employees' actions after working hours.
III. The actions of the law firm were not a cause in fact of Nora's injuries.
IV. Edgar Beaver, the driver, is liable not the law firm.

(A) I and II only
(B) II and III only
(C) III and IV only
(D) I, II, III and IV

Questions 123–124 are based on the following fact situation.

Putnam Peck worked as a delivery person for Horowitz's Drug Store in Perth Amboy. As part of Putnam's duties and responsibilities he would regularly deliver prescriptions and other items (such as toiletries, cosmetics, vitamins and gift products) to customers. One afternoon while Putnam was on duty he remembered that it was his girlfriend, Crystal's, birthday. He went ahead and bought her a bottle her a bottle of perfume from the pharmacy's cosmetic department. Putnam paid the full price of $79.95 for the perfume which he had gift wrapped. He then drove to Crystal's house in the company van to personally deliver the birthday present. This trip took place during Putnam's regular working hours. As he was traveling to Crystal's house, he was in such a hurry that he drove through a red light and collided with a vehicle owned and operated by Wendell Kim. Wendell, who had entered the intersection on the green light, tried unsuccessfully to swerve and stop but was unable to avoid Putnam's vehicle. Wendell was injured in the accident which also caused extensive damage to both vehicles.

123. If Wendell brings suit against Horowitz's Drug Store to recover damages arising from the accident, Wendell will probably

(A) prevail, because Putnam paid for the perfume
(B) prevail, if Putnam was under the control and direction of the drug store at the time of the accident
(C) not prevail, because Putnam was acting outside the scope of the employment relationship at the time of the accident
(D) not prevail, unless the drug store was negligent in hiring Putnam

124. Assume for the purposes of this question only that Wendell was successful in his suit against Horowitz's Drug Store and recovered $25,000 in damages. Suppose, too, that this jurisdiction has applicable statutes for contribution and indemnity. In the event that Horowitz's now brings suit against Putnam to recover for its losses, Horowitz will recover

(A) nothing, because the drug store was primarily liable for the entire amount of damages
(B) nothing, unless Putnam's delivery to Crystal's house was unauthorized
(C) $25,000, because Putnam was at fault in causing the accident
(D) $25,000, unless the drug store was fully insured against such losses

Questions 125–126 are based on the following fact situation.

At approximately 9:00 a.m. on October 12, an Ozark Airline DC 10 jetliner departed from Cincinnati to its scheduled destination of Los Angeles. The airplane made a refueling stop in Denver three hours later. The refueling was performed by the Mile High Fuel Comp. which, in turn, purchased the fuel from Xenon Oil Comp. Unknown to either Mile High or Xenon, the fuel was contaminated. Shortly after the plane took off in Denver it started to sputter over Colorado Springs. The pilot was forced to make an emergency landing on Interstate Highway 15. The plane landed safely on the highway and none of the passengers were injured. However, as the plane was touching down, one of its wings stretched across Pieffer's property. The wing happened to hit Pieffer's car. The auto, a classic 1956 T-Bird which was parked in his driveway, was demolished. A subsequent investigation by the FAA concluded that under the circumstances the pilot had made a skilled and expert landing in preventing a near catastrophe.

Pieffer's auto which was valued at $35,000 was insured for that amount by McGuinnes Insurance Company. An FAA investigation conclusively proved that the contaminated fuel caused the jetliner's mechanical problems.

125. In a tort action by Pieffer against Ozark Airlines, Pieffer will most likely

(A) prevail, under the doctrine of *res ipsa loquitur*
(B) prevail, since the airline is strictly liable
(C) not prevail, unless Ozark failed to inspect the fuel which it purchased from the Mile High Fuel Comp.
(D) not prevail, because the pilot exercised due care in making the emergency landing

126. Assume for the purposes of this question only that McGuinnes Insurance Comp. pays Pieffer for the insured value of his car. If Pieffer brings suit against Xenon Comp., will Pieffer prevail?

(A) No, because since his car was insured, Pieffer suffered no loss.
(B) No, if Xenon Comp. was not aware that the fuel was contaminated when they sold it to the Mile High Comp.
(C) Yes, because Xenon Comp. sold the fuel to Mile High Comp.
(D) Yes, if Xenon failed to inspect the fuel before selling it to the Mile High Comp.

Questions 127–128 are based on the following fact situation.

Reynolds owned a sporting goods store specializing in hunting and camping supplies. His friend Robinson had often cautioned him that he should not leave so much of his merchandise out in the open. One day as Robinson entered the store to pay a visit he decided he'd put his unheeded warnings into action by playing a joke on his friend. Robinson took a hatchet that was lying on a display case and picked it up over his head as if he were going to strike Reynolds, who was standing at the register with his back turned. Also in the store at that time was Haden, an elderly man who Robinson knew had a weak heart. Robinson noticed Haden standing there. Robinson then said, "All right buddy, one false move and it's over." Haden, thinking Robinson meant what he said, suffered a heart attack and collapsed.

127. If Reynolds asserts a claim against Robinson the most likely result is that he will

    (A) recover, if Robinson was negligent
    (B) recover, if he feared Robinson would hit him
    (C) not recover, if he suffered no harm
    (D) not recover, because Robinson was only joking

128. If Haden brings suit against Robinson for damages arising from the heart attack the most likely result is that he will

    (A) prevail, since Robinson knew Haden was present and had a weak heart
    (B) prevail, because Robinson assaulted Reynolds
    (C) not prevail, unless Haden was a member of Reynold's immediate family
    (D) not prevail, because the resulting harm was unforeseeable

Question 129 is based on the following fact situation.

Gloria, a New York City resident, commuted to work each day by subway. After purchasing her token, Gloria entered the subway at the Grand Central Station for her ride downtown to Wall Street where she was employed. Looking for a seat, Gloria was walking toward the rear of the subway when it came to an abrupt halt. As a result of the sudden stop, Gloria fell into Arthur, an elderly gentleman, injuring him.

129. If Arthur asserts a claim against the subway company to recover for his personal injuries, Arthur will probably

    (A) prevail, because a special duty of care was owed him
    (B) prevail, because the sudden stop caused Gloria to fall into him
    (C) not prevail, if the operator of the subway was not negligent in making the stop
    (D) not prevail, if Gloria was negligent in not holding onto the hand rail

Questions 130–131 are based on the following fact situation.

Hunter was on his property one day looking for rabbits and other small game which he shot occasionally for sport. As he rounded a clump of bushes he spotted Caine, whom he thought was a man wanted by the police. Caine, who had his back facing Hunter, was carrying a rifle on his shoulder. Hunter called out to Caine to stop. Caine was startled as he turned around and his rifle fell forward so that it pointed directly at Hunter. Hunter, thinking Caine was about to shoot him, fired his rifle at Caine. The bullet missed Caine and hit Able, a trespasser. Hunter was aware that people often walked onto his land since there was a pond adjoining the property which provided boating and fishing activities.

130. If Able asserts a claim against Hunter for battery, Able will

(A) recover, because Hunter intended to hit Caine
(B) recover, because Able suffered a harmful and offensive contact
(C) not recover, because Hunter accidentally shot Able
(D) not recover, because Hunter reasonably acted in self-defense

131. Hunter asserts a claim for assault against Caine. In his action the most likely result is that Hunter will

(A) recover, because Caine pointed the rifle at him
(B) recover, because Caine's act of turning around was voluntary
(C) not recover, unless Caine intended to scare Hunter
(D) not recover, if Caine did not intend to shoot Hunter

Question 132 is based on the following fact situation.

Tracy and Mary were sitting at a booth in the ice cream parlor one evening when Rocky and Butch, two football players on the local high school team, walked in and asked if they could join the girls for a milkshake. The girls agreed. They hoped they might impress the football players enough to get a date. Candy, one of Tracy's friends who was sitting at the counter with her boyfriend, called out to Tracy. Tracy turned around and the two began talking. Rocky then picked up his straw, bit off a piece of the paper at the tip, and blew the wrapper at Tracy. It hit her in the head and fell back into her milkshake. She turned around and reached into the drink to pull out the paper, but clumsily she ended up spilling chocolate all over the place and making a mess. Embarrassed, she got up and walked out.

132. If Tracy asserts a tort action against Rocky can she recover?

(A) No, because Rocky's behavior was not socially unacceptable in the situation.
(B) No, because the girls consented to allow Rocky to sit with them.
(C) Yes, if Tracy reasonably apprehended the contact with the straw as being harmful or offensive.
(D) Yes, if Tracy was offended by Rocky's act.

Question 133 is based on the following fact situation.

Chester Chessman was employed by Bar Review of America (hereafter referred to as BRA) as its New York regional director. Chester's responsibilities included lecturing and overseeing BRA's promotional activities at the various New York law schools. Chessman, who was a member of the New York Bar, worked for BRA for ten years and was a well known figure in the bar review business. Following the conclusion of the summer bar review classes, Chessman was fired by BRA.

Since Chessman was such a popular and well respected individual in the bar review industry, there was much speculation and interest concerning his termination. Fanny Finkelstein, a reporter for the *Gotham Law Journal*, telephoned Sheldon Skibby, BRA's administrative director, and inquired why Chessman had been fired. Skibby told Finkelstein that Chessman was fired because Mario Marino, BRA's president, believed that Chessman had embezzled money. The next day, Finkelstein wrote an article that was published by the *Gotham Law Journal* which quoted Skibby and stated that "Chessman was fired because BRA's president believed that he had embezzled money." It was later learned that Chessman was not responsible for any unlawful conduct and had not embezzled funds.

133. If Chessman asserts a defamation action against the *Gotham Law Journal*, he will most likely

(A) prevail, if Chessman proves malice
(B) prevail, if the newspaper was negligent in not ascertaining whether Chessman had actually embezzled any funds
(C) not prevail, because, Skibby, a BRA employee, was merely providing Marino's opinion regarding the reason for Chessman's termination
(D) not prevail, if Marino's belief that Chessman had embezzled funds from the company was reasonable

Questions 134–135 are based on the following fact situation.

At 1:00 AM one night, two police officers from the city of Montecello were driving past Malone's Tavern when they noticed Zonker vomiting outside. They stopped their patrol car and walked over to Zonker who they recognized as a troublemaker from the neighboring town of Yonkers. Realizing that Zonker was extremely intoxicated, they grabbed him and shoved him into their patrol car.

They drove Zonker around in the police car for a few minutes and told him he had two choices. They would either take him to jail for the night or drive him to the Montecello city limits and drop him off there. Zonker indicated that he didn't want to go to jail. One of the officers then said, "Does that mean you want us to drop you off at the city limits?" Zonker replied, "Yes". They then drove him to the outskirts of Montecello and left him along a busy highway. Moments later, Zonker staggered onto the street and was struck by a car driven by Motorist. He suffered multiple injuries.

134. If Zonker asserts a claim against the Montecello Police Department for false imprisonment, he will most likely

(A) prevail, unless the police made a valid arrest
(B) prevail, if he consented to the confinement because he was intoxicated
(C) not prevail, if Zonker was legally subject to arrest for being intoxicated in a public place
(D) not prevail, because Zonker told the police that he wanted to be taken to the city limits

135. If Zonker asserts a claim against the Montecello Police Department based on negligence, he will most likely

(A) recover, because the police should have realized it was dangerous to drop him off where they did
(B) recover, because the police knew that Zonker was intoxicated when they dropped him off
(C) not recover, because Zonker chose to be driven to the city limits
(D) not recover, because Motorist's act was a superseding cause

Question 136 is based on the following fact situation.

Monk, a 35-year-old man with some experience as a truck driver, owned a lumber truck. One day he set out driving his truck, heavily loaded with lumber, down a mountain road. Sitting next to Monk in the passenger seat was Sloan, his 19-year old helper. During the course of the trip, when the truck was going down a long hill, the brakes failed. Monk shouted to Sloan to jump, but the teenager refused to do so and shouted back to Monk that he should try to steer the truck down. Monk then opened the door on the passenger's side of the truck and pushed Sloan out. Sloan, who suffered a broken leg, was rushed to the hospital where he was treated for his injury. As Sloan was recuperating, Nurse Nitwit inadvertently mixed-up his chart with that of the female patient in the next room. Nurse Nitwit gave Sloan a fertility pill that made him sterile.

136. If Sloan brings suit against Monk to recover damages for his sterility Sloan will

(A) recover, because it is foreseeable that a hospital can be negligent in its care of patients
(B) recover, if Monk was negligent in pushing Sloan out of the truck
(C) not recover, because Nurse Nitwit's act was a supervening cause
(D) not recover, because it is not foreseeable that a patient would be injured in such a manner

Questions 137–139 are based on the following fact situation.

Otis Elevator Company installed an elevator in Duncan's apartment building. The apartment building, which was thirty stories high, was located in Quincy, a suburb of Boston. Under the terms of its contract with Duncan, Otis agreed to carry out regular monthly inspections of the elevator and to make all necessary repairs. The elevator was installed in the apartment complex in January. For the next ten months, Otis made regular inspections. However, in November Otis began to have some difficulties with its employees and failed to send inspectors out for three successive months.

On February 20, Doris, a friend of Rebecca, who was a tenant on the twentieth floor, entered the elevator on a planned social visit to Rebecca's apartment. A number of persons entered with her, including Grubby, a dubious-looking man who seemed out of place. By the twelfth floor, only four persons were left, including Doris and Grubby. At that floor the other two people left, leaving Doris and Grubby alone on the elevator. Apprehensive at finding herself alone with such an unkempt stranger, Doris pressed the thirteenth floor button, intending to step out and hoping to find other persons on that floor. Unfortunately, the elevator stalled, and came to a stop between the twelfth and thirteenth floors. Doris' fears were justified as Grubby suddenly grabbed at her purse. When Doris resisted, Grubby struck her and she fell unconscious. When Doris recovered consciousness, she found herself in a hospital with a concussion and multiple contusions on her body. She later learned that the elevator had remained stalled for fifty minutes. Thereafter, it moved to the twentieth floor where she was found by her friend Rebecca who took her to the hospital. Two weeks later, the police arrested Grubby and found Doris' purse in his possession. The elevator's stalling was caused by a defective cable that a routine inspection would have discovered. Prior to the stalling, Otis had last inspected the elevator November 20.

137. If Doris brings suit against Duncan for negligence, she will most likely

(A) recover, because she was an invitee of a tenant in the building
(B) recover, because Duncan would be vicariously liable for Otis' failure to inspect the elevator
(C) recover, only if Duncan actually knew that the elevator had been malfunctioning
(D) not recover, if Duncan was unaware of any previous assaults in the apartment building

138. If Doris asserts a claim against Duncan for false imprisonment, she will most likely

(A) prevail, because she was confined in the elevator for an unreasonably long period of time
(B) prevail, because she was injured during her confinement in the elevator
(C) not prevail, because Duncan did not intentionally cause Doris to be confined
(D) not prevail, because Doris was unaware of the confinement period

139. If Doris asserts a claim against Otis Elevator Company, she will most likely

(A) prevail, because Otis failed to inspect the elevator in a timely manner
(B) prevail, because Otis is liable for permitting a dangerous condition to exist in an area of public use
(C) not prevail, because Otis was an independent contractor
(D) not prevail, because Otis' nonfeasance was not the cause of her injuries

Question 140 is based on the following fact situation.

Henshey's Department Store had suffered a succession of thefts of merchandise over a period of months. From reports by employees and customers, Henshey's manager, Hana Lai, concluded that the losses were due, wholly or in large part, to the depredations of a female shoplifter, aged 30-40 years, about 5' 5" in height, with red hair and green eyes, who usually wore a suit. This information was passed on to all Henshey employees.

One day, Monica Bay entered the store to purchase underwear. Monica was 5' 5" in height, 37 years old, red-haired and green eyed, and dressed in a smartly tailored suit. She carried a large shopping bag. Hana noticed her as she picked up, examined and put down a number of panties and bras. After a while, she looked about tentatively, then started to walk out, swinging her bag. Hana intercepted her and, standing in front of her, politely asked Monica if she would accompany her to her office. When Monica asked for an explanation, Hana told her of the store's recent experience, and her consequent fear that she might be concealing pilfered merchandise in her bag. Flushing angrily, she replied, "Very well", and followed her to the office.

Once there, Hana began to question Monica quite intensively. After the questioning, Hana then asked Monica's permission to inspect the contents of her shopping bag. At first, Monica curtly refused and announced that she had enough of this nonsense. When she rose to go, Hana told her, "Listen, unless you let me look inside that bag, I'm going to call the police." Monica replied, "Very well", and handed her the bag. Hana inspected the contents of the bag thoroughly, but did not find any pilfered merchandise. Finally, after detaining Monica for thirty minutes, Hana gave her permission to leave.

140. If Monica asserts a claim for false imprisonment against Henshey's, she will most likely

(A) prevail, because she was detained for an unreasonably long period of time
(B) prevail, because Hana did not have reasonable grounds to suspect that Monica had committed a theft
(C) not prevail, because under the circumstances Hana had reasonable grounds to suspect that Monica had committed a theft
(D) not prevail, because Hana gave Monica permission to leave after conducting her investigation

Questions 141–143 are based on the following fact situation.

Tod, on a winter ski holiday at Lake Tahoe, visited a ski lift operated by the Mogel Co. in a private park owned by Oscar. Mogel Co. had installed and operated the lift pursuant to a concession agreement with Oscar. Visitors gained entry to the park on payment of a $5 fee, which entitled them to go ice skating, tobogganing or sledding. A ski lift ticket cost an additional $7 per day. At the top of the ski lift, there was a platform for embarking and disembarking passengers. Mogel Co. paid Oscar a stipulated rental plus 15 per cent of the net proceeds from the lift.

Two employees of Mogel Co. operated the lift, one from a station at the bottom and the other from a station at the top of the hill. When Tod boarded the ski lift, it was late afternoon and most of the skiers had left. He was the sole passenger on the lift. Meanwhile Jerry, the employee at the top, had left his post to go to the bathroom, asking his friend Gary to keep watch on the lift and to stop it to allow any passengers to disembark. Gary consented and Jerry showed him how to use the control switch.

When Tod approached the top, Jerry was still away. Instead of stopping the lift to permit Tod to get off, Gary allowed the lift to keep moving. Tod was carried past the platform and he was swung violently from side to side as the ski lift started downward. When Jerry returned and sized up the situation, he threw the switch, stopping the lift. Tod, severely bruised and badly frightened, jumped off the ski lift and completed his descent by foot.

141. In a personal injury action by Tod against Oscar, Tod will rely on the basis of

(A) *respondeat superior*
(B) vicarious liability
(C) joint venture
(D) imputed negligence

142. If Tod asserts a claim against the Mogel Co. for personal injuries, Tod will most likely

(A) prevail, since Mogel would be vicariously liable for Jerry's unauthorized actions
(B) prevail, since Gary's negligence would be imputed to Mogel
(C) not prevail, since Jerry acted outside the scope of employment by entrusting the operation of the ski lift to Gary
(D) not prevail, since Gary's inaction did not impose any tort liability on Mogel

143. Assume for the purposes of this question only that as Tod was ascending on the ski lift, the lift suddenly broke down due to a power failure in the area. Tod was suspended in his lift chair, one third of the way up the hill and 50 feet above the ground. Tod remained on the lift for five hours until power was restored. He was then returned uninjured to the bottom of the hill. In a suit against Mogel and Oscar, Tod is likely to have action(s) for:

(A) false imprisonment
(B) negligence
(C) assault
(D) no cause of action

Questions 144–145 are based on the following fact situation.

Defense Systems Company (hereinafter referred to as Defense) provided home security protection to property owners in the San Diego and La Jolla area. Chuck Munchkin, who owned a summer cottage in La Jolla, hired Defense to provide 24-hour protection during the winter months when his home was unoccupied. According to the security arrangement, Defense's uniformed guards would periodically patrol the property and, if necessary, provide an "armed response" to any unauthorized individuals who were found trespassing on the property.

Defense provided security protection to Munchkin's property for two years. Then on December 7, 1983 Munchkin notified Defense that he was planning to sell the cottage. As a result, he requested that Defense discontinue its home protection service effective immediately. Two weeks later, Kelly Winslow, a burglar, broke into the cottage and was ransacking it. As Kelly was running across the front lawn (of Munchkin's property) carrying a portable television set, he was seen by Doug Fauts, a Defense security guard. Fauts, who was driving past the home on secu-rity patrol, had not been informed that Munchkin had discontinued protection service. Fauts suddenly stopped his patrol vehicle and ran toward Winslow shouting, "Stop ... Don't move or I'll shoot." Startled, Winslow dropped the television set and began to flee. Believing that the suspected burglar was about to escape, Fauts pulled out his service revolver and fired a bullet at Winslow. The shots struck Winslow in the leg, seriously wounding him.

144. If Winslow asserts a claim against Defense Systems for damages for his injuries, Winslow will

(A) prevail, because Fauts used unreasonable force to protect Munchkin's property
(B) prevail, because Munchkin had notified Defense to discontinue its security protection service
(C) not prevail, because Winslow was trespassing on Munchkin's property
(D) not prevail, because Winslow was burglarizing on Munchkin's cottage when he was shot

145. If Winslow asserts a claim against Munchkin for damages for his injuries, Winslow will probably

(A) prevail, because Winslow was unarmed when he was shot
(B) prevail, if he did not know nor had reason to know that Defense provided an "armed response" to suspected trespassers
(C) not prevail, because Winslow was committing a criminal act when he was shot
(D) not prevail, because Munchkin had discontinued his protection service from Defense when the shooting occurred

Questions 146–148 are based on the following fact situation.

At 10:00 P.M. on November 14th, Driver was operating his automobile down Sunset Boulevard in Beaver Falls. As Driver was approaching the intersection of Sunset Boulevard and Vine Street, Motorist, who was driving straight through a red light, suddenly appeared before him. Trying to avoid Motorist, Driver veered his car onto the sidewalk. The car landed in a deep hole in the sidewalk. This hole had been dug by the Fall-Tee Construction Company which had been repairing a water main break earlier in the day. Fall-Tee had been hired by the Beaver Falls Municipal Water Department. Although Fall-Tee had erected a warning sign advising pedestrians about the hole, there was no fence or barrier surrounding it.

When Driver's car fell into the hole, it ruptured the water main, engulfing the car with water. Within a short time, Driver, unable to escape, drowned in his car which rapidly filled with water.

Fifteen minutes later, Walker was proceeding down Vine Street. The warning sign had been knocked down by Driver's car after it veered onto the sidewalk. As a result, Walker was unaware of the dangerous condition as he approached the gaping hole. In the darkness, Walker, not seeing the hole, fell in. As Walker was attempting to stay afloat, he began screaming, "Help! Help! I can't swim. I'm drowning." His screams attracted the attention of Rescuer, who immediately hurried to assist Walker. As Rescuer was leaning over the hole attempting to pull Walker out, he lost his balance and plunged into the hole himself. Both Walker and Rescuer suffered serious bodily injuries before they were pulled out of the hole by the Beaver Falls Rescue Squad.

146. In a wrongful death action by Driver's estate against the Beaver Falls Municipal Water Department, they will most probably

(A) prevail, since sovereign immunity would not attach to non-delegable duties which are proprietary in nature
(B) prevail, only if Fall-Tee was negligent in failing to enclose the hole
(C) not prevail, since the Water Department would not be liable for the negligence of its independent contractor
(D) not prevail, since sovereign immunity attaches to functions that are governmental in nature

147. Which of the following facts or inferences, if true, would be most helpful in a wrongful death action by Driver's estate against Motorist?

(A) Fall-Tee's work crew failed to post the warning sign on the day of the accident.
(B) The Municipal Water Department had instructed Fall-Tee to erect a fence or barrier around the hole.
(C) The traffic signal at Sunset and Vine had been inspected the day before the accident and found to be functioning properly.
(D) Motorist was operating his vehicle without his driver's license in violation of the State Motor Vehicle Code.

148. In a negligence action by Rescuer to recover for his personal injuries, the Municipal Water Department will most probably

(A) be held liable, since there is an independent duty of care owed to the rescuer
(B) be held liable, since the hole constituted an unreasonably dangerous artificial condition
(C) not be held liable, since Rescuer assumed the risk by leaning over the hole
(D) not be held liable, since the Water Department would be immune from such personal injury actions

Question 149 is based on the following fact situation.

Ozark, an avid Philadelphia Phillies baseball fan, wanted to purchase tickets for the World Series games being held in Philadelphia. He contacted the Phillies' ticket sales office which advised him that all tickets were to be placed on sale at the stadium at 9:00 a.m. the following day. Ozark, who was employed as a bricklayer, realized that he could not leave work to purchase the tickets. Consequently, Ozark telephoned his next-door neighbor, Smitty, and asked him if he would be interested in going to the stadium to purchase the World Series tickets. Smitty told Ozark that he would be happy to purchase the tickets for him, and that he (Smitty) also wanted to buy tickets for himself. However, Smitty said that his car had broken down and that he didn't have available transportation to get to the stadium. Ozark suggested that Smitty could "borrow" his car. Smitty agreed, and the following morning the two men met in front of Ozark's home.

Ozark gave Smitty the keys to his car and also $50 with which to buy his World Series tickets. Thereafter, Smitty drove Ozark's car to the stadium where he purchased the tickets for Ozark and (using his own money) also bought a set of tickets for himself. Ozark had instructed Smitty to return the car to Ozark's home after his trip to the stadium. After Smitty left the stadium, however, he decided to visit a friend in West Chester, a town located 12 miles from his home. As Smitty was driving towards West Chester, an automobile driven by Maddox crashed into his (Ozark's) car. The cost of repairing Ozark's car was determined to be more than the blue-book value of the auto.

149. In an action by Ozark against Smitty to recover damages resulting from the accident, Ozark will most likely

(A) recover nothing, since Smitty was on a joint venture when the accident occurred
(B) recover, the cost of repairing the car
(C) recover, the blue-book value of the car
(D) recover, only if Smitty was negligently operating the auto at the time of the accident

Question 150 is based on the following fact situation.

Flutie was the star quarterback on the Venice High School football team. Nicknamed the "Gondoliers", the team won the state championship beating the Capistrano Valley Christian "Crusaders" 61 - 5 in the title game.

After the game the "Gondoliers" held a victory rally at the high school gym. As the team was being honored, Flutie approached Suzie, one of the cheerleaders, and asked her out for a date. Suzie, who had a "crush" on Flutie, said she'd love to go out with him. Flutie told her, "Great, I'll pick you up at eight."

Later that evening Flutie was getting ready to drive to Suzie's when his car wouldn't start. Flutie then called his next door neighbor, Mooch, and asked him if he could borrow his car. Mooch, who was an old friend of Flutie's, agreed but told him, "O.K. but make sure you return it by 2:00 a.m." Flutie assented and then went to Suzie's house.

After picking her up, they drove to Le Hot Tub Club where they spent the night making love and watching XXX-rated movies. Losing track of time, Flutie and Suzie didn't leave Le Club until 3:00 a.m. After returning home around 4:00 a.m., Flutie decided that it was too late to return the car so he parked it in his driveway. He intended to return the car to Mooch in the morning.

A short while later a thief stole Mooch's car from outside Flutie's home. The police found the car three months later undamaged. Mooch, however, refused to accept the car and brought a claim against Flutie for conversion.

150. In his claim Mooch will

(A) succeed, because Flutie could have returned the car and failed to do so
(B) succeed, because Flutie left the car in his driveway and it was stolen
(C) not succeed, because Flutie intended to return the identical property he borrowed in an undamaged condition
(D) not succeed, because the criminal act of the thief was unforeseeable

Question 151 is based on the following fact situation.

Pedestrian was walking in front of The Brown Palace Hotel in downtown Denver when a chair was thrown from an unidentified hotel window. The chair struck Pedestrian on the head, knocking her unconscious. When Pedestrian recovered consciousness, she found herself in a nearby hospital with a doctor in attendance. An examination revealed that Pedestrian had suffered a concussion and severe head lacerations. A subsequent investigation revealed that the chair had, in fact, been thrown from a window at The Brown Palace Hotel. None of the hotel's employees or guests, however, admitted culpability for the incident.

151. If Pedestrian asserts a claim against The Brown Palace Hotel for negligence, will the doctrine of res ipsa loquitur enable her to recover?

(A) Yes, because the chair was within the control of the hotel.
(B) Yes, because a chair is not usually thrown from a window in the absence of someone's negligence.
(C) No, because the chair wasn't within the control of the hotel at the time Pedestrian was injured.
(D) No, because the hotel is not vicariously liable for the tortious conduct of its employees and guests.

Question 152 is based on the following fact situation.

A statute in the state of Lahaina makes it a misdemeanor for any motor vehicle to travel to the left of the center line of any two-way highway, road, or street.

Late for a business appointment, Velma was driving north on Bayshore Drive. Suddenly, she decided to pass the car in front of her. As she swung across the center line into the southbound lane, her vehicle collided with a fire engine. As a result of the accident, the fire engine was delayed in reaching Kareem's house, which was entirely destroyed by fire. Kareem's home was located on Memorial Way approximately one mile from the accident scene.

152. If Kareem asserts a claim against Velma, he will most likely

(A) recover the value of the house before the fire
(B) recover that part of his loss that would have been prevented if the accident had not occurred
(C) recover nothing because Velma was not responsible for causing the fire
(D) recover nothing because the statute was not designed to protect against the harm that resulted

Questions 153–155 are based on the following fact situation.

In June 2004, Hondo Kim, a Japanese businessman, opened an Oriental health and massage parlor known as The Pleasure Temple which was located at 6969 Frye Street in San Francisco. The Pleasure Temple featured attractive Oriental masseuses who specialized in the art of body massage. In addition, the Temple provided health club facilities such as saunas, steam rooms, and whirlpool baths.

Prudence Beck, a seventy-five-year-old spinster, resided across the street from the Temple. Prudence opposed the opening of the Temple because she believed that it was a "cover" for a bawdy house. During the day Prudence sat in her rocking chair on her front porch and observed a constant stream of businessmen entering the Pleasure Temple.

On the evening of June 29th, Prudence, disguising her voice, called The Temple and told Mr. Kim, "You pimp, you purveyor of sluts, why don't you take your dirty trade elsewhere." Without paying any attention to the call, Mr. Kim hung up.

Prudence then began making repeated obscene telephone calls to Mr. Kim's establishment. Every hour on the hour for the next three weeks, Prudence made her crank calls harassing Mr. Kim and his employees. As a result of the hourly phone calls, the Temple business was constantly disrupted causing Mr. Kim to suffer a decline in the volume of customers. After contacting the police, Mr. Kim discovered that Prudence was the person making the harassing phone calls.

153. If Mr. Kim asserts a claim against Prudence, the theory on which he will most likely prevail is

(A) public nuisance
(B) private nuisance
(C) intentional infliction of emotional distress
(D) negligence

154. If Mr. Kim asserts a claim based on invasion of privacy against Prudence for the telephone calls, the most likely outcome is that Mr. Kim will

(A) prevail, since the telephone calls intruded upon his seclusion and solitude
(B) prevail, only if Mr. Kim was able to prove malice on the defendant's part
(C) prevail, since the telephone calls caused Mr. Kim to suffer economic hardship
(D) not prevail, since Prudence believed that her actions were in the public interest

155. If Mr. Kim asserts a claim for defamation against Prudence based on the June 29th telephone call, he will most likely

(A) succeed, since Prudence's remarks constituted slander per se
(B) succeed on the theory of slander if Mr. Kim is able to prove by way of colloquium, that the defamatory meaning attached to him
(C) succeed, since Prudence's remarks constituted libel per quod
(D) not succeed, since Prudence's remarks were not published or communicated to anyone but the plaintiff

Questions 156–157 are based on the following fact situation.

Mr. Zimmer, a resident of Wealthy Heights, an exclusive residential area, is a marine biologist. To aid in his study of sharks, he had a large tank built in his backyard in which he placed a great white shark.

Due to a problem in the filter system, the tank emitted a pungent smell. As a result, many neighbors were concerned and afraid to let their children outside, for fear that they would wander onto Mr. Zimmer's property. In order to convince his next-door neighbors, Mr. and Mrs. Nervous and Mr. and Mrs. Darvon, that they had nothing to fear, Mr. Zimmer invited them over to view the shark tank. While Mrs. Nervous was standing near the tank, the shark splashed its tail and Mrs. Nervous got very wet. Mrs. Nervous, who had a cold, developed bronchitis.

156. If Mrs. Nervous sues Mr. Zimmer for damages incurred from being drenched by the shark, and bases her suit on strict liability in tort, she will most likely:

(A) recover, because the possessor of wild animals is strictly liable for all injuries caused to others by the animals
(B) recover, because she was an invitee
(C) not recover, because she was a licensee
(D) not recover, because she did not sustain the type of harm normally inflicted by a shark

157. Assume for the purposes of this question only that although Mr. and Mrs. Darvon owned the property next to Mr. Zimmer's house, they lived in Malibu while another family lived on the property under a long-term lease. If Mr. and Mrs. Darvon assert an action in nuisance, Mr. Zimmer's best defense would be:

(A) that he (Zimmer) kept the shark tank for the purpose of studying an endangered species
(B) that his keeping the tank did not violate any zoning ordinance
(C) since the Darvons did not live on the property (next to Zimmer's), they did not have actual possession or the right to immediate possession of the land
(D) Mr. and Mrs. Darvon purchased the property (next to Zimmer's) with knowledge of the shark tank

Questions 158–160 are based on the following fact situation.

Richard Levin, a third-year student at Tower Hill Law School, applied to take the Delaware Bar examination. Upon receiving Richard's application, the Delaware Board of Bar Examiners sent a letter to the Tower Hill Law School requesting that they forward Richard Levin's academic file. Upon receiving this request, Holly Donavan, an administrative secretary at Tower Hill Law School, inadvertently pulled the file of another third year student named Richard Levine, and forwarded the latter's file to the Board of Bar Examiners.

Richard Levine's file contains a letter written by Professor Kingsfield, which accused Levine as being "an unscrupulous individual who cavorts with the most unchaste women in town."

When Vicky Vinton, secretary of the Board of Bar Examiners, received this information, she did not notice that the file was that of Richard Levine rather than Richard Levin. Consequently, she attached Levine's academic file to Levin's bar application and forwarded it to the Board for their review. Without the Board's knowledge, Vicky, who had been jilted by Levin, read the contents of this file. After reading Professor Kingsfield's letter, Vicky telephoned the editor of the local newspaper, *The Delaware Daily*. She informed him that a prospective bar applicant named Richard Levin was a "high class pimp".

The following day *The Delaware Daily* ran a front page story about Levin. The headline read "Will Board of Bar Examiners approve Pimp's Bar Application?" The Board of Bar Examiners promptly rejected Levin's bar application upon reading this newspaper account.

158. In a defamation action by Levine against Professor Kingsfield for the remarks contained in the letter, the most likely result is that Levine will

(A) recover for libel, since the statement was defamatory on its face
(B) recover for libel per quod if special damages are pleaded and proved
(C) not recover, since a qualified privilege would extend to all internal communications made within an educational institution
(D) not recover, since it was unforeseeable that Professor Kingsfield's statement would be republished

159. If Levin were to institute a defamation action against Vicky, in all likelihood he will

(A) prevail on the basis of libel only if he can prove malice on Vicky's part
(B) prevail on the basis of slander per se without proof of special damages
(C) prevail on the basis of slander despite any wrongful intent or improper motive on Vicky's part
(D) not prevail, since Vicky was privileged in the public interest to inform the newspaper

160. In a defamation action by Levin against *The Delaware Daily*, which of the following arguments would be most controlling in the court's determination of the outcome?

(A) As a public figure, Levin would be required to show "actual malice" on the part of the newspaper.
(B) Since Levin was a private figure, the newspaper's qualified privilege would be defeated by its negligence in failing to check its source.
(C) The newspaper would be privileged to report the story because it was newsworthy and a matter of public concern.
(D) Since the publication was defamatory on its face, Levin would be required to plead and prove special damages.

Questions 161–163 are based on the following fact situation.

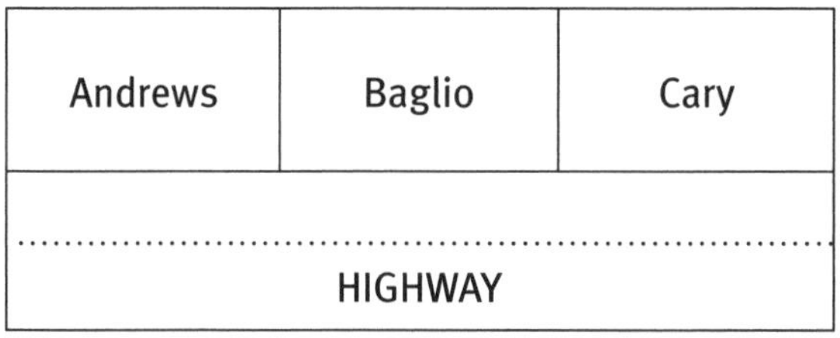

Andrews owned parcel 1; Baglio owned parcel 2; and Cary owned parcel 3. Each owner and his family lived on the property units in single-family dwellings. One afternoon Baglio and his thirteen-year-old son, Sal, were raking leaves in their front yard. After raking the leaves into a large pile, Sal and his father scooped the leaves into two large metal containers. Before burning the leaves, Baglio telephoned the local weather bureau to determine which direction the wind would be blowing. Since a highway was located on the southern edge of Baglio's property, he was aware that it would be unsafe to burn the leaves if the wind were blowing in that direction. The weather bureau, however, indicated that the wind would be gusting in a northerly direction. As a result, Baglio told Sal that it would be safe to burn the leaves.

After Baglio set the leaves on fire, the wind current unexpectantly shifted and started gusting in a southerly direction. As a consequence, the smoke and ashes blew over the highway resulting in poor visibility. After starting the fire, Baglio and his son went inside to watch the Army and Navy football game. Moments later, Sprinks was driving his automobile in a westerly direction. The posted speed limit was 45 miles per hour, although Sprinks was traveling about 55 mph. Because of the smoke, Sprinks could not see the highway clearly and crashed his vehicle into a medial strip.

Shortly thereafter, a wind gust blew some burning leaves onto Andrews' property causing a small fire amid some brush. Andrews quickly extinguished the fire and telephoned Baglio telling him what had occurred. Baglio immediately ran outside and doused the smoldering leaves with water. The dousing caused giant billows of smoke to pass over Cary's property, which caused his home to become discolored. This jurisdiction follows the common law principles of contributory negligence and assumption of risk.

161. If Sprinks asserts a claim against Baglio, Baglio's best defense is that

(A) the weather bureau assured him that the wind would be blowing in a northerly direction
(B) he used reasonable care by burning the leaves in metal cans
(C) Sprinks was driving in excess of the speed limit
(D) Sprinks was contributorily negligent under the circumstances

162. If Andrews asserts a claim against Baglio, Andrews will most likely

(A) recover, because Baglio is strictly liable for the spread of the fire
(B) recover, because Baglio was negligent in leaving the fire unattended
(C) recover, because Baglio created a public nuisance in failing to control the fire
(D) not recover, because Baglio is not liable for an unforeseeable act of God

163. If Cary asserts a claim against Baglio, Cary will probably

(A) recover for strict liability
(B) recover for negligence
(C) recover for nuisance
(D) recover for trespass

Question 164 is based on the following fact situation.

Lois Childs was employed as a legal secretary for Jay Ewing, a Dallas attorney. After Ewing terminated Childs' employment, she sent a job application and resume' to another Dallas attorney named Pat Duffy. In her resume' to Duffy, Childs listed her former employment with Ewing. After receiving Childs' resume', Duffy telephoned Ewing for his opinion of her qualifications. Ewing replied that he dismissed Childs "because she was unprofessional and incompetent." Ewing's assessment was based on one malpractice incident for which he blamed Childs, but which in fact was attributable to another secretary in his law firm. Although Ewing believed that his low rating of Childs was a fair reflection of her performance, he wrongfully held her responsible for the malpractice incident. Based on Ewing's poor recommendation, Duffy did not hire Childs.

164. In a defamation action by Childs against Ewing, the plaintiff will most likely

(A) prevail, because Ewing's statement reflected adversely on Childs' professional competence
(B) prevail, because Ewing was mistaken in the facts upon which he based his opinion of Childs' performance
(C) not prevail, if Ewing had reasonable grounds for his belief that Childs was incompetent
(D) not prevail, because Childs listed her former employment with Ewing in her resume' to Duffy

Questions 165–166 are based on the following fact situation.

Russell had noticed a peculiar "shimmy" in the steering wheel of his automobile, which appeared to him to have been getting progressively worse in the course of the preceding week. As a result, Russell decided to take his car to a service garage for inspection and repair. He was about to leave his home for this purpose when his wife, Heidi, ran in from the kitchen explaining that their 4-year-old son Justin, had just swallowed some medicine which had been prescribed for use as a skin lotion. Dashing to the car, Russell then drove his wife and ailing son to the nearest hospital. As he drove north on Kingman Street, his wheel began to shimmy crazily and his car went out of control, swinging across the center line into the southbound lane, where it collided with Johncock, who was driving south.

In this jurisdiction a statute makes it a misdemeanor for any motor vehicle to travel to the left of the center line of any two-way highway, road or street.

165. If Johncock asserts a claim against Russell, the most likely result is that plaintiff will

(A) prevail, because Russell is strictly liable for violating the statute
(B) prevail, because the statute was designed to protect motorists such as Johncock
(C) prevail, because Russell was aware that the steering was faulty
(D) not prevail, because Russell was acting in an emergency situation

166. Assume for the purposes of this question only that a few days after Russell discovered the "shimmy" in the steering wheel, he loaned his automobile to his next-door neighbor, Oscar. When Oscar picked up the car, Russell forgot to tell him about the "shimmy". Oscar was driving Russell's car at a reasonable rate of speed within the posted speed limit when the car began to swerve across the highway. Oscar turned the steering wheel to the right in an attempt to drive the car onto the shoulder of the highway. The steering failed, however, and the car drifted in the opposite direction into the path of Clark's car. The two cars collided and both Oscar and Clark were injured. If Oscar initiates suit against Russell, the former will most likely

(A) prevail, because Russell knew the steering was faulty and failed to tell Oscar
(B) prevail, because Russell is strictly liable under the circumstances
C) not prevail, because the faulty steering was the cause in fact of Oscar's harm
(D) not prevail, because Russell was a gratuitous lender

Question 167 is based on the following fact situation.

On May 19, Irma, a telephone operator for the Mid-Atlantic Telephone Co., received a call in which a male voice said: "I want to report that the Sansom Sporting Arena is going to be blown up tonight." The caller then hung up. The line on which the call was made was a two party line shared by a Miss Tomlin and a Mrs. Anderson. Immediately after receiving the call, Irma reported the threatening conversation to the police. About half an hour later, during which time she had handled a number of other calls, Irma received a call from a police officer who was at Miss Tomlin's home. He asked her to listen to a voice. After she did, the officer asked Irma if she could identify it. Irma responded that she was positive that it was the original voice who had made the threat. As a result of Irma's identification, Miss Tomlin's boyfriend, Mouthy, was arrested and charged with the crime of terroristic threatening.

As a consequence of the arrest, Mouthy lost his job and suffered embarassment and ridicule in the community. At trial, however, Irma's identification proved to be erroneous and Mouthy was exonerated.

167. In a defamation action for slander by Mouthy against Irma and the Mid-Atlantic Telephone Co., he will most likely

(A) succeed, since Irma's erroneous identification constituted slander per se
(B) succeed, since Irma's erroneous identification re-sulted in the loss of his good reputation in the community
(C) not succeed, since Irma's erroneous identification was made without actual malice
(D) not succeed, since Irma's erroneous identification constituted a qualified privilege in the public interest

Question 168 is based on the following fact situation.

Homeowner was planning to construct a new pool in her backyard. She hired Anthony, a well-known pool contractor, to design and construct the pool. Anthony in turn hired Dozer to dig the hole and plaster the pool area. After Dozer completed his job, Anthony then hired Electrician to install the heater and wiring for the pool. While Electrician was performing his work, the wiring became disjointed and had to be replaced at a substantial expense to Homeowner.

168. If Homeowner sues Electrician in tort to recover the damages she suffered because of this occurrence, will Homeowner prevail?

(A) Yes, if the wiring became disjointed because Electrician's plans departed from established standards in the electrical industry.
(B) No, unless the electrical wiring that became disjointed was defective.
(C) No, if Electrician used his best professional judgment in performing the electrical work.
(D) No, unless Homeowner knew that Anthony had hired Electrician to perform the electrical work.

Questions 169–170 are based on the following fact situation.

Crum purchased a new 2005 Jaguar XJS convertible from Cougar Motors. After driving it 1,000 miles, Crum began smelling a pungent gasoline odor in the vehicle. Crum immediately took the car to Cougar and told the service manager what was wrong. The service manager, indicated that he would take care of the problem and contact Crum when the car was ready. The next day, Crum was informed that the problem had been corrected and the car was available for pick-up. Crum then went to the dealership, took possession of his car and drove off. After traveling about five miles, Crum again smelled gasoline fumes. Aggravated that the problem had not been corrected, Crum decided to drive back to Cougar. As he was doing so, the car suddenly exploded and Crum suffered third-degree burns over ninety percent of his body.

A subsequent investigation revealed that the explosion was caused by a defective gas tank which had ruptured. This produced a gasoline leak that was ignited by sparks from the car's underbody. A reasonable inspection would have disclosed the defective gas tank. The trouble Crum had described to the service manager was indicative of such a problem.

169. If Crum asserts a claim against the manufacturer of the Jaguar for damages for his injuries, will Crum prevail?

(A) Yes, if Cougar should have replaced the gas tank.
(B) Yes, because Crum's injury was caused by the defective gas tank.
(C) No, if Crum should have realized the gasoline smell presented a hazardous condition and stopped the car before the explosion occurred.
(D) No, unless the gas tank was defective when the car left the manufacturer's plant.

170. If Crum asserts a claim against Cougar Motors for damages for his injuries, will Crum prevail?

(A) Yes, if the gas tank was defective when it was sold by Cougar to Crum.
(B) Yes, because Cougar is strictly liable for defective repairs on cars it has sold.
(C) No, because the car had been driven 1,000 miles.
(D) No, unless Cougar was negligent in repairing the gas tank.

Question 171 is based on the following fact situation.

Agnes was employed as a bankteller at the Bowery Savings Bank. One morning Deke, a customer, entered the bank to make a deposit. As Deke handed the deposit to Agnes, she saw that he had a misprinted $5 bill in his possession. Agnes knew that the $5 bill, which had President Lincoln's picture upside down, was worth $500 to bill collectors. Agnes then asked Deke if he would like to exchange "that old $5 bill for a new bill". Deke accepted Agnes' offer and handed her the misprinted bill for a new one. One week later, Deke learned that the $5 bill which he gave Agnes was valued at $500.

171. If Deke asserts a claim against Agnes for deceit, will he prevail?

(A) Yes, because Deke was the true owner of the misprinted bill, and therefore he was entitled to the benefit of the bargain.
(B) Yes, because Agnes did not disclose the true value of the misprinted bill.
(C) No, because Agnes made no false representation of fact.
(D) No, because Deke was not justified in relying on Agnes' offer.

Question 172 is based on the following fact situation.

Franklin Stubbs held title in fee simple to a tract of 20 acres located outside the boundaries of Durham. Thereafter Franklin constructed a shopping center on the property and leased commercial buildings and parking facilities to various tenants. The shopping center which was located near a public high school attracted many teenagers who often loitered in the parking lot. The youths frequently harassed shoppers and damaged autos by breaking off windshield wipers and radio antennas.

Customarily, the local police department patrol the shopping center and drive-by three or four times each day. This, however, has not prevented the teenagers from hanging out at the shopping center. One afternoon Bette was shopping at the center when an unidentified youth damaged her car by throwing a rock through the back window.

172. Bette brings an action against Stubbs to recover for the damage to her auto. She will most likely

(A) prevail, unless the person who was responsible for damaging her car can be identified
(B) prevail, if the damage to her car could have been prevented had Stubbs taken reasonable security measures
(C) not prevail, because the car was damaged by the malicious acts of an independent third person
(D) not prevail, because the local police had the primary duty to provide security protection at the shopping area

Questions 173–175 are based on the following fact situation.

Buddy Carrelli, legislative assistant to Senator William Harrison, approached various wealthy Arab lobbyists without the Senator's knowledge, to solicit illegal campaign contributions for the Senator's upcoming re-election campaign in the State of South Jersey. Buddy dictated several letters requesting such contributions which Senator Harrison signed without reading, along with a pile of other correspondence. Before the letters were mailed, however, the Senator discovered what had happened and then immediately terminated Buddy's employment.

Later that same evening after being notified that he was fired, Buddy returned to Capitol Hill and used his keys which had not yet been returned, to enter the Senator's office. Buddy then proceeded to the correspondence files in the office. Since the original letters in question were destroyed, he removed copies of the letters from the file cabinets.

The following day Buddy turned over the copies of the letters to Bob Bernfield, an investigative reporter from the *Washington Planet*, the largest newspaper in the Washington, D.C. area. Bob had heard about Buddy's dismissal from another staff member, and was curious about all the underlying circumstances. After Buddy provided Bob with all of the pertinent facts, Bob wrote a news story regarding Senator Harrison's solicitation of illegal campaign contributions from various wealthy Arabs. Although Bob's story was printed in *The Planet*, he did not reveal the source of his information. As soon as the publication was made, the FBI initiated an investigation of Senator Harrison's campaign finances.

173. If Senator Harrison asserts a claim based on invasion of privacy against *The Planet* for the publication of the article concerning the solicitation of illegal campaign contributions, the most likely result is that the Senator will

    (A) prevail, only if the Senator is able to prove malice on the defendant's part
    (B) prevail, since the newspaper story placed the Senator in a "false light in the public eye"
    (C) prevail, since the newspaper disclosed private facts about the plaintiff
    (D) not prevail, since the newspaper was acting in the public interest by printing the news story

174. In a defamation action by Senator Harrison against the *Washington Planet* and Bob Bernfield for the publication of the news story, which of the following is the most accurate statement with regard to the defendants' -liability?

    (A) A qualified privilege of fair comment existed since the defendants were reporting on a matter of public interest.
    (B) Since the Senator was a public figure, he has the -burden of proof to show malice on the part of the defendants.
    (C) The defendants would not be liable because under the First Amendment freedom of press, the newspaper was privileged to publish the story.
    (D) The defendants would be relieved of any liability for defamation since an absolute privilege existed, regardless of the malice requirement.

175. If Senator Harrison brings suit in defamation against Buddy Carrelli for turning over the copies of the letters in question to Bob Bernfield, the Senator will most likely

    (A) recover on the basis of libel per se, since Buddy was aware of the false statements in the letters
    (B) recover on the basis of libel, since the letters were defamatory on their face
    (C) recover on the basis of slander, even though Buddy did not have a malicious intent or improper motive for turning the letters over to Bernfield
    (D) not recover

1. **(A)** As previously mentioned in the outline, **Restatement of Torts,** 2d, Section 402A provides that "one who sells any product in a defective condition unreasonably dangerous to the user or consumer or to his property is (strictly) liable for the physical harm thereby caused... if the seller is engaged in the business of selling such a product." Based on the stated rule, Cummings Motors will be subject to strict liability ***if the car was defective at the time it left the seller's hands.***

2. **(C)** Note that the rule stated in the aforementioned section applies to any person engaged in the business of selling products for use or consumption. It therefore applies to any manufacturer of such a product, to any wholesale or retail dealer or distributor, and to the operator of a restaurant. ***The rule does not, however, apply to the occasional seller of food or other products who is not engaged in that activity as a part of his (or her) business.*** According to comment (f) of Section 402A, this rule "does not apply to the owner of an automobile who, on one occasion, sells it to his neighbor, or even sells it to a dealer in used cars, and this even though he is fully aware that the dealer plans to resell it." Thus, since Tresh was not engaged in the business of selling automobiles, choice (C) is the best answer.

3. **(B)** Prosser states that "the storage in quantity of explosives or inflammable liquids, or blasting, or the accumulation of sewage, or the emission of creosote fumes, or pile driving which sets up excessive vibration, all have been considered "non natural" uses, leading to strict liability when they result in harm to another." Note that choice (C) is incorrect because **Restatement of Torts,** 2d, Section 522 provides, "One carrying on an abnormally dangerous activity is subject to strict liability for the resulting harm although it is caused by the unexpectable operation of a force of nature." The rationale for imposing strict liability upon those who carry on abnormally dangerous activities is that they have for their own purposes created a risk that is not a usual incident of the ordinary life of the community.

4. **(C)** Once again, it is necessary for students to recognize the "fine line" distinctions tested on the MBE. Here, for example, you must distinguish this fact situation from the one presented in the next question. In this hypo, Rosebud's conduct was "extreme" and "outrageous" because it occurred at a Hall of Fame induction in front of hundreds of onlookers. As a consequence, Rosebud will be held liable for intentional infliction of mental distress rather than battery. ***Examination Tip:*** Remember that a plaintiff can recover for infliction of mental distress even though he or she did not suffer any physical injuries. According to Prosser, "there are a substantial number of decisions which have found liability for mere mental disturbance (e.g., humiliation or embarrassment) without any evidence of physical consequences." **Law of Torts,** pg. 59.

5. **(B)** Prosser tells us that freedom from intentional and unpermitted contacts with the plaintiff's person is protected by an action for the tort of battery. The protection extends to any part of the body, or to anything which is attached to it and practically identified with it. Thus, contact with the plaintiff's clothing, or with a cane, a paper, or any other object held in his hand, will be sufficient; and the same is true of the chair in which he sits, the horse or the car which he is riding or driving, or the person against whom he is leaning. Therefore, where defendant acts, intending to offend plaintiff's sense of dignity, as by pulling out the chair in which plaintiff is about to sit, he (defendant) is liable for battery.

Multistate Nuance Chart:

TORTS

Question 4		Question 5
Rosebud's conduct was **EXTREME & OUTRAGEOUS** which is the basis for tortious **INFLICTION OF MENTAL DISTRESS**	← **Degree of Tortious Conduct** →	Carlos' conduct was **OFFENSIVE** which is the basis for tortious **BATTERY**

6. **(A)** Under the doctrine of "transferred intent," if the defendant shoots or strikes at A, intending to wound or kill him, and ***un***foreseeably hits B instead, he is held liable to B for an intentional tort. The intent to commit a battery upon A is pieced together with the resulting injury to B; it is "transferred" from A to B. Prosser in **Law of Torts** points out that "the intention follows the bullet." Similarly, since "Happy" intended to hit Rita, he would be liable for committing a tortious battery upon Paul under the aforementioned doctrine.

7. **(C)** In accordance with the **Restatement of Torts,** 2d, Section 435 (2), the defendant is not liable for consequences which, looking backward after the event with full knowledge of all that has occurred, would appear to be "highly extraordinary." In other words, it was "unforeseeable" that one would fire a weapon at someone who refused to service them.

8. **(D)** Students should be aware that an actor is subject to liability to another for battery if he acts ***intending to cause*** a harmful or offensive contact with the person of another. In the present hypothetical, Granny did ***not*** act intending to cause a harmful or offensive contact, and therefore, liability for battery would not attach.

9. **(B)** Note that an actor is subject to liability for battery if he acts intending to cause a harmful *or* offensive contact with the person of another. Since the essence of the plaintiff's grievance consists in the offense to the dignity involved in the unpermitted and intentional invasion of the inviolability of his person and not in any physical harm done to his body, it is *not necessary* that the plaintiff's actual body be disturbed.

10. **(B)** Since Ellen did not imminently apprehend being hit by the tennis ball, Patsy would not be subject to liability for assault. However, Patsy would be liable of battery for operating the tennis machine intending to "hit" Ellen with the balls.

11. **(A)** In answering this question, it is necessary to know that elephants are classified as wild animals. According to **Restatement of Torts,** 2d, Section 507, "A possessor of a wild animal is subject to (strict) liability for trespass to another for harm done" even though the possessor has exercised the utmost care to confine the animal. As a result, choice (A) is the best answer. Be advised that the rule involving ***strict liability for trespass*** should not be confused with strict liability for harm done by wild animals that results from the dangerous propensities that are characteristic of that particular class of animals.

Multistate Nuance Chart:

TORTS

WILD ANIMALS		DOMESTICATED ANIMALS	
Lions	Rattlesnakes	Cattle	Bulls
Tigers	Alligators	Sheep	Stallions
Bears	Ostriches	Horses	Parrots
Elephants	Tsetse flies	Dogs	Bees
Wolves	"Killer" bees	Cats	Goats
Monkeys	Guard dogs	Mules	

Multistate Exam Tip: Note that the possessor of "livestock" (including cattle, horses, sheep, hogs, and such wandering fowls as turkeys, chickens and pigeons), however, is held ***strictly liable for their trespasses.***

12. **(C)** According to **Restatement of Torts** 2d, Section 19, "a bodily contact is offensive if it offends a reasonable sense of personal dignity." Comment (a) further states that "in order that a contact be offensive to a reasonable sense of personal dignity it must be one which would offend the ordinary person and as such one not unduly sensitive as to his personal dignity." Thus, the contact must be unwarranted by the social usages prevalent at the time and place at which it is inflicted. Under the circumstances presented here, Rider's conduct would be socially acceptable and therefore, he would not be liable for any offensive touching or harmful contact.

13. **(C)** This question presents a very difficult interplay between the torts of negligence and battery, and it must be answered by process of elimination. Choice (D) is the easiest response to eliminate because it is inconclusive. The fact that a firearm, a dangerous instrumentality, is used in the commission of a tort does not by itself impose either strict liability, negligence, or an intentional tort. Choice (A) is also incorrect. According to Prosser, a "servant's conduct is within the scope of his employment if it is of the kind which he is employed to perform, occurs substantially within the authorized limits of time and space, and is actuated, at least in part, by a purpose to serve the master". **Prosser and Keeton, Torts,** p. 502. Silver's conduct in shooting at Dugan, although forbidden by Conroy's, was undertaken during the time of employment to protect Conroy's interests, and would likely be deemed "within the scope", due to the nature of employment in that Silver was a security guard. Choices (B) and (C) are very close, the former basing Howser's claim on negligence ***only,*** and the latter basing the claim on the intentional tort of battery. Choice (B) is incorrect because it is too narrow since it disallows the possibility of battery and is based solely on a claim of negligence. Conversely, choice (C) is the correct answer because it is merely stating that plaintiff will prevail ***if*** a battery occurred — if any of the shattered glass touched Howser — but it does not prelude the existence of a possible negligence claim. Students should note that this type of "if-unless" wording analysis is tested very commonly on the Multistate.

14. **(A)** In accordance with **Restatement of Torts,** 2d, Section 158, "One is subject to liability to another for trespass, irrespective of whether he thereby causes harm to any legally protected interest of the other, if he ***intentionally*** (a) enters the land in the possession of the other, or causes a thing or a third person to do so, or (b) remains on the land, or (c) fails to remove from the land a thing which he is under a duty to move." Students should also be cognizant that one may also be liable for trespass for intrusions resulting from ***reckless or negligent conduct*** and ***abnormally dangerous activities.*** In this regard, **Restatement of Torts,** 2d, Section 165, provides that "One who recklessly or negligently, or as a result of an abnormally dangerous activity, enters land in the possession of another or causes a thing or third person so to enter is subject to liability (for trespass)." Note that choice (B) is wrong because the facts do not indicate that Marty either ***intentionally or negligently*** caused the ball to enter onto Dickie's property.

15. **(D)** Students should be aware that no battery occurred. In accordance with **Restatement of Torts,** 2d, Section 18, "an actor is subject to liability to another for battery if (a) he acts intending to cause a harmful or offensive contact with the person of the other and (b) an offensive contact with the person of the other directly or indirectly results." It is important to point out, however, that an act which is not done with the intention stated in subsection (b) does not make the actor liable to the other for a mere offensive contact with the other's person. Thus, Marty, *not* intending to strike Dickie with the golf ball, would not be held liable for battery. Similarly, Marty would not be liable for assault since he did not intend to cause a harmful or offensive contact to Dickie's person, nor did he intend to put Dickie in imminent apprehension of such conduct.

16. **(D)** In light of the preceding explanation, Marty would not be subject to tort liability to either.

17. **(C)** Approximately 15 of the 34 Torts questions deal with ***negligence****. Foreseeability and proximate causation are specific areas that are highly tested. Students must be able to analyze multiple negligent acts which follow *directly* (i.e., an uninterrupted chain-of-events) or *indirectly* (i.e., where a period of time passes between intervening events) from the initial negligent conduct of the defendant, and then determine, by applying a test of foreseeability, whether or not the defendant's initial conduct remains as the proximate, or legal, cause of plaintiff's harm. In this question, it must be determined whether Cepeda, the plaintiff, was a ***foreseeable plaintiff*** to whom Laurie owed a duty. According to the majority (Cardozo) view, a defendant owes a duty of care only to those plaintiffs who are foreseeably within the risk of harm created by defendant's conduct (i.e., within the "zone of danger"). If Laurie could not reasonably have been expected to foresee injury to a person in Cepeda's position, then ***no duty would be owed***, and therefore, Laurie's negligence could not be the proximate cause of Cepeda's harm. *Beginning with the July, 1997 MBE there will be 34 Torts questions rather than 40 as in previous years.

18. **(C)** Violation of a statutory standard of care imposing a criminal penalty is held by the majority of jurisdictions to be presumption of negligence. Breach of such a statutory duty is ***negligence per se*** only if two requirements are met: (1) the plaintiff must be a member of the class of persons intended to be protected, and (2) the

plaintiff's harm must be of the type the statute was designed to prevent. If Wagner, the defendant, can show that Cepeda's injuries were not of the type intended to be prevented by enactment of an ordinance prohibiting parking within 50 feet of a fire hydrant, he will have a valid defense. Therefore, choice (C) is correct. ***Note:*** A small minority of jurisdictions follow the rule that violation of a criminal statute is ***only evidence of negligence.*** Students should follow the majority rule on the MBE, unless the facts say otherwise.

19. **(B)** One who by extreme and outrageous conduct intentionally or recklessly causes severe emotional distress to another is subject to liability for such emotional distress, if bodily harm to the other results from it, for such bodily harm. See **Restatement of Torts** 2d, Section 46. In short, the rule stated in this section imposes liability for intentionally causing severe emotional distress in those situations, as in the present illustration, in which the actor's conduct had gone beyond all reasonable bounds of decency. Generally, the cause is one in which the recitation of the facts to an average member of the community would arouse his resentment against the actor and lead him to exclaim, "Outrageous." Students should know that choice (A), though a correct statement, is the less preferred alternative because defendant's actions must, in addition to being the cause in fact, also be the proximate, or legal, cause of plaintiff's harm in order for defendant to incur civil liability.

20. **(C)** In conjunction with **Restatement of Torts** 2d, Section 35, an actor is subject to liability to another for false imprisonment if (a) he acts ***intending*** to confine the other or a third person within the boundaries fixed by the actor, and (b) his act directly or indirectly results in such a confinement of the other, and (c) the other is conscious of the confinement or is harmed by it. **NOTE:** An act which is not done with the intention stated in subsection (a) does not make the actor liable. Here, since Mr. Reel's intention was to have Tillie leave her home and return to the group, he did not possess the requisite intent to seek Tillie's confinement to her home. Although choices (B) and (D) are also correct, alternative (C) is the best answer since there is no false imprisonment unless the defendant *intends* to cause a confinement. It has been held that a mere incidental confinement due to acts directed at another purpose—as, for instance, locking the door with the plaintiff inside for the sole purpose of keeping others out—is not a sufficient basis for an action for false imprisonment.

21. **(B)** According to Dean Prosser, **Law of Torts** 3rd Ed. (1964) "the essence of a private nuisance is an interference with the use and enjoyment of the land. The ownership or rightful possession of land necessarily involves the right not only to unimpaired condition of the property itself, but also to some reasonable comfort and convenience in its occupation." Thus, in determining whether the billboard would constitute a private nuisance, the court will consider enumerated factors II and III. Here, it is important to distinguish between nuisance, which is an interference with one's use and enjoyment of his land and trespass, which is an invasion of plaintiff's interest in the exclusive possession of his land. Therefore, factor I is incorrect because the court will consider the billboard's invasion (of the exclusive possession of plaintiff's land) as the basis for a trespass, not nuisance action.

22. **(A)** The complex tort of invasion of right to privacy is not one tort, but comprises the four distinct wrongs of: (a) appropriation by the defendant of plaintiff's picture or name for defendant's commercial advantage; (b) intrusion by the defendant upon plaintiff's affairs or seclusion; (c) publication of facts by defendant which place plaintiff in a false light; or (d) public disclosure of private facts about the plaintiff by the defendant. In the present case, alternative (A) is correct since the billboard would clearly be viewed as an intrusion upon Tillie's physical solitude or seclusion. Note that the principle has been carried beyond such physical intrusion, and extended to eavesdropping upon private conversations by means of wire tapping and microphones; and there are decisions indicating that it is to be applied to peering into the windows of a home, as well as persistent and unwanted telephone calls. Hence, students should note that the intrusion must be something which would be offensive or objectionable to a reasonable man, and that there is no tort when the landlord stops by on Sunday morning to ask for the rent.

23. **(D)** Whether this is an action for defamation (choices A or C) or intentional infliction of emotional distress (choice B), answer choice (D) is correct because Sofie did not suffer sufficient damages. In order to recover for slander, plaintiff must plead and prove special damages (i.e., pecuniary loss). For infliction of emotional distress, the plaintiff must suffer severe emotional distress. If Sofie only suffered hurt feelings, then (D) obviously "trumps" all other possible answers.

24. **(C)** A popular Multistate testing area deals with proximate or legal cause. In order to be liable for negligence, defendant's conduct must constitute the legal or proximate cause of plaintiff's harm or injury. According to the rule enunciated in the *Palsgraf* case, Judge Cardozo stated that a defendant's duty of care is owed only to foreseeable plaintiffs (i.e., those individuals who are within the risk of harm created by defendant's unreasonable conduct). Choice (C) is the best answer because it addresses the fact that Bush was an unforeseeable plaintiff to whom no duty of care was owed.

25. **(C)** **Restatement of Torts** 2d, Section 63, defines self-defense as follows: "An actor is privileged to use reasonable force, not intended or likely to cause death or serious bodily harm, to defend himself against unprivileged harmful or offensive contact or other bodily harm which he reasonably believes that another is about to inflict intentionally upon him." Furthermore, a reasonable mistake as to the existence of the danger does not vitiate the defense. Even though Bush mistakenly thought he was being attacked by drug smugglers when he fired his gun, his belief as to the imminence of the danger was reasonable, since the facts state that he was hiding out to watch a trail frequently used by drug smugglers when he heard the shot from Lloyd's gun.

26. **(B)** Under Section 46 **Restatement of Torts** 2d, one who by extreme and outrageous conduct intentionally or recklessly causes severe emotional distress to another is subject to liability for such emotional distress. Moreover, where such conduct is directed at a third person, the actor is subject to liability if he intentionally or recklessly causes severe emotional distress to a member of such person's immediate family who is present at the time.

27. **(C)** Where the extreme and outrageous conduct is directed at a third person, the cases thus far decided have limited such liability to plaintiffs who were present at the time, as distinguished from those who discover later what has occurred.

28. **(D)** An actor is subject to liability to another for battery if (a) he acts intending to cause a harmful *or* offensive contact with the person of the other or a third person, or an imminent apprehension of such a contact, and (b) an offensive contact with the person of the other directly or indirectly results. Since Lester intended to douse Judge Cooch with water (from the sprinkling device), he would be liable for a battery. In addition, by directing water over Judge Cooch's property, Lester would be liable for trespass. Under **Restatement of Torts**, 2d, Section 158, "one is subject to liability to another for trespass, irrespective of whether he thereby causes harm to any legally protected interest of the other, if he ***intentionally*** (a) enters the land in the possession of the other, or causes a thing or a third person to do so.

29. **(C)** The elements of the tort action for deceit may be summarized as follows: (1) a false representation made by the defendant (usually this representation must be one of fact); (2) knowledge or belief on the part of the defendant that the representation is false; (3) an intention to induce the plaintiff to act or to refrain from action in reliance upon the misrepresentation; (4) justifiable reliance upon the representation on the part of the plaintiff; and (5) damage to the plaintiff, resulting from such reliance. In the present hypothetical, since the defendant did not make any false representation of fact, the correct answer is choice (C).

30. **(D)** Here's a classic Multistate example dealing with ***non-liability for "accidental" entries on land.*** In accordance with **Restatement of Torts 2d,** Section 166, "Except where the actor is engaged in an abnormally dangerous activity, an unintentional and non-negligent entry on land in the possession of another, or causing a thing or third person to enter the land, does *not* subject the actor to liability to the possessor, even though the entry causes harm to the possessor or to a thing or third person in whose security the possessor has a legally protected interest."

31. **(C)** This example illustrates the major problem most students encounter on the Multistate, namely choosing between two conceivably correct answers. Here, choices (A) and (B) are clearly incorrect because the cases thus far decided have found liability (for emotional distress) only where the ***defendant's conduct has been extreme and outrageous.*** Certainly, Cox's conduct was ***not*** *so* extreme in degree or so outrageous in character to go beyond all possible bounds of decency to be regarded as atrocious. Thus, most students will be able to narrow the correct answer down to choices (C) and (D). Here, the *test maker* knows that many students will incorrectly choose alternative (D) because they are aware that the extreme and outrageous character of the conduct may arise from the actor's knowledge that the other is peculiarly susceptible to emotional distress, by reason of some physical or mental condition or peculiarity. The conduct may become heartless, flagrant, and outrageous when the actor proceeds in the face of such knowledge, where it would not be so if he did not know. ***It must be emphasized, however, that major outrage is essential to the tort; and the mere fact that the actor knows that the other will regard the conduct as insulting, or will have his feelings hurt is not enough.*** Consequently, the correct answer is choice (C) rather than (D) for that reason.

32. **(C)** Under the "rescue doctrine" efforts to protect the personal safety of another have been held not to supersede the liability for the original negligence which has endangered it. As Judge Cardozo stated in *Wagner v. International R. Co.*, 232 N.Y. 176, 133 N.E. 437 (1921), "The risk of rescue, if only it be not wanton, is born of the occasion. The emergency begets the man." There is thus an independent duty of care owed to the rescuer himself, ***which arises even when the defendant endangers no one's safety but his own.*** Students must also remember that whether the rescuer succeeds in injuring himself, or the person rescued, or a stranger, ***the original wrongdoer is still liable.*** Prosser, pg. 277.

33. **(A)** Another popular testing area on the Multistate deals with situations involving an ***arrest without a warrant.*** As a general rule, either an officer or a private citizen may arrest without a warrant to prevent a felony or breach of peace which is being committed, or reasonably appears about to be committed, ***in his presence.*** Once the crime has been committed, however, the private person may still arrest but his authority depends upon the fact of the crime, and he must take the full risk that none has been committed. In the present case, the killing of the Riverdale police officers did ***not*** occur in Nelson's presence. As a result, he must take the full risk for falsely arresting Jones. Therefore, by pointing the pistol at Jones, Nelson would be liable for assault.

34. **(B)** A private person may arrest if a felony has in fact been committed, and she has reasonable grounds to suspect the man whom she arrests has committed the crime. Here, the facts state that the killings were committed by an individual who was a paraplegic and Caucasian. As a consequence, ***Nelson did not have reasonable grounds*** to believe that Jones was the suspected felon since he was a black man walking down the street. Note that (B) is a better answer than (A) because Nelson would have been privileged to detain Jones had his belief been reasonable.

35. **(C)** According to Section 197 (a) **Restatement of Torts** 2d, where the actor is acting for the protection of himself or his property he is privileged to enter another's property to prevent a threatened harm from taking effect.

36. **(B)** Under Section 197 (2) **Restatement of Torts** 2d Allen is not liable for his mere entry, although he is subject to liability for any harm caused in the exercise of the privilege stated in subsection (1).

37. **(A)** With respect to the defense of consent, Prosser in **Law of Torts** pg. 103, notes that consent is to the plaintiff's conduct rather than to its consequences. Thus, if the plaintiff willingly engages in a boxing match, he does not consent to be killed, although he does consent to the defendant's striking at him, and hitting him if he can; and consequently if death unexpectedly results, his consent to the act will defeat any action for the invasion of his interests. He does not, on the contrary, consent to being hit with brass knuckles, which is the same invasion by an act of a different character. In sum, defendant's privilege is limited to the conduct to which the plaintiff consents.

38. **(C)** The consent of the person damaged will ordinarily avoid liability for intentional interference with person or property. It is a fundamental principle of the common law that ***volenti non fit injuria***—to one who is willing, no wrong is done. Consent to

an act is simply willingness that it shall occur. Actual willingness, established by competent evidence, will prevent liability. Since Carlos consented to being punched in the chest, Hymie is not liable for battery. ***Examination Tip*:** The consent is to the plaintiff's conduct, rather than the consequences. If the plaintiff willingly engages in a boxing match, he does not of course consent to be killed, but he does consent to the defendant's striking at him, and hitting him if he can; and if death unexpectedly results, his consent to the act will defeat any action for the resulting invasion of his interests. Note that choice (B) is incorrect because Prosser points out that a ***"minor acquires capacity to consent to different kinds of invasions and conduct at different stages in his/her development."*** In other words, a 14 year-old boy who plays a tackle football game consents to physical contact. By the same token, teenage youngsters may consent to engage in fistfights or similar physical encounters.

39. **(A)** This question which deals with burden of proof requires a two-step analysis. First, it is necessary to recognize that lorg is bringing a negligence action against Dix. Certainly, lorg cannot be suing Dix for strict liability because Dix was the purchaser not the seller of the automobile. Next, on the issue of negligence is the sufficiency of evidence to permit a finding of the facts. In civil suits, unlike criminal prosecutions, the burden of proof does not require that the jury be convinced beyond all reasonable doubt, but only that they be persuaded that a preponderance of the evidence is in favor of the party sustaining the burden. Thus, the burden of proof of the defendant's negligence is quite uniformly upon the plaintiff, since he is asking the court for relief, and must lose if his case does not outweigh of proof (that Dix was driving negligently), choice (A) is correct.

40. **(B)** The tort of defamation requires the plaintiff to prove that the defendant intentionally communicated (i.e., published) a defamatory matter to some third person who reasonably understands that the plaintiff's reputation is lowered in the estimation of at least a substantial minority of the community or such that third persons are deterred from associating with the person to whom the matter refers. Additionally, since the First Amendment constitutional privileges likely encompass all ***pure opinions,*** whether false or not, the expression of pure opinions is not actionable. Prosser and Keeton, **Prosser and Keeton on Torts,** p. 813. Therefore, ***only statements of fact can be actionable as being defamatory.*** If Charlotte is suing Newman for calling her a "deadbeat," she will not prevail, unless reasonable third persons regard his statement as one of fact, not of opinion. Choice (B) is therefore correct. Choice (D) is not as precise since even if Newman's letter was highly offensive to reasonable persons, it would not be defamatory if it were merely a statement of opinion. Likewise, choice (C) is incorrect for failing to reach the more fundamental requirement that only statements of fact are actionable, regardless of malice. Choice (A) is incorrect because under the common law, ***a conditional privilege was extended for fair comment on matters of general public interest.*** Newman's letter regarding failure of one single homeowner to pay annual maintenance dues for her townhome is certainly devoid of such public concern as to reasonably permit publication to 20,000 newspaper subscribers.

41. **(C)** Students should note that in accordance with **Restatement of Torts,** 2d, Section 402A, "one who sells any product in a defective condition unreasonably dangerous to the user or consumer or to his property is subject to (strict) liability for physical harm to the ultimate user or consumer, or to his property, if (a) the seller

is engaged in the business of selling such a product, and (b) it is expected to and does reach the user or consumer without substantial change in the condition in which it is sold." In the present case, the removal of the speed regulators ***would constitute a substantial change*** in the character of the snowmobiles, so that, Aspen would not be held strictly liable under the provisions of this section.

42. **(C)** In light of the previous explanation, the Ski and Snow Shop only would be strictly liable under the provisions of the aforementioned section. Since Aspen manufactured the snowmobiles with the speed regulators, they would not be liable for the subsequent modification by the Ski and Snow Shop.

43. **(C)** One is subject to liability for trespass, irrespective of whether he causes harm to any legally protected interest of the other, if he ***intentionally*** enters the land in possession of the other. Based upon the given facts, Vic did not intentionally drive his vehicle onto Edna's property. Rather he lost control of his vehicle while trying to negotiate a sharp curve in the highway. In this regard, Vic may be liable for trespass because he was operating his car in a ***reckless*** manner. However, where a person enters the land of another through negligence, recklessness or as a result of an abnormally dangerous activity, ***in order to be liable for trespass he must cause damage to the land.*** Therefore, choice (C) is a better answer than (A) because even though Vic was reckless, he will not be liable unless he damaged Edna's property. Note that choice (B) is not correct because Vic's entry was not intentional.

Multistate Nuance Chart:

TORTS

TRESPASS

Intentional Entrees	**Negligent or Reckless Entrees**
1. One is subject to liability, regardless of whether he thereby causes harm to the land, if he ***intentionally*** enters the land in the possession of another. 2. A trespass covers intrusions upon, beneath and above the surface of the earth. 3. Mistake is no defense. It is the intent to enter, not the intent to trespass that determines liability.	One who negligently or recklessly enters the land of another is subject to liability if, but only if, ***he causes harm to the land or to a thing on the land.***

44. **(C)** Mistake is no defense for intentional trespass. Ott erroneously believed the channel was a public waterway when, in fact, it was owned by Carr. Choice (C) is correct because it addresses Ott's intentional entry onto the channel. Note that choice (D) is wrong because the facts do suggest that an easement by necessity was created since there was no conveyance of land.

45. **(B)** Pharmy's best defense would be that he was merely an employee, and not a seller within the context of **Restatement** Section 402(A) which provides: "One who sells any product in a defective condition unreasonably dangerous to the user or consumer is subject to (strict) liability for physical harm thereby caused to the ultimate user or consumer if (1) the seller is engaged in the business of selling

such a product, and (2) it is expected to and does reach the user or consumer without substantial change in the condition in which it is sold".

46. **(B)** As Pharmy's best defense, he would want to argue that Kathy had previously taken Clinoril. If so, she should have been aware of the appearance and taste of the drug and should have discovered that Pharmy had not given her Clinoril in filling her prescription. In which case, Kathy was contributorily negligent in failing to realize that she had not been given Clinoril.

47. **(C)** Based on the holding in *Sullivan v. H. R Hood & Sons,* 168 N. E. 2d 80 (1960), ***no recovery will be allowed for mental disturbance alone unaccompanied by physical injury*** upon finding a dead mouse in a milk bottle. Where the defendant's negligence causes only mental disturbance, without accompanying physical injury, illness or other physical consequences, and in the absence of some independent basis for tort liability, the great majority of courts still hold that there can be no recovery. Prosser, **Torts, 5th Ed.,** p. 361. The policy for denying such recovery is based upon the notion that such mental harm is often temporary and relatively trivial. Since claims may easily be falsified or exaggerated, merely negligent, rather than intentional, conduct should not be the basis for imposing a disproportionate financial burden on a defendant. Choice (C) is thus correct. Choice (A) is incorrect since severe emotional distress is not compensable under negligence principles. Choice (D) is incorrect because Trent's cause of action may be for negligent infliction of emotional distress not intentional infliction. Choice (B) is incorrect because *res ipsa loquitur* is a negligence-based doctrine which requires physical injury.

48. **(B)** These two questions typify the new format of Torts questions on the MBE. In years past, the Torts problems would commonly specify the particular cause of action (e.g., negligence, strict liability, nuisance, etc.) in the call of the question. Recently, however, there has been a shift to this new format wherein the cause of action is *not* designated and the question simply reads: "If A asserts a claim against B, judgment for whom?" As a consequence, ***you must first determine what is the proper cause of action.*** Here, Chase is suing Laid Back, the manufacturer of the traction device. In accordance with **Restatement of Torts, 2d,** Section 402A, a manufacturer or seller of goods (such as Laid Back) will be strictly liable for a "defective condition unreasonably dangerous" existing at the time of sale which causes harm to the user or consumer. Thus, if the traction apparatus ***was defective*** for failure to include a safety latch, Chase will prevail. Choice (B) is therefore the best answer. Choice (A) is wrong because the mere fact that the apparatus broke during normal use does not by itself make it defective nor does it prove that Laid Back was negligent. Choice (C) is incorrect because a seller of a defective product remains strictly liable even ***after*** it leaves his control. Choice (D) is wrong because a negligent act of a non-party cannot limit a defendant's strict liability.

49. **(A)** Once again, this question simply states that the plaintiff is asserting ***a claim*** against the defendants. In the previous question, Chase was bringing suit against Laid Back, the manufacturer of the traction apparatus. Here, Chase is suing Dr. Derneral and the Jerri Ford Hospital. As a general rule of thumb, if the defendant (in a tort action) is a seller, manufacturer or distributor of defective products, then the proper cause of action is strict liability. Otherwise, it will generally be a negligence

action (unless, of course, the facts indicate some other tort basis). In the present case, Chase will prevail against Dr. Demeral and the Jerri Ford Hospital if either defendant was negligent. Choice (A) is correct because if Dr. Demeral failed to securely fasten the stirrup, that would lead to an inference of negligence.

50. **(B)** According to **Restatement of Torts,** 2d, Section 402A, "One who sells any product in a defective condition unreasonably dangerous to the user or consumer or to his property is subject to (strict) liability for physical harm thereby caused to the ultimate user or consumer, or to his property, if (a) the seller is engaged in the business of selling such a product, and (b) it is expected to and does reach the user or consumer without substantial change in the condition in which it is sold." Thus, if the car was sold with defective brakes, Santa Monica Import Motors will be strictly liable for Garp's injuries. Consequently, choice (B) is the best answer.

51. **(D)** Here, it is necessary for students to distinguish between negligence and strict liability. Whereas the preceding question dealt with strict liability, this one pertains to negligence. Obviously, a seller's negligence may take a number of forms. Most frequently, it consists merely in failing to exercise reasonable care to inspect the goods to discover defects, or in preparing them for sale. When the action is for negligence, it is of course agreed that the care required of the seller is only that of a reasonable man under the circumstances. In this regard, there has been a dispute as to whether the retailer of goods manufactured by another is under a "duty" to inspect them before sale, to discover defects of which he does not know. According to Prosser, "in any case where the nature of the goods themselves makes it more likely that defects will lead to serious injury—as for example on the sale of an automobile—something more careful than such casual examination will be required, and if there is any special reason to believe that the particular product may be defective, very thorough inspection may be required before it is sold." **Law of Torts,** pg. 633. Therefore, since Santa Monica Import Motors had a duty to exercise reasonable care to inspect the auto before selling it to Garp, choice (D) is correct.

52. **(D)** A popular Multistate testing area deals with the extent of strict liability and the limitations upon it. Clearly, the type of damage threatened by the conduct which entails strict liability usually is well defined. For example, the keeping of vicious animals involves the risk that human beings or other animals will be attacked; the risk of abnormally dangerous things and activities, such as high tension electricity or blasting, is sufficiently obvious. In general, Prosser notes that "strict liability has been confined to consequences which lie within the extraordinary risk whose existence calls for such special responsibility." **Law of Torts,** pg. 518. As a result, choice (D) is correct because Garp will only be liable for the normal or foreseeable consequences of transporting highly flammable petroleum in his car. Since slipping on the petroleum was not within the recognizable risk, Dr. Jay will be denied recovery.

53. **(C)** Prosser points out that in most jurisdictions the keeper of animals of a kind likely to roam (e.g., cattle, horses, sheep, chickens and pigeons) is strictly liable for their trespasses. On the other hand, in the case of such domestic favorites as dogs and cats, nearly all courts have refused to impose strict liability for trespass. ***Examination tip:*** Don't confuse this rule involving ***strict liability for trespass*** with strict liability for damage or injuries caused by "dangerous" or wild animals.

54. **(B)** In regard to the question of liability apart from trespass, students should be aware that a distinction has been made between animals which, by reason of their species, are by nature ferocious, mischievous or intractable and those of a species normally harmless. In the first category are lions, bears, tigers, elephants, monkeys, and other similar animals. No animal of such a species, however domesticated, can ever be regarded as safe. Conversely, in the second class are cattle, sheep, horses, dogs, cats and other creatures regarded as usually harmless.

55. **(B)** **Restatement of Torts, 2d,** § 314A deals with special relations giving rise to a duty to aid or protect: (1) "A common carrier is under a duty to its passengers to take reasonable action (a) to protect them against unreasonable risk of physical harm." This duty to protect extends not only to risks arising out of the common carrier's own conduct, but also to risks arising from ***acts of third persons***, whether they be innocent, negligent, intentional, or even criminal. Dottie's failure to stop serving drinks to Martin in light of his inebriated state and abusive behavior posed an unreasonable risk of harm to Tippi. Repulsive Airlines will be vicariously liable for Dottie's negligent conduct under the doctrine of ***respondeat superior***. Tippi will therefore prevail. Choice (B) is the correct answer. Since first-class passengers are accorded no special legal duty over other passengers, choice (A) is incorrect.

56. **(C)** Choice (A) is incorrect because even though Dottie's conduct may have involved a high degree of negligence or recklessness, it would not constitute an actionable basis for battery. By the same token, choice (B) addresses the foreseeability of harm requirement for negligence. Since this is an action for the intentional tort of battery, choice (B) is incorrect. In this regard, students should not confuse intentional tort actions with negligence. Choice (D) is not correct because a common carrier may be held vicariously liable for the intentional torts of its passengers.

57. **(B)** Under **Restatement of Torts, 2d.** §876, dealing with persons acting in concert, "For harm" resulting to a third person from the tortious conduct of another, one is subject to liability if he (a) does a tortious act in concert with the other or pursuant to a common design with him; or (b) knows that the other's conduct constitutes a breach of duty and gives substantial assistance or encouragement to the other so to conduct himself, or (c) gives substantial assistance to the other in accomplishing a tortious result and his own conduct separately considered, constitutes a breach of duty to the third person." Whenever two or more persons commit tortious acts in concert, each becomes subject to liability for the acts of the others, as well as for his own acts. If Tripuka and the three other men were acting in concert, Tripuka would be liable even though he himself did not strike Flores with the bottle. Based on this analysis, choices (C) and (D) are incorrect statements (since Tripuka could still be liable). Thus, choice (B) is the best answer.

58. **(A)** According to **Restatement of Torts,** Section 402(A) "One who sells any product in a defective condition unreasonably dangerous to the user or consumer or his property is subject to ***(strict) liability for physical harm thereby caused to the ultimate user or consumer, or to his property,*** if (a) the seller is engaged in the business of selling such a product, and (b) it is expected to and does reach the user or consumer without substantial change in the condition in which it is sold." Based on **Restatement** Section 402(A), choice (A) is correct because Monica can recover for the damage to her property (namely, the china set) even though she herself was not physically injured by the defective dishwasher.

59. **(B)** Students must be cognizant of the distinction between "modified" comparative negligence and "pure" comparative negligence. Generally speaking, in a modified comparative negligence jurisdiction ***plaintiff's degree of fault must not be equal to or greater than that of the defendant***. In other words, plaintiffs negligence must be less than 50% as a general rule. On the other hand, in a pure comparative negligence jurisdiction plaintiff may still recover damages despite the fact that her negligence exceeds that of the defendant (e.g., plaintiff s degree of fault is greater than 50%). In the present case, since the plaintiff-Pedestrian's negligence did not exceed that of Motorist, Pedestrian is entitled to recover in a modified comparative negligence jurisdiction. Note that choice (B) is correct because her recovery will be $30,000 (or total amount of damages of $50,000 reduced by 40% which is the percentage of fault attributable to the plaintiff). Be aware that the "collateral sources" rule is applicable in that the $10,000 paid by ***plaintiff's insurance company will not reduce her recovery***.

60. **(B)** As a patron in a restaurant, Liz should be classified as an ***invitee***. According to **Restatement of Torts 2d**, §34(A), "A possessor of land is subject to liability to his invitees for physical harm caused to them by his failure to carry on his activities with reasonable care for their safety if, but only if, he should expect that they will not discover or realize the danger, or will fail to protect themselves against it." This obligation of reasonable care extends to everything that threatens the invitee with an unreasonable risk of harm — care against negligent activities, warning of known latent dangers, as well as inspection of the premises to discover possible dangerous conditions that are not known, and precautions against foreseeable dangers. See Prosser, **Law of Torts,** p. 393. In this very tricky Torts question, students must choose the precise answer choice which is neither overinclusive — choice (A) — nor underinclusive — choice (C). Choice (B) is correct because Wong's ***duty to inspect*** implies "reasonable" inspection as to time. An invitor cannot be expected to know of every unsafe condition — or every banana peel on the floor — immediately, but such inspection must be made within a reasonable time. Therefore, if the egg roll has been on the floor for a substantial period of time, Wong, the restaurant owner, would be liable. Note that choice (C) is incorrect because the duty to warn of ***known dangerous conditions applies to licensees,*** whereas the duty to an invitee is expanded to inspect and make the premises safe. Choice (D) is incorrect because the act of a third person will not relieve the defendant's negligent conduct unless it is unforeseeable (i.e., supervening).

Multistate Nuance Chart:

Duties Owed To Entrants Coming Onto The Land

Status	Duty Owed
Trespasser, undiscovered	no duty
Trespasser, known or anticipated	ordinary care; duty to warn of dangerous conditions which are known to possessor (no liability for obvious dangerous conditions)
Licensee	ordinary care; duty to warn of dangerous conditions which are known to possessor
Invitee	ordinary care; duty to (1) inspect premises and/or land, and (2) make safe for protection of invitees who enter

61. **(D)** **Restatement of Torts 2d,** Section 519, provides that "(1) One who carries on an abnormally dangerous activity is subject to liability for the harm to the person, land or chattels of another resulting from the activity, although he has exercised the utmost care to prevent the harm. (2) Thus strict liability is limited to the kind of harm, the possibility of which makes the activity normally dangerous." Since strict liability arises out of the abnormal danger of the activity itself and the risk that it creates, it follows that the defendant's use of extraordinary care is irrelevant. Therefore, Statement I will not be a valid defense for Linden. Furthermore, Statement III is no defense in light of **Restatement of Torts 2d,** Section 522, which states that "One carrying on an abnormally dangerous activity is subject to strict liability for the resulting harm although it is caused by the unexpectable (a) innocent, negligent or reckless conduct of a third person, or (b) action of an animal, or (c) operation of a force of nature." Even unexpected lightning, therefore, would not relieve Linden of strict liability for the explosion. Since Statements I and III are not applicable defenses, choice (D) has to be the correct answer.

62. **(B)** This same issue was tested on the February, 1997 Multistate Bar Examination. The issue presented is whether a plaintiff may recover for infliction of emotional distress for injury caused to a third person. The older decided cases held that recovery was allowed where (1) the plaintiff was present and witnessed defendant's extreme and outrageous conduct and (2) where the plaintiff was a close family member of the person attacked. With respect to non-family members, it is necessary of course that they be present, but, in addition, their distress must result in bodily harm. As between answer choices (A) and (B), note that (A) is wrong because Connie did in fact suffer bodily injury by having a miscarriage. Note that choice (C) is not the best answer because breach of duty is an element in a negligence action not in an infliction of mental distress case. Likewise, choice (D) is incorrect because "foreseeability" applies in determining proximate cause for negligence. In emotional distress cases where defendant's conduct is directed at a third person, it is only necessary that the plaintiff ***be present at the time of the incident. Exam Tip:*** To be sure, this is an extremely difficult Multistate question. Once again, when you are confronted by similarly worded answer choices, it is necessary to proceed by process of elimination and not confuse the elements of one cause of action (such as negligence) with another (as in this cause with infliction of emotional distress).

INFLICTION OF EMOTIONAL DISTRESS CHART:

INFLICTION OF EMOTIONAL DISTRESS CHART:

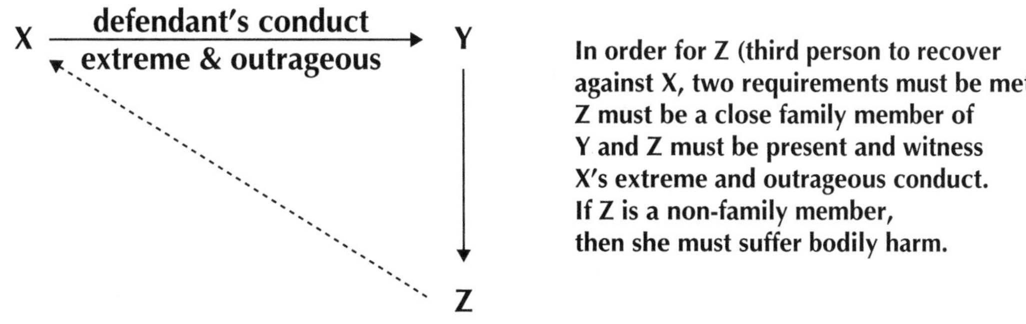

X
defendant's conduct
extreme & outrageous
Y
Z
In order for Z (third person to recover against X, two requirements must be met: Z must be a close family member of Y and Z must be present and witness X's extreme and outrageous conduct. If Z is a non-family member, then she must suffer bodily harm.

63. **(C)** It is important to note that strict products liability only applies to ***sellers of defective goods.*** Since Patsy and Thomas Jefferson High School were not engaged in the sale of the tennis machine, they would not be held strictly liable. Even though Patsy may have used the machine to commit an assault (which resulted in a battery when Ellen was actually struck by the ball), there is no indication that her mishandling of the machine caused it to become defective. As such, it must be assumed that the tennis machine was sold in a defective condition.

64. **(D)** Choice (D) is the best answer. None of the other choices should prevail as a defense to the strict liability action.

65. **(B)** According to Prosser, certain results, by their very nature, are obviously incapable of any logical, reasonable, or practical division. Death is such a result, and so is a broken leg or any single wound, the destruction of a house by fire, or the sinking of a barge. Where two or more causes combine to produce such a single result, incapable of any logical division, each may be a substantial factor in bringing about the loss, and if so, ***each must be charged with all of it.*** In this situation, most courts place the burden of proof on the issue of causation upon the two defendants. Unless the innocent defendant can prove that he or she is not culpable, liability will be imposed. This is the rule enunciated in the case of *Summers v. Tice,* 199 P.2d I (1948). Choice (B) is therefore correct.

66. **(B)** As a general rule, comparative negligence statutes have the effect of apportioning damages based on the parties' respective degrees of fault. For example, if the defendant's fault is found to be twice as great as that of the plaintiff, the latter will recover two-thirds of his damages, and himself bear the remainder of his loss. In the present case, Driver was negligent in failing to keep a proper lookout while driving. By the same token, defendant was also at fault since he left an abandoned auto in the middle of the highway. As a consequence, plaintiff's recovery will be diminished in proportion to his negligence. Note that choice (C) is wrong because the "last clear chance" doctrine is applied in contributory, not comparative, negligence jurisdictions.

Multistate Nuance Chart:

TORTS	**COMPARATIVE NEGLIGENCE**	**CONTRIBUTORY NEGLIGENCE**
Where Plaintiff is Negligent:	He still recovers but his damages are reduced in proportion to his negligence.	He is barred from recovering as a matter of law.
"Last Clear Chance" Doctrine:	Not Applicable.	Applicable.
Essay Exam:	Majority View.	Minority View.
"MBE" Exam:	Applied unless otherwise directed.	Not applied unless directed by specific question.

67. **(D)** Students should be aware that a necessary element in a negligence action is the *requirement* that the plaintiff suffer actual loss or damage. Since the action for negligence developed chiefly out of the old form of action on the case, it retained the rule of that action that *proof of damage* was an essential part of the plaintiff's case. Consequently, since Norton did not sustain any injuries from the electrical shock, he would be defeated in his negligence action.

68. **(C)** Norton's legal status is that of a public invitee. **The Restatement of Torts**, 2d, Section 332, defines a public invitee as a person who is invited to enter or remain on land as a member of the public for a purpose for which the land is held open to the public. Comment (a) under this section provides that "invitees are limited to those persons who enter or remain on land upon an invitation which carries with it an implied representation, assurance, or understanding that reasonable care has been used to prepare the premises and make them safe for their reception."

69. **(C)** First, Trixie is a licensee who in its broadest sense includes anyone who comes upon the land with a privilege arising from the consent of the possessor. Next, what duty of care does a possessor owe to a licensee? As to passive conditions on the land, it is still the settled rule that the possessor is under no obligation to the licensee with respect to anything that the possessor does not know. The duty is not to maintain the land in a safe condition, but to exercise reasonable care to see that the licensee is aware of the danger.

70. **(D)** In accordance with **Restatement of Torts** 2d, Section 356, a lessor of land is not liable to his lessee or to others on the land for physical harm caused by any dangerous condition whether natural or artificial, which existed when the lessee took possession. Exceptions to this general rule include situations (1) where the lessor contracts to repair; (2) undisclosed dangerous conditions known to lessor; (3) land leased for purposes involving admission of the public; (4) parts of land retained in lessor's control which lessee is entitled to use or (5) where lessor makes negligent repairs.

71. **(A)** As a general rule, most states have enacted statutes which to a greater or less extent permit contribution among tortfeasors. Prosser points out that a more difficult question is whether a tortfeasor who has settled with the original plaintiff shall be entitled to contribution. It is for this reason that statutes of several jurisdictions limit contribution to those against whom judgments have been rendered, which fix both liability and amount. It is important to note, however, where there is no such provision it is almost invariably held that one who settles without judgment can recover contribution. See *Hargar v. Caputo,* 1966, 420 Pa. 528.

72. **(D)** Section 402(A) of the **Restatement** provides that "one who sells any product in a defective condition unreasonably dangerous to the user or consumer is subject to (strict) liability for physical harm thereby caused to the ultimate user or consumer, if (a) the seller is engaged in the business of selling such a product, and (b) it is expected to and does reach the user or consumer without substantial change in the condition in which it is sold." Students should be cognizant that in order for the rule stated in this Section to apply, it is not necessary that the ultimate user or consumer have acquired the product directly from the seller. Note that it is not even necessary that the consumer have purchased the product at all. The **Restatement** Section 402(A)(1) provides that the user may be a member of the family of the final purchaser, or his employee, or a guest at his table, or a mere donee from the purchaser.

73. **(A)** Obviously, Peggy is a licensee. Prosser states that "nearly all of the decisions are agreed that a social guest, however cordially he (or she) may have been invited and urged to come, is *not* an invitee—a distinction which has puzzled generations of law students, and even some lawyers." The guest is legally nothing more than a licensee, to whom the possessor owes no duty of inspection and affirmative care to make the premises safe for his visit. Usually, the guest understands when he comes that he is to be placed on the same footing as one of the family, and must take the premises as the occupier himself uses them, without any inspection or preparation for his safety; and that he also understands that he must take his chances as to any defective conditions unknown to the occupier, and *is entitled at most to a warning of dangers that are known*. **Law of Torts,** pg. 378.

74. **(C)** In the famous case of *Wagner v. International R. Co.,* 1921, 232 N.Y. 176, Judge Cardozo noted that "the risk of rescue, if only it be not wanton, is born of the occasion; the emergency begets the man." Under the prevailing view, there is an independent duty of care owed to the rescuer himself, which arises even when the rescuer endangers no one's safety but his own. Remember that the rule is not limited to spontaneous or instinctive action, but applies even when there is time for thought. In addition, whether the rescuer succeeds in injuring himself, or the person rescued, or a stranger, the original wrongdoer is still liable.

75. **(D)** In modern day society, flying an airplane is so commonplace as *not* to be regarded as an abnormally dangerous activity. Therefore, alternative (D) is the **LEAST** accurate statement. Historically, flying was of course regarded at its outset as a questionable and highly dangerous enterprise. This view was encouraged by the fact that the first cases arose in New York, where there was strict liability for any physical invasion of land. In fact, Prosser notes that the **First Restatement of Torts** in 1939 took the position that aviation had not reached such a stage of safety as to justify treating it by analogy to the railroads, and classified it as an "ultrahazardous activity" upon which strict liability for ground damage was imposed. However, with the further development of the industry, later years witnessed a definite reversal of this trend. See Prosser, **Law of Torts,** 4th Ed., pg. 515.

76. **(C)** In the present case, Reggie's reckless operation of his aircraft would be viewed as a superseding cause terminating the Andersons' liability. Students should note that ***a superseding cause is an unforeseeable intervening cause which relieves defendant from liability for his antecedent negligence.*** In effect, the superseding event, in itself, becomes the proximate, or legal cause of plaintiff's injury. Simply, if the defendant can foresee neither any danger of direct injury, nor any risk from an intervening cause, he is not negligent.

77. **(C)** Violation of a statute imposing criminal liability may create a presumption of negligence (i.e., negligence per se) according to the majority of jurisdictions where (1) the plaintiff is a member of the class of persons sought to be protected, and (2) ***the harm suffered is of the type the statute was designed to prevent.*** Pedestrian will not prevail against Sonoma's Liquor Store if the purpose of the statute prohibiting the sale of liquor on Sundays was to aid in the observance of the Sabbath. Choice (C) is correct. Had the statute been enacted to prevent injuries caused by drunk drivers on Sundays, the result would be different. Choice (A) is incorrect because it is too broad. Again, defendant cannot be presumed to be negligent per se by

selling the wine unless the statute was designed to prevent the type of harm that was suffered. Choice (B) is incorrect because "but for" causation is insufficient to impose liability absent a showing of legal, or proximate, causation. Choice (D) is incorrect because the liquor prohibition ordinance was a strict liability statute requiring no mens rea, so mistake is no defense.

78. **(A)** **Restatement of Torts 2d,** Section 402(A) states that "One who sells any product in a defective condition unreasonably dangerous to the user or consumer, or to his property, is subject to liability for physical harm thereby caused if (1) the seller is engaged in the business of selling such a product, and (2) it is expected to and does reach the user or consumer without substantial change in the condition in which it is sold." When the call of the question asks for strict liability as the basis of recovery, students must learn to eliminate all answers which address some other cause of action. Choice (B) deals with misrepresentation, whereas choices (C) and (D) focus on negligence. All three will be incorrect because if the plate glass were defective when purchased, the seller, defendant Glass, will be strictly liable. Therefore, choice (A) is correct.

79. **(C)** Liability under **Restatement** Section 402(A) is limited to ***persons engaged in the business of selling products*** for use or consumption. It therefore applies to any manufacturer, wholesaler, retailer, distributor, supplier as well as to the operator of a restaurant. In this question, Culver is an independent contractor who simply installed the plate glass door. He is not engaged in the sale of the product. As a consequence, Culver cannot be held strictly liable. Choice (C) is therefore correct.

80. **(C)** Products liability based on negligence requires the existence of a defect which would have been discoverable upon reasonable inspection (i.e. breach of duty), actually and proximately causing harm to the plaintiff. This question deals with negligence in a situation where negligent manufacture has already been established. Therefore, to find the defendant, Lee, negligent, the plaintiff will have to show that Lee could reasonably have been expected to discover the defect prior to installation. Choice (C) is correct. Choice (A) is incorrect because negligence is not imputed in the case of seller and supplier. Choice (B) is incorrect because plate glass is generally safe, even though this particular piece was not. Choice (D) is incorrect since Lee would additionally have to show a "substantial identity of material circumstances"—i.e., did other people hit the door "faster than walking" and have their hands slip off the pedal-handle without breaking the door.

81. **(A)** Under the theory of express warranty under **UCC** 2-313, any affirmation of fact or promise made by the seller to the buyer relating to the goods that becomes "part of the basis of the bargain" creates an express warranty. Such a warranty is breached where actual and proximate damages are caused. Mr. Glass' representation to Lee that plate glass was "super safe" constituted an express warranty that was breached when the glass door shattered injuring Victor. Lee will prevail, and choice (A) is correct. Choices (B) and (C), using the words "only if," are too restrictive since they each consider only one possible basis of liability. Choice (D) is incorrect because contributory negligence is generally no defense in express warranty cases. Note: Misrepresentation is another basis of liability often used in this type of situation.

82. **(B)** The courts have been compelled to recognize that an actor who is confronted with an emergency is not to be held to the standard of conduct normally applied to one who is in no such situation. There are, however, a number of limitations which have hedged the "emergency" rule. It does not mean that any different standard is to be applied in the emergency. According to Prosser, "the conduct required is still that of a reasonable man under the circumstances". Prosser further states that one "may still be found to be negligent if, notwithstanding the emergency, his acts are found to be unreasonable". **Law of Torts,** pg. 169. Based on this rule, choice (B) is the best answer. Even though Veronica was confronted with an emergency situation, she would, nevertheless, be liable for negligence if she acted unreasonably in pushing Lucinda off the sled.

83. **(D)** This series of Torts examples is designed to develop and sharpen your "test-wiseness" for the Multistate exam. As you can now see, merely reading and memorizing outlines is not the best way to prepare for the MBE. It is necessary to supplement your outline review by practicing on our Multistate examples. Remember practice makes perfect. In this particular question Lucinda's parents are asserting a claim against Jenner, the driver of the auto that struck Lucinda. Here, you must determine what is the cause of action. Obviously, negligence would provide the plaintiffs with their best theory of relief. Therefore, choice (D) is correct because Jenner will be liable if he was driving negligently.

84. **(C)** In the previous question Lucinda's parents were asserting a tort action against Jenner. Now Veronica's parents, on behalf of their daughter, are bringing suit against Jenner. Here, too, the plaintiffs will recover if Jenner were driving his car negligently. Note that choice (A) is wrong because even though Jenner was driving within the posted speed limit, he may still be liable if he was operating his vehicle in a negligent manner. Choice (B) is also wrong because Veronica may recover against Jenner regardless of whether Lucinda was negligent. To be sure, if Jenner's negligence was subsequent to Lucinda's, then he would remain liable for Veronica's injuries. Note that choice (D) is not the best answer because the "last clear chance" doctrine applies in contributory negligence situations where the defendant is the last human wrongdoer. According to the given facts, there is no showing that Veronica was negligent, thus alternative (D) is incorrect.

85. **(C)** As a general rule of law, a parent is not vicariously liable for the conduct of the child. Apart from any basis of the family relationship, however, a parent may be liable for the tortious act of his son or daughter if he has directed, encouraged or ratified it. In the present case, Lucinda's parents gave her permission to sled down Hill Street. As a result, her parents may be negligent in permitting her to sled along a public thoroughfare. Certainly, there was a recognizable risk that Lucinda could be injured by automobiles traveling along the street where she was sledding. Consequently, in a contributory negligence jurisdiction Lucinda's parents will be barred from recovering if either they or Lucinda is found to be negligent.

86. **(C)** As noted previously, a key area repetitively tested on the Multistate deals with your ability to recognize and understand the ***distinction between comparative and contributory negligence.*** As a general rule, remember that a typical comparative negligence statute (as in this example) has the effect of apportioning damages between the parties according to their respective degrees of fault. In contributory

negligence jurisdictions, on the other hand, the plaintiff is precluded from recovering because his own conduct falls below the standard to which he is required to conform. As a result, in contributory negligence jurisdictions, the entire burden of the loss falls on the plaintiff since the defendant goes scot free of all liability, and the plaintiff bears it all. In this comparative negligence example, students must first determine the measure of damages suffered by each party, and then diminish that amount by their respective degrees of fault. To illustrate, plaintiff-Hall suffered damages in the amount of $5,000 which would then be diminished by 70% (or the degree of fault attributable to him). Therefore, Hall's recovery would be $1,500. Similarly, defendant-Oats, who was 30% at fault, would recover $700 because his damages of $1,000 would be reduced by $300 in proportion to his degree of fault.

87. **(C)** This apportionment statute has the effect of limiting recovery to cases where the plaintiff's negligence is "not as great" as that of the defendant. Since Hall's negligence was 70% (which would be greater than Oats' negligence), he would be precluded from recovering anything. Conversely, since Oats' negligence was "not as great" as that of Hall, he (Oats) may recover (although his damages will be reduced in proportion to the negligence attributed to him). Consequently, choice (C) is correct because Oats recovers $700; while Hall recovers nothing.

88. **(A)** According to the "last clear chance" doctrine, the last wrongdoer is viewed as the worst wrongdoer, or at least the decisive one, and should pay. As such, it merely transfers from the plaintiff to the defendant the entire loss due to the fault of both. As a consequence, plaintiff Hall should recover the full amount of damages if defendant-Oats had the last chance to avoid the accident.

89. **(C)** In this example, students are required to make a fineline distinction between an invitee-father who entered the premises upon business which concerned the occupier and a licensee-son who was viewed as a social guest. Here, the father is a potential customer. He is entering the defendant's apartment to purchase a painting. Thus, he is classified as an invitee. On the other hand, Felix (the defendant) "invited" Scott to come along so that he could play with his son, Junior. Scott, therefore, is viewed as a social guest or a licensee.

90. **(C)** It is a well settled rule that the possessor of land (or premises) is only under a *duty to warn* a licensee of dangerous conditions known to the occupier. Note that the possessor is under no obligation to the licensee with respect to anything that the possessor does not know. Moreover, he is not required to inspect his land for unknown dangers. Here, a sliding glass door is not normally viewed as a dangerous condition. Thus, Felix was under no obligation to warn Scott of the glass door. Choice (B) is therefore incorrect. Note that choice (D) is wrong because assumption of risk is a defense when a person *knowingly* exposes himself to a known dangerous condition. Scott did not knowingly run into the glass door.

91. **(C)** According to **Restatement of Torts 2d,** Section 46, "One who by extreme and outrageous conduct intentionally or recklessly causes severe emotional distress to another is subject to liability for emotional distress, and if bodily harm to the other results from it, for such bodily harm." Generally speaking, liability has been found only where the conduct has been so ***outrageous*** in character, and so ***extreme*** in

degree, as to go beyond all possible bounds of decency. In the present case, PMBR filed a criminal complaint against Missy charging her with larceny. Moreover, an arrest warrant was issued. Under the circumstances, PMBR was reckless in its deliberate disregard by failing to notify the police that the (criminal) matter had been resolved. Prosser points out that "there are a few cases which indicate that liability for extreme outrage is broader than intent, and that it extends to situations in which there is no certainty, ***but merely a high degree of probability that the mental distress will follow,*** and defendant goes ahead in conscious disregard of it. **Law of Torts,** pg. 60.

92. **(D)** "An actor is subject to liability to another for false imprisonment if (1) he acts intending to confine the other or a third person within the boundaries fixed by the actor, and (2) his act directly or indirectly results in such a confinement of the other, and (3) the other is conscious of the confinement or is harmed by it." **Restatement of Torts 2d,** Section 35. The restraint sufficient for false imprisonment may consist in the intentional breach of a duty to take active steps to release the plaintiff from a confinement in which he has already properly been placed. Prosser, **Law of Torts,** pp. 46-47. This rationale would certainly be effective if Missy were suing PMBR; however, note that she is suing the arresting officers instead. Prosser goes on to say that "one who participates in an unlawful arrest, or procures or instigates the making of one without proper authority, will be liable" if he has "taken some active part in bringing about the unlawful arrest itself, by some 'affirmative direction', persuasion, request, or voluntary participation." Ibid., p.47. Therefore, to avoid liability, the arresting officers must show not just that Missy was arrested pursuant to a warrant—choice (C)—but that the arrest was lawfully made with probable cause, reasonably relying upon PMBR's honest belief that a felony had in fact been committed. Choice (D) is therefore the correct answer.

93. **(B)** In accordance with Section 343 of the **Restatement of Torts,** 2d, "a possessor of land is subject to liability for physical harm caused to his invitees by a condition on the land, but only if, he (a) knows or by the exercise of reasonable care would discover the condition, and should realize that it involves an unreasonable risk of harm to such invitees, and (b) should expect that they will not discover or realize the danger and (c) fails to exercise reasonable care to protect them against the danger." It is important to point out that in any case where the occupier, as a reasonable man, should anticipate an unreasonable risk of harm to the invitee notwithstanding his (the invitee's) knowledge, warning, or the obvious nature of the condition, something *more* in the way of precaution is necessary. This is the case in our factual situation. Although Mike posted a warning sign in the potentially dangerous area of the supermarket, more adequate precautions should have been taken under the circumstances. Consequently, Becky would be entitled to recover damages in negligence against Safeway Supermarket. Choice (D) is incorrect since it is generally agreed that the obligation as to the condition of the premises is of such importance that it cannot be delegated. Furthermore, the occupier will be liable for the negligence of an independent contractor to whom he entrusts maintenance and repair work.

94. **(B)** Becky must prove by a preponderance of the evidence that AAA was negligent. In civil actions, unlike criminal prosecutions, the burden of proof does *not* require that the jury be convinced beyond all reasonable doubt, but only that the jury be

persuaded that a preponderance of the evidence is in favor of the party sustaining the burden. Please note that Choice (C) is incorrect since the burden of proof in a negligence action is upon the plaintiff since he is asking the court for relief damages. Choice (D) is also wrong since *res Ipsa loquitur* is a type of circumstantial evidence that is merely an inference that the defendant was negligent. The plaintiff, however, still has the burden to prove negligence by a preponderance of the evidence.

95. **(A)** The owner or occupier of land is under an affirmative duty to protect his business invitees not only against dangers of which he is aware, but also against those which with reasonable care he might discover. The basis of liability to the invitee is the implied representation made to the public by holding the land open to them, e.g., that it has been prepared for their reception. Under this theory of liability, even a person who comes onto the premises without the intention of conferring an economic benefit upon the occupier/owner, is classified as an invitee. In this regard, even though Driver did not intend to purchase any items at the supermarket, he would be classified as an invitee, since the supermarket is open to the public. Therefore, Driver would recover in negligence as a result of the supermarket's failure to take adequate safety precautions to protect its business invitees.

96. **(B)** is important for students to differentiate between negligence and strict liability. In the present case, Perez, the injured pedestrian, is suing Cycle Company, the manufacturer, based on negligence theory. In the event that Cycle Company failed to exercise reasonable care (or failed to make a reasonable inspection) to discover the defect, that would establish negligence on the part of the manufacturer. Note that choice (A) is incorrect because it addresses strict liability. Since privity of contract is not a requisite for asserting negligence, choice (C) is incorrect. Likewise, choice (D) is wrong because Roth was not contributorily negligent but rather he was privileged to take such action in an emergency situation.

97. **(B)** Rancher's installation of the electrical wiring device would constitute a cause-in-fact, not the legal cause of Cowboy's death. It is important to understand the difference between proximate/legal cause and causation in fact. We suggest that you ask yourself, "Has the conduct of the defendant caused plaintiff's injury?" This is a question of fact. In the present case, clearly Rancher's installation of the electrical device was the cause-in-fact of Cowboy's death. Next, once it is established that the defendant's conduct has in fact been one of the causes of plaintiff's injury, there remains the question whether the defendant should be legally responsible for what he has caused. In other words, was the defendant under a duty to protect the plaintiff against the event which did, in fact, occur? In the present example, Cowboy is an "unforeseeable" plaintiff outside the zone of any obvious danger from the defendant's conduct. The facts state that the electrical device was of such low intensity that it posed no risk of injury to a human being. Therefore, Rancher would not owe a special duty of care to a trespasser with a pacemaker. **CAVEAT:** If presented with a question where a city dweller installs an electrical device on a fence bordering along the sidewalk with heavy pedestrian traffic, then choice (C) is correct because the "pacemaker pedestrian" becomes a foreseeable plaintiff.

98. **(A)** or **(C)** In the famous case *Palsgraf v. Long Island Railroad Co.*, 248 N.Y. 339, 162 N.E. 99 (1928) Judge Andrews in his dissent stated that "Due care is a duty imposed upon each one of us to protect society from unnecessary danger, not to protect A, B, or C alone. Every one owes to the world at large the duty of refraining from those acts which unreasonably threaten the safety of others. Not only is he wronged to whom harm might reasonably be expected to result, but to him also who is in fact injured, even if he be outside what would generally be thought the danger zone." It is important to note that Judge Andrews' view is a minority one. The **Restatement of Torts** almost immediately afterward accepted the view of the Palsgraf case, that there is no duty, and hence no negligence, and so never any liability to the unforeseeable plaintiff.

99. **(D)** **Restatement of Torts 2d,** Section 282, defines ***negligence as "conduct which falls below the standard established by law for the protection of others against unreasonable risk of harm."*** In this question, Repulski will not prevail if the Golden Nugget used reasonable care in selecting the lock. In other words, plaintiff will not prevail if defendant was not negligent. Choice (D) is the best answer because, by process of elimination, it is the only correct statement given. Choice (A) is incorrect because Golden Nugget is a hotel, not a commercial seller for which strict products liability would attach. Choice (B) is incorrect because the duty owed a business invitee is not an ***absolute*** one, but merely a ***reasonable*** duty to inspect and remedy unsafe conditions existing on the premises. Since the lock complied with the local security ordinance, Golden Nugget, absent some prior notice, would have no reason to discover that the lock on room 1213 was otherwise defective. Choice (C) is incorrect because hotel theft is a foreseeable occurrence, and the duty of an innkeeper towards its guests requires the use of reasonable care to prevent not only conduct which is negligent but also physical attacks and thefts of property. Prosser and Keeton, **Torts,** p. 383. Only ***supervening*** acts break the chain of proximate causation and relieve the defendant of liability.

100. **(B)** **Restatement of Torts 2d,** Section 652B, states that "One who intentionally intrudes, physically or otherwise, upon the solitude or seclusion of another or his private affairs or concerns, is subject to liability to the other for invasion of his privacy, if the intrusion would be highly offensive to a reasonable person." It may be by physical intrusion into a place in which the plaintiff has secluded himself such as forcing himself into the plaintiffs room in a hotel, or it may be by the use of the defendant's senses, with or without mechanical aids, to oversee or overhear the plaintiff's private affairs. Comment to Section 652b. In this situation, by electronically recording Colavito's conversations as to team strategy for the National Volleyball Championship, Repulski unlawfully intruded upon Colavito's private affairs and will be liable. Choice (B) states the correct rationale.

101. **(C)** One who by extreme and outrageous conduct intentionally or recklessly causes ***severe emotional distress*** to another is subject to liability for such emotional distress, and if bodily harm to the other results from it, for such bodily harm. According to the majority view, this rule applies only where the emotional distress has in fact resulted, and where it is severe. Emotional distress passes under various names, such as mental suffering, mental anguish, mental or nervous shock, or the like. It includes all highly unpleasant mental reactions, such as fright, horror, grief, shame, humiliation, embarrassment, anger, chagrin, disappointment,

worry and nausea. However, it is only where it is extreme that liability arises. In the present example, the facts do *not* indicate that the Snodgrasses suffered severe emotional distress. The facts simply state that the Snodgrasses were "outraged by Pearlman's actions." As such, choice (C) is correct because the Snodgrasses will not recover unless they suffered severe emotional distress. Choice (A) is wrong because even though Pearlman's conduct was "extreme" and "outrageous", there can be no recovery unless the plaintiffs suffered severe emotional distress. Choice (B) is wrong because merely trying to take unfair advantage of an individual does not establish infliction of mental distress. Furthermore, choice (D) is incorrect because it is irrelevant whether the Snodgrasses received a settlement. The question presented herein relates to whether Pearlman's conduct caused the Snodgrasses to suffer emotional distress; and, if so, was the distress suffered severe?

102. **(C)** "One who makes a fraudulent misrepresentation is subject to liability to the person or class of persons whom he intends or has reason to expect to act or to refrain from action in reliance upon the misrepresentation, for pecuniary loss suffered by them through their justifiable reliance in the type of transaction in which he intends or has reason to expect their conduct to be influenced." **Restatement of Torts**, Sec. 531. The tort of ***misrepresentation*** requires ***a false representation of a material fact known by the defendant to be false, which induces actual and justifiable reliance by the plaintiff, resulting in monetary loss.***

103. **(B)** It is important to note that the defendant would not recover for nuisance if her business was ***abnormally sensitive*** to harm caused by high frequency sound waves. To be considered public, the nuisance must affect an interest common to the general public, rather than the peculiar sensitivities of one individual. Note choice (A) is wrong because "coming to the nuisance" is not an absolute defense. It is merely one factor the court will consider in weighing the equities. Choice (C) is incorrect because trespass requires the entry of something tangible (although invisible gases and microscopic particles will suffice) onto the land of another. Alternative (D) is wrong because in order to be considered a nuisance the disturbance must ***substantially and unreasonably*** interfere with the use and enjoyment of one's land. Here, Petsky's testing the whistles at his factory was *not* unreasonable even though the sound waves substantially interfered with Rula's business.

104. **(D)** Choice (A) is incorrect because the facts do not indicate that Anderson either had knowledge or conspired with Liddy to steal copies of the documents pertaining to Moose's "dirty tricks". Choice (B) is wrong because although under the rationale of *Time v. Hill* there is a constitutional privilege to publish private facts if the matter is one of ***legitimate public interest,*** it is not an absolute privilege. Prosser points out that an action for invasion of privacy may still exist where there is publication of a picture which is taken without the plaintiff's consent from a private place, or where it is stolen, or obtained by bribery or other inducement of breach of trust. Therefore, choice (D) is the best answer because Anderson will not be liable unless there is a showing that he engaged in wrongful conduct.

105. **(B)** In accordance with the **Restatement of Torts 2d,** Section 435, an actor's conduct may be held not to be the legal cause (i.e., the proximate cause) of harm of another where after the event, and looking back from the harm to the actor's negligent conduct, it appears to the court highly extraordinary that it should have brought about

the harm. For example, in the present case, Nancy's injection of the morphine overdose would constitute a superseding force, or an independent intervening cause, which would serve to break the causal connection between the initial wrongful act (i.e., Bob's serving of the liquor to Rudy) and the ultimate injury (i.e., Rudy's death). Thus, the superseding force becomes the proximate cause of such injury, and, hence, the first actor, Bob, would be relieved of liability for the consequences of his antecedent conduct. It is important to point out that Nurse Nancy's conduct was ***grossly negligent*** (not ordinarily negligent) because she should have been aware of the excessive dosage.

106. **(C)** Here, the (mis)performance of the hernia operation would be viewed as a superseding cause (or an unforeseeable intervening force). As a consequence, looking backwards, the intervention of the hernia operation would be so unrelated and extraordinary, as to fall outside the class of normal intervening events, that Bob, the original tortfeasor, would be relieved of responsibility for the operation and resulting complications.

107. **(C)** Clearly, Nurse Nancy's injection of the fatal dosage of morphine would be (1) the cause in fact and (2) the legal, or proximate, cause of Rudy's death. In this regard, it is helpful to understand the difference between proximate/legal cause and causation in fact. First, ask yourself, "Has the conduct of defendant caused plaintiff's injury?" This is a question of fact. **NOTE:** although defendant's conduct may be the cause in fact of plaintiff's harm, it (the tortious conduct) may or may not be the proximate cause. However, if defendant's actions constitute the proximate cause, then, it must, also, always be the cause in fact (of plaintiff's injury).

108. **(A)** In the present illustration, Bartender Bob should have reasonably foreseen that by continuing to serve alcohol to Rudy, the intoxicated patron might endanger himself and others (especially in the operation of his motor vehicle). As a result, Bob's conduct (in violation of his master's order and in breach of the local dramshop statute) would be viewed as the proximate cause of Butch's injuries since the automobile accident was a foreseeable intervening force for which Bob must bear responsibility.

109. **(D)** It is not unreasonable to find that a 15 year-old boy who had been sledding on this pathway for a number of previous months, should have realized the risk, if any, involved while sledding. In order to recover under the "attractive nuisance" or "infant trespasser" doctrine, it is necessary that the children because of their youth do not discover the "dangerous" condition or realize the risk involved.

110. **(D)** Choices (A), (B) and (C) each state elements of the "attractive nuisance" or "trespassing children's" doctrine.

111. **(C)** Prosser points out that "conduct which is indecent, such as breeding animals before the plaintiff's windows, or destructive of the general welfare, as in the case of house of prostitution, is nearly always a private nuisance when it interferes with the enjoyment of the plaintiff's property." **Law of Torts,** pg. 598. Moreover, loud noises also constitute a nuisance where they unreasonably and substantially interfere with the use and enjoyment of plaintiff's land.

112. **(A)** Recently, questions dealing with ***directed verdicts and summary judgments*** have appeared on the Multistate. Note that although Civil Procedure is still not a primary Multistate subject, it can be tested in a "cross-over" or secondary fashion. A motion for summary judgment is a ***pretrial procedure*** of "going behind the pleadings" to determine whether a genuine dispute actually exists. To obtain a summary judgment the moving party must show that ***no genuine issue of material fact exists.*** A directed verdict, on the other hand, may be requested at the end of a plaintiff's case or after all the evidence is completed. In brief, the moving party is arguing that the evidence clearly reveals that he must prevail and there is no reason to send the case to the jury. In deciding whether a directed verdict should be granted, all the evidence is viewed in the light most favorable to the non-moving party. In the present example, Strawbridge is asserting a claim against Merryweather to recover damages caused by the tree falling on his property. In all likelihood, the proper cause of action would be for trespass. In order to prevail, Strawbridge must prove that Merryweather either intentionally, negligently or as a result of an abnormally dangerous activity caused the tree to enter his land. Obviously, Merryweather did not intentionally cause the tree to fall since it was uprooted during a storm. Next, Merryweather was not engaged in an ultrahazardous or abnormally dangerous activity. Therefore, in order for Strawbridge to prevail he must prove that Merryweather negligently caused the tree to fall. Since Strawbridge did not produce such evidence, choice (A) is correct.

113. **(C)** As a general rule, a surviving child has a right to recover for tortiously inflicted prenatal injuries. While foreseeability of future injury alone does not establish the existence of a duty owing to an unborn infant by its mother's physicians, it is now beyond dispute that in the case of negligence resulting in prenatal injuries, both the mother and the child in utero may be directly injured and are owed a duty. See *Albala v. City of* New York 429 N.E. 2d 786 (1981). Furthermore, the case of *Highson v. St. Frances Hospital* 459 N.Y. 2d 814 (1983) followed these principles in holding that a cognizable and independent cause of action exists on behalf of the infant in utero, who is born alive, against a physician for prenatal injuries. Since the discoloration of Milton's teeth was proximately caused by Dr. Dork's failure to administer a pregnancy test and prescription of Tetracycline to his pregnant mother, Marla, Milton may successfully maintain a cause of action for malpractice against Dr. Dork. Therefore, choice (C) is correct.

114. **(C)** A person is subject to liability for battery if he or she acts ***intending to cause*** a harmful or offensive contact with the person of the other and an offensive or harmful contact directly or indirectly results. An act which is not done with such an intention does not make the actor liable for mere offensive contact. Since Keiki vomited involuntarily, she would lack the requisite intent to be liable for tortious battery.

115. **(C)** According to Prosser, the conditions necessary for the application of the principle of res ipsa loquitur are as follows: 1) the event must be of a kind which ordinarily does not occur in the absence of someone's negligence; 2) it must be caused by an agency or instrumentality within the exclusive control of the defendant, 3) it must not have been due to any voluntary action or contribution on the part of the plaintiff. **Law of Torts,** 5th Edition, p. 244. In applying the doctrine of res ipsa loquitur to the issue of the toy store's liability for Cassie's

fall, the second requirement is crucial, namely "Was the 'Buffalo Bob' doll within the ***exclusive control*** of the defendant?" A general statement that the toy store was in control of the premises—choice (B)—is insufficient to establish ***exclusive*** control. Similarly, the fact that the toy store owed a ***duty*** to plaintiff to inspect and make the premises safe—choice (A)—is insufficient to ***infer*** negligence using res ipsa as a basis. Choices (C) and (D) are tricky. Choice (D) is saying res ipsa will apply ***only if*** the doll had been negligently placed on the edge of the shelf by defendant. It fails to address the possibility that even if defendant was negligent in this manner, the actual and proximate cause of harm may have been brought about by the conduct of ***another customer***, not defendant, in dislodging the doll. If so, then the doll would not have been within the exclusive control of the toy store at the time of Cassie's injury. Choice (C) is the correct answer.

116. **(C)** The key to, Multistate (or multiple-choice) testing is always to remember that the ***test maker's main goal is to hide the correct answer!*** Here, for example, the test maker is trying to mislead students into thinking that this hypo involves either trespass to chattels or conversion. On the other hand, this is simply a straightforward negligence question. It is important to point out that the facts simply state "Blackman lent Dykstra his car to attend a Moody Blues concert". Dykstra drove the car to the concert where it was struck. The distractor or "red herring" intended to confuse students is that Dykstra went on a diversion and purchased marijuana. However, the accident did not occur while he was making unauthorized use of the vehicle. As such, there is no liability for either conversion or trespass to chattels. ***Examination Tip:*** In analyzing Torts questions, always remember that an essential element of the plaintiff's cause of action for negligence, or for that matter for any other tort, is that there must be some reasonable connection (i.e., causation) between defendant's act and the damage which the plaintiff has suffered. In sum, Dykstra's diversion was not the cause of the accident.

117. **(D)** Note that choice (B) is incorrect because a public utility company is not strictly liable in tort. However, when the city performs a service which might as well be provided by a private corporation, and particularly when it collects revenue from it, the function is considered a "proprietary" one, as to which there may be liability for the torts of municipal agents within the scope of their employment. This is true where it supplies water, gas, or electricity, or where it operates a ferry, an airport or a public market. Note that choice (C) is wrong because a rescuer is entitled to recover even though his conduct is negligent. This is true so long as the rescuer is not grossly or wantonly negligent. Where the rescuer's conduct is reckless or wanton, then the rescuer will be liable (and his liability will supersede that of the original wrongdoer). As between alternatives (A) and (D), the latter answer is preferred because if the "rescue doctrine" is to apply then it is necessary to show that Felipe (the workman) was the original wrongdoer and his negligence endangered himself. Thus, it would be foreseeable for Matty to attempt to rescue Felipe, and in such a situation Matty's negligence would not supersede the liability of the original wrongdoer. Choice (D) is therefore correct because if Felipe were not negligent then Matty would be held liable for his own injuries.

118. **(A)** In accordance with the **Restatement of Torts** 2d, Section 158, one is subject to liability to another for trespass, irrespective of whether he thereby causes harm to any legally protected interest of the other, if he intentionally (a) enters land

in the possession of the other, or causes a thing or a third person to do so, or; (b) remains on the land, or; (c) fails to remove from the land a thing which he is under a duty to remove. In the present case, Pedestrian would be classified as a trespasser since he entered the premises without the Club's permission.

119. **(C)** As a general rule, a possessor of land owes ***no duty of care to undiscovered or unanticipated trespassers.*** However, once a landowner discovers the presence of a trespasser (or should know of the likelihood of trespassers), then there is a duty ***to warn the trespasser of any dangerous conditions known to the occupier or owner of the property.*** In the present case, the dinner club knew of the existence of a dangerous condition (namely, the malfunctioning of the electric dryer in the restroom). As a result, the defendant owed a duty to warn trespassers of this dangerous condition. It is important to point out that choice (C) is a better answer than (A) because trespassers can be anticipated to enter the premises of a private club (especially to make use of restroom facilities or telephone services).

120. **(D)** It is important to note that invitees are among those who enter the premises upon business which concerns the occupier and upon his invitation (express or implied), the latter is under an affirmative duty to protect them not only against dangers of which he knows, but also against those which with reasonable care he might discover. The invitee is sometimes called a business visitor; the typical example is the customer in a store or patron(s) of restaurants, banks, theatres, fairs and other places of amusement. The occupier is not an insurer of the safety of invitees; he must not only warn of latent dangers which the occupier knows, but he must also inspect the premises to discover possible dangerous conditions of which he does not know. Choice (B) is incorrect because Patron will not recover only if the Club had prior knowledge but rather Patron will succeed if the Club failed to make reasonable inspection of the premises. In this respect, the Club has an affirmative duty to inspect the premises and to make the same reasonably safe for the protection of its customers.

121. **(A)** In accordance with **Restatement of Torts** 2d, Section 400, one who puts out as his own product a chattel manufactured by another is subject to the same liability (i.e., strict liability) as though he were its manufacturer. Thus, one puts out a chattel as his own product when he promotes or advertises it under his name or affixes to it his trade name or trademark. When such identification is referred to as an indication of the quality or wholesomeness of the chattel, there is an added emphasis that the user can rely upon the reputation of the person so identified. As a consequence, choice (A) is correct because the Supper Club represented the chowder as its own "homemade" soup. Therefore, the Supper Club would remain strictly liable to the ultimate consumer even though there was no showing of negligence on the part of the seller.

122. **(D)** Arguably, each statement presents a valid defense for the law firm. First, the law firm did not breach any duty of care owed to the general public simply by requiring one of its employees to work overtime. Next, statement II presents a legally persuasive defense since the accident occurred after "working hours". Thus, the law firm will contend that when Edgar started to drive home, he was acting ***outside the scope of the employment relationship.*** Likewise, statement III presents a persuasive argument because an essential element in any tort action is causation. If,

in fact, defendant's act was not the cause of plaintiff's injury; then no tort liability will attach. Lastly, statement IV is a valid defense because the law firm should not be vicariously liable for Edgar's negligent operation of ***his own*** motor vehicle.

123. **(B)** Under the doctrine of ***respondeat superior***, a master is vicariously liable for the torts of a servant committed within the scope of employment. The servant's conduct is within the scope of employment if it is of the kind the servant is employed to perform, occurs substantially within the authorized limit of time and space, and is actuated, at least in part, by a purpose to serve the master. Generally, it appears that "the master will be liable at least for those slight departures from the performance of the work which might reasonably have been expected on the part of servants similarly employed, and that the ***foreseeability*** of such deviations is an important factor in determining the scope of employment." Prosser, **Torts**, p. 502, 504-5. Even though Putnam was making an unauthorized delivery to his girlfriend at the time he drove through the red light and injured Wendell, he was still en route from the drug store to make another separate, authorized delivery. Choice (C) is incorrect because Putnam was not definitely acting outside the scope of employment based on the unresolved issue of foreseeability of his deviation.

124. **(C)** **Restatement of Torts, 2d** § 886B defines the rule for ***indemnity between tortfeasors*** as follows: "(1) if two persons are liable in tort to a third person for the same harm and one of them discharges the liability of both, he is entitled to indemnity from the other if the other would be unjustly enriched at his expense by the discharge of the liability." Indemnity is granted under this principle where (a) "the indemnitee was liable only vicariously for the conduct of the indemnitor." In the question, the basis for Horowitz's liability would be vicarious, under the doctrine of respondeat superior. Therefore, the entire burden of loss ($25,000) may be shifted to the party who was at fault in causing the accident, Putnam. Choice (C) is correct.

125. **(B)** According to **Restatement of Torts, 2d,** Section 520A, "If physical harm to land or to persons or chattels on the ground is caused by the ascent, descent or flight of aircraft, or by the dropping or failing of an object from the aircraft, the operator of the aircraft is subject to strict liability for the harm, even though he has exercised the utmost care to prevent it." The rationale for this rule is that the risk of harm to those or the ground is sufficiently obvious if anything goes wrong with the flight; and while the safety record is greatly improved for aircraft it still cannot be reduced that the ordinary rules of negligence law should be applied.

126. **(C)** Choice (A) is wrong because a tortious defendant is liable for damages even though the plaintiff may have an insurable interest in the property damaged. Note that choices (B) and (D) are wrong because each alternative addresses the issue of negligence. Here, Xenon is strictly liable for selling contaminated fuel to the airline company. According to **Restatement** Section 402 A, one who sells a product in a defective condition is (strictly) liable for the harm or injury suffered.

127. **(B)** In this situation Robinson would be liable for tortious assault if Reynolds feared that he would hit him. Simply defined, assault is an act by the defendant creating a ***reasonable apprehension*** in plaintiff of immediate harmful or offensive contact to plaintiff's person. Choice (A) is wrong because Robinson is liable for the

intentional tort of assault not negligence. Choice (C) is likewise incorrect because it is *not* necessary to prove actual damages to sustain an action for assault. Note that choice (D) is wrong because once apprehension has been intentionally created, it is no defense that the defendant meant to play a joke or changed his mind.

128. **(A)** Here's a *tricky* Multistate example in which most students will narrow the correct answer down to alternatives (A) or (C). Where the mental distress is caused by the defendant's conduct which is not directed at the plaintiff, but at a third person, certain problems result. In order for the plaintiff to recover in such cases, three requirements generally must be established: (1) the plaintiff was present at the time; (2) the defendant knew that the plaintiff was present; and (3) the plaintiff was a close relative of the person attacked. However, with respect to the third requirement that recovery should be limited to near relatives, Prosser states that although most cases allowing recovery have involved members of the immediate family, there are a few which have not. More importantly, Prosser indicates the *modern trend* "appears to be moving in the direction of liability" and, thus, permitting recovery for non-family members. Based on the *modern trend*, the correct answer is choice (A) rather than (C). **Law of Torts,** pg. 62.

129. **(C)** In order that a negligent actor shall be liable for another's harm, it is necessary not only that the actor's conduct be negligent toward the other, but also that the negligence of the actor be a legal cause of the other's harm. In the present case, if the subway was not negligent, then it cannot be held liable. With respect to choice (A), there are situations in which the actor is under a ***special responsibility*** to protect the plaintiff from the intentional, or even criminal, misconduct of others. Among such relations are those of (1) carrier and passenger, (2) innkeeper and guest, (3) employer and employee, (4) invitor and business visitor, (5) school district and pupil, and (6) bailee and bailor among others. However, in such situations the defendant is under a ***duty to exercise reasonable care.*** Choice (A) is wrong because if the subway was not negligent, then it did not fail to exercise reasonable care.

130. **(D)** When a person has reasonable grounds to believe that he is being or is about to be attacked, he may use such force as is reasonably necessary for protection against the potential injury. Remember that the actor need only have a reasonable belief as to the other party's actions, i.e., apparent necessity, not actual necessity, is sufficient. As a result, reasonable mistake as to the existence of the danger does not vitiate the defense. Choice (D) is therefore correct because Hunter reasonably acted in self-defense when he shot at Caine. ***Caveat:*** If, in the course of reasonably defending himself, one accidentally injures a bystander, he is nevertheless protected by the defense.

131. **(C)** Here's another difficult Multistate example where both alternatives (C) and (D) are arguably correct. To be liable for assault, the defendant must have intended to interfere with the plaintiff's personal integrity — which is to say that he must have intended to bring about an assault or a battery. But the intent need not necessarily be to inflict physical injury, and it is enough that there is an intent to arouse apprehension. Thus, Prosser points out that "it is an assault to fire a gun not aimed at the plaintiff for the purpose of frightening him, or to point it at him when the

defendant knows that it is unloaded, and the plaintiff does not." **Law of Torts,** pg. 41. Therefore, Caine will be liable for assault if he intended to frighten Hunter regardless of whether he actually intended to shoot him.

132. **(D)** In order to be liable for battery, the defendant must do some positive and affirmative act which causes an ***unpermitted or offensive contact*** with the plaintiff's person. Here, Rocky is liable for battery for causing an offensive touching by hitting Tracy with the wrapper. Note that choice (C) is wrong because it provides the rationale for assault not battery. Choice (B) is incorrect because even though the girls allowed Rocky to join them, they didn't consent to be hit by the wrapper(s). Similarly, choice (A) is not correct because the gist of the action for battery is not the hostile intent of the defendant, but rather the absence of consent to the contact on the part of the plaintiff.

133. **(B)** The "key" issue is determining whether Chessman is a public or private figure. A public figure is an individual who has (a) achieved pervasive fame or notoriety (e.g., a movie star or celebrity sports figure) or (b) has voluntarily injected himself/herself into a public controversy. Here, Chessman is viewed as a private figure even though he may be well-known within the bar review industry. As such, choice (B) is correct because he will be required to prove negligence on the part of the news media.

134. **(A)** As a general rule, a detainee may recover for false imprisonment unless there is a lawful arrest. Prosser and Keeton discuss this same problem and point out that restraint upon the plaintiff's freedom may be imposed by the assertion of legal authority. Thus, "if the plaintiff submits, or if there is even a momentary taking into the custody of the law, there is an arrest; and if it is without proper legal authority, it is a false arrest, and so false imprisonment." **Law of Torts,** 5th Edition, pg. 50.

135. **(A)** Quite clearly, the police were negligent by dropping Zonker off at a busy intersection. Negligence is a matter of risk, that is to say, of recognizable danger or injury. It has been defined as "conduct which involves an unreasonable great risk of causing damage," or, more fully, conduct "which falls below the standard established by law for the protection of others against unreasonable risk of harm." Prosser, pg. 169. Based upon the given facts, it was foreseeable that Zonker might be in such a manner since the police knew he was intoxicated when they left him along a busy highway. Thus, the police's conduct may properly be viewed as the legal or "proximate" cause of the harm which resulted.

136. **(B)** This is a "tricky" question dealing with intervening causation. Nurse Nitwit's mix-up of the charts was a foreseeable intervening act. Many students will thus choose (A) as correct. The reason why (B) is better is because Monk is the defendant in the lawsuit. In order for Monk to be held liable (for the hospital's negligence), it must be shown that he was at fault or negligent in causing Sloan's original injury. Choice (B) is preferred because if Monk was *not* negligent in pushing Sloan, then he would not be liable for the intervening negligence of the hospital.

137. **(D)** In this question your natural inclination is to find Duncan liable for failing to have the elevator inspected. However, in any negligence action it is necessary that the defendant's misfeasance (or nonfeasance) be the "legal" cause of plaintiff's harm.

Here, Doris was injured when she was assaulted by Grubby. She was not injured by the stalling of the elevator. Therefore, Grubby's action would be viewed as a superseding cause (or unforeseeable intervening force). In this regard, **Restatement** Section 448 advises that "the act of a third person in committing an intentional tort or crime is a superseding cause of harm to another resulting therefrom, although the actor's negligent conduct created a situation which afforded an opportunity to the third person to commit such a tort or crime unless the actor at the time of his negligent conduct realized or should have realized the likelihood that such a situation might be created, and that the third person might avail himself of the opportunity to commit such a tort or crime." Based on the given facts, since Duncan had no reason to realize the likelihood that Doris would be injured in such a manner, he should not be held liable for the intentional tortious conduct of Grubby.

138. **(C)** **Restatement** Section 35 states, "An actor is subject to liability to another for false imprisonment if (a) he acts intending to confine the other within boundaries fixed by the actor, and (b) his act directly or indirectly results in such a confinement of the other, and (c) the other is conscious of the confinement or is harmed by it". According to the majority view, an actor is not liable unless his act is done for the purpose of imposing confinement, upon the other (i.e., he acts intentionally), or with knowledge that such a confinement will, to a substantial certainty, result from it. Since Duncan did not act intending to confine Doris, choice (C) is the best answer. Moreover, there was not a substantial certainty that the elevator would stall. Note that choice (D) is wrong because there is a split of authority on whether the plaintiff must be aware of the imprisonment. The Restatement has taken the position that since the interest is in a sense a mental one (resembling the apprehension of contact in assault cases), there can be no imprisonment unless the plaintiff is aware of it at the time. However, there are a number of American decisions where there was imprisonment apparently without consciousness of it. See Prosser, 5th Edition, pg. 48.

139. **(D)** As noted previously, Doris' injuries were not proximately related to the malfunctioning of the elevator. Therefore, neither Duncan nor Otis will be vicariously liable for Grubby's tortious conduct. Surely, it is not improbable that Grubby may have attacked Doris even if the elevator was operating properly.

140. **(A)** Another highly tested Multistate area deals with false imprisonment. With respect to the shopkeeper's privilege, a department store may make a reasonable detention for a reasonable period of time of a shopper suspected of theft. Prosser notes, however, that a ***thirty minute detention may be an unreasonably long period of time*** to question a shopper. In fact, there are a number of recent decisions holding department stores liable for false imprisonment involving thirty minute detentions.

141. **(C)** In Todd's personal injury action against Oscar, the owner of the park, he will rely principally upon the doctrine of joint venture. The elements which are essential to a joint enterprise are commonly stated to be four: (1) an agreement, express or implied, among the members of the group; (2) a common purpose to be carried out by the group; (3) a community of pecuniary interest in that purpose, among the members; and (4) an equal right to a voice in the direction of the enterprise, which gives an equal right of control. The law then considers that each (member of the joint enterprise) is the agent or servant of the others, and that the act of any one within the scope of the enterprise is to be charged vicariously against the rest.

142. **(A)** Mogul would be vicariously liable for Jerry's unauthorized acts since under the doctrine of respondeat superior a master is liable for the torts of servants which are committed within the scope of employment. Students should take note that questions of fact of unusual difficulty arise in determining whether the servant's conduct is an entire departure from the master's business or only a roundabout way of doing it, and likewise, the point at which the departure is terminated, and the servant may be said to have reentered the employment. Essentially, so long as there is an intent on the part of the servant to serve the master's purpose, the master may be liable if what is done is otherwise within the service.

143. **(D)** Todd would not have any cause of action against Mogul for the intentional torts of false imprisonment or assault. Moreover, Mogul would not be liable for negligence since the power failure was wholly an independent cause which was beyond Mogul's control and responsibility.

144. **(A)** Under the majority view, since the law has always placed a higher value upon human safety than upon mere rights in property, it is the accepted rule that ***there is no privilege to use any force calculated to cause death or serious bodily injury to repel the threat to land or chattels,*** unless there is also such a threat to the defendant's personal safety as to justify self-defense. Prosser points out that "even the tradition that a man's house is his castle, and that one may kill in defense of his dwelling, has given way in most jurisdictions to the view that such force is not justified unless the intrusion threatens the personal safety of the occupants". Prosser, pg. 115.

145. **(D)** A possessor of land owes a duty to warn trespassers of ***known dangerous conditions*** which are not obvious to the trespasser. In the present hypo, Munchkin was under no duty to warn trespasser-Winslow of Defense's use of deadly force since Munchkin had ordered Defense to discontinue its protection service. Consequently, Defense was not authorized to use deadly force under the circumstances. Choice (C) is wrong because this question hinges on the issue of whether Munchkin knew or had reason to know that Defense would be continuing to provide protection service for his property. If he had reason to know, then Munchkin would have been under a duty to warn trespassers of Defense's "armed response" policy. Note that choice (B) is wrong because it is irrelevant whether Winslow knew that Defense provided an "armed response". On the contrary, the "key" issue is whether Munchkin, as landowner, was aware of the danger presented. If so, then he would be liable for not warning trespassers of the dangerous condition (namely, Defense's "armed response").

146. **(A)** Here, Driver's estate should in all likelihood prevail, because sovereign immunity does not attach to non-delegable duties which are "proprietary" in nature. Students should be aware that when the city performs a service which might as well be provided by a private corporation, and particularly when it collects revenue from it, the function is considered a "proprietary" one, as to which there may be liability for the torts of municipal agents within the scope of their employment. On the other hand, immunity from tort liability does attach to those functions in their "governmental", "political" or "public" capacity. The following are, examples of "proprietary" functions: where a city supplies water, gas, electricity or where it operates a ferry, wharves, docks, an airport or public market.

147. **(C)** In establishing a wrongful death action against Motorist, Driver's estate must prove wrongful or negligent conduct on the part of Motorist. In general, on the issue of the fact of causation in a negligence action, the plaintiff has the burden of proof. He must introduce evidence which affords a reasonable basis for the conclusion that it is more likely than not that the conduct of the defendant was a substantial factor in bringing about the result. Therefore, proof that the traffic signal was functioning properly is most helpful for plaintiff's case. Ostensibly, this fact, if true, would establish that Motorist was negligent per se in driving through the red light.

148. **(A)** Under the "rescue doctrine", efforts to protect the personal safety of another have been held not to supersede the liability for the original negligence which has endangered it. As Judge Cardozo stated in *Wagner v. International R. Co.*, 133 N.E. 437 (1921), "The risk of rescue, if only it be not wanton, is born of the occasion. The emergency begets the man." It is important to remember that whether the rescuer succeeds in injuring himself, or the person rescued, or a stranger, the original wrongdoer is still liable.

149. **(C)** A commonly tested Multistate area deals with situations where an agent or bailee is authorized to make some use of a chattel, but exceeds or departs from what is permitted. In general, any ***major and serious departure will be held to be a conversion,*** while minor ones which do no harm will not. Choice (C) is therefore correct because Smitty committed a conversion by his unauthorized use of the motor vehicle (i.e., driving an additional 120 miles to visit a friend). As a result, Smitty will be liable for the full value of the auto since the accident occurred during the course of this deviation.

150. **(B)** According to **Restatement of Torts,** 2d, Section 228, "One who is authorized to make a particular use of a chattel, and uses it in a manner exceeding the authorization, is subject to liability for conversion to another whose right to control the use of the chattel is thereby seriously violated." In this regard, note that even where there is a clear breach of the agreement, the unpermitted use is not a conversion ***unless*** it amounts to such a serious violation of the other's right of control as to justify requiring the user to pay the full value of the chattel. In the present case, Flutie will be liable for conversion because his failure to return the car on time resulted in it being stolen. Moreover, the fact that Mooch was deprived of the use of the vehicle for three months was sufficiently serious to constitute a material violation of his ownership rights.

151. **(C)** Prosser in **Law of Torts** points out that it is never enough for the plaintiff to prove merely that he or she has been injured by the negligence of someone unidentified. Even though there is beyond all possible doubt negligence in the air, it is still necessary to bring it home to the defendant. See **Prosser,** pg. 218. On this too the plaintiff has the burden of proof by a preponderance of the evidence; and in any case where it is clear that it is at least equally probable that the negligence was that of another, the court must direct the jury that the plaintiff has not proved his case. Accordingly, *re ipsa loquitur* is held not to apply where a chair is thrown from an unidentified person in the defendant's hotel. Refer to *Larson v. St. Francis Hotel*, 188 P.2d 513 (1948).

Multistate Nuance Chart:

TORTS

RES IPSA LOQUITUR

Byrne v. Boadle (1863)	*Larson v. St. Francis Hotel* (1948)
Facts: barrel of flour tossed out *warehouse* window and fell upon a passing pedestrian	Facts: chair thrown from an unidentified window in defendant's *hotel*
1. ***inference of negligence*** (i.e., reason able inference) that defendant's employee was negligent	1. ***no inference of negligence*** on the part of defendant's employee because it is just as probable that the chair was thrown by a guest
2. instrumentality (i.e., barrel) was within the exclusive control of the defendant	2. instrumentality (i.e., chair) was not within the exclusive control of the defendant
3. defendant (warehouse owner) vicariously liable for tortious conduct of employee-servant committed within the scope of the employment relationship	3. defendant (hotel owner) not vicariously liable for the independent torts of its guests

152. **(B)** Another popular Multistate testing area deals with apportionment of damages in tort law. Once it is determined that the defendant's conduct has been a cause of some damage suffered by the plaintiff, a further question may arise as to the portion of the total damage sustained which may properly be assigned to the defendant, as distinguished from other causes. According to Prosser, the question is primarily not one of the fact of causation, but of splitting up the total harm into separate parts which may be attributed to each of two or more causes. Where a logical basis can be found for some rough practical apportionment, which limits a defendant's liability to that part of the harm which he has in fact caused, it may be expected that the division will be made. Upon this basis, Velma will be liable for that part of the damage to Kareem's home caused by her negligence in colliding with the fire engine. As a result, choice (B) is the best answer. See **Law of Torts**, pp. 313-314.

153. **(B)** The essence of a private nuisance is an interference with the *use* and *enjoyment* of land. According to Prosser, a private nuisance may consist of an interference with the physical condition of the land itself, as by vibration or blasting which damages a house, the destruction of crops, flooding, raising the water table, or the pollution of a stream. Also, it may consist of a disturbance of the comfort or convenience of the occupant as, in the present hypo, by repeated telephone calls (See 55 Mich. L. Rev. 310) or by unpleasant odors, smoke or dust or gas, loud noises or excessive light or high temperatures. For a more complete analysis refer to Prosser, **Law of Torts**, pg. 592.

154. **(A)** Students should note that the complex tort of invasion to right of privacy is not a single tort, but rather comprises the four distinct torts of (a) the appropriation, for defendant's benefit or advantages, of the plaintiff's name or likeness, (b) intrusion upon plaintiff's physical solitude or seclusion (c) public disclosure of private facts about the plaintiff or (d) placing the plaintiff in a false light in the public eye. In the case at bar, Mr. Kim under subsection (b) would succeed in an invasion to right of privacy action against Prudence. The tort has been extended to include persistent and unwanted telephone calls. See *Carey v. Statewide Finance Co.*, 223 A 20 405 (1966). Also, the tort has been applied to peering into windows of a home and eavesdropping upon private conversations by means of wiretapping and microphones.

155. **(D)** It is essential to tort liability for either libel or slander that the defamation be communicated to some one other than the person defamed. Note that where there is no communication to anyone but the plaintiff, there may be a possible action for intentional infliction of mental suffering, but no tort action can be maintained upon the theory of defamation. Thus, Prudence's June 29th telephone call to Mr. Kim would not be actionable as defamatory. Also, Prudence's subsequent crank calls to Mr. Kim's employees would not furnish a basis for defamation, unless supported by additional facts reciting the content (or defining with more specificity) the slanderous remarks.

156. **(D)** A possessor of wild animals is strictly liable for injuries to others, which result from the animals' normally dangerous propensities. Since sharks do not normally harm people by splashing them, Mr. Zimmer would not be strictly liable, therefore choice (A) is incorrect. Alternatives (B) and (C) are wrong, because if strict liability had applied, it would extend to injuries suffered by licensees as well those suffered by invitees.

157. **(C)** To recover for the tort of nuisance, the conduct of the defendant must constitute an invasion of one's possessory interest in land. Mr. Zimmer's strongest defense would be that the property was occupied by another family (under a long-term lease) and, therefore, Mr. and Mrs. Darvon were not entitled to actual or immediate possession. Thus, there wasn't an invasion of the Darvon's present possessory interest in the land.

158. **(C)** Where the libelous, or slanderous, statement imputes (a) criminal conduct, (b) loathsome disease, (c) improper conduct in business, trade, or profession or (d) unchastity (on the part of plaintiff), it is actionable without proof of special damages. In the present hypothetical, Professor Kingsfield's statement referring to Levine as "an unscrupulous individual" would constitute libel *per se* under category (c). It is clearly actionable (without proof of special damages) to remark that a potential lawyer is unscrupulous (literal meaning "unprincipled" or "conscience less"). Certainly, the likelihood of "temporal" damage in such a case is sufficiently obvious.

159. **(B)** In the same light, ***slander, in general, is not actionable unless actual damage is proved.*** To this, the courts very early established certain specific exceptions: the imputation of crime, of a loathsome disease, and those affecting the plaintiff in business, trade, profession or calling—which required no proof of damage. Students should note that even though Vicky did not originate the defamatory statement, she nevertheless would be liable for its republication. ***Every repetition of the defamation is a publication in itself,*** even though the repeater states the source, or resorts to the customary newspaper evasion that "it is alleged" or makes clear that he does not himself believe the imputation.

160. **(B)** Generally, the press has a qualified privilege of enlightening the public in the dissemination of news in the sense of current events. The condition attached to all such qualified privileges is that they must be exercised in a ***reasonable manner and for a proper purpose.*** The immunity is forfeited if the defendant steps outside the scope of the privilege, or abuses the occasion. Here, the *Delaware Daily* is not free to publish a story accusing a prospective bar examinee of being a "pimp". Moreover, students should note that as a private person, Levin would only be required to show the newspaper was *negligent* in publishing such an irresponsible story. On the other hand, in *New York Times v. Sullivan*, 376 U.S. 254 (1964) the First Amendment was interpreted to require defamatory statements made about ***public figures*** not be actionable, unless there is a showing of ***"malice" which means "knowledge of the statement's falsity" or "reckless disregard as to its truth."***

161. **(D)** The two most common defenses in a negligence action are contributory negligence and assumption of risk. Contributory negligence is conduct on the part of plaintiff, contributing as a legal cause to the harm he has suffered, which falls below the standard to which he is required to conform for his own protection. Certainly, Sprinks contributed to his own injury by driving over the speed limit while knowing that visibility was poor. Though choice (C) is a correct statement of fact, alternative (D) is correct because it is the correct rule of law.

162. **(B)** At early common law, something approaching strict liability for fire was imposed upon landholders. Under the modern view, however, in the absence of legislation, there is no liability for the escape of fire where the defendant was not negligent. There may, as in the present case, be liability for negligence in failing to control it (or take adequate precautions) after it is stated.

163. **(B)** In the present case, Baglio was negligent by leaving the fire unattended. Note that plaintiff-Cary has suffered actual harm since his home became discolored from the smoke. Choice (C) is incorrect because the disturbance is not of a continuing nature. On the other hand, if a factory emits smoke or dust on a ***daily basis*** then an action for nuisance may arise. Choice (D) is wrong because smoke related disturbances are generally not decided under trespass grounds.

Multistate Nuance Chart:

TORTS

TRESPASS ON LAND	NUISANCE
1. one who (1) intentionally, (2) negligently or (3) recklessly enters land in the possession of another or causes a thing or a third person to do so is subject to liability 2. consists of intrusions upon, beneath and above the surface of the earth 3. intentional intrusions which cause no harm to the land as well as intrusions made under a mistaken belief of law or fact, nevertheless, subject the actor to liability	1. substantial and unreasonable interference with one's use and enjoyment of the land 2. consists of interference with the (1) physical condition of the land (such as by vibrations or blasting which damages a house, the destruction of crops, flooding or pollution of a stream); or it may consist of (2) a disturbance of the comfort or convenience of the occupant (such as by unpleasant odors, smoke, dust, loud noises, excessive light or even repeated telephone calls)

164. **(C)** Prosser points out "it is permissible to warn a present or prospective employer of the misconduct or bad character of an employee." Prosser further notes that **"the *qualified privilege*** includes false statements of fact concerning the plaintiff made in good faith". Choice (C) is therefore correct. **Law of Torts,** pg. 790.

165. **(D)** Under the prevailing view, one who is confronted with an emergency is not to be held to the standard of conduct normally applied to one who is in no such situation. An emergency has been defined as a sudden or unexpected event or combination of circumstances which calls for immediate action. Under such conditions, the actor cannot reasonably be held to the same conduct as one who has had full opportunity to reflect, even though it later appears that he made the wrong decision. In this situation, the actor's choice "may be mistaken and yet prudent." See Prosser, **Law of Torts,** pg. 169.

166. **(A)** In the case of gratuitous bailments, the majority of courts have treated the guest as a licensee on personal property, in essentially the same position as one entering by permission upon the land of another. Prosser notes that the application of the analogy has led to decisions in several states holding that, while the driver or owner is under a duty to exercise reasonable care for the protection of the guest in his active operation of the car, ***and is required to disclose to him any defects in the vehicle of which he has knowledge,*** he is not required to inspect the automobile to make sure it is safe.

167. **(D)** The privilege involved in this case usually has been called one of "public interest." Actually the privilege here is a rather narrow one, of communication to those public officers or others who may reasonably be expected to take some effective action on a matter of public, rather than purely private, importance. Thus, anyone has a qualified privilege to give information to proper authorities for the prevention or detection of crime.

168. **(A)** Choice (A) is the best answer because it shows that Electrician's conduct fell below that of a reasonable man or the standard required by members of his profession. Alternative (B) is clearly incorrect because it states that the ***only*** basis of recovery would be for strict liability. Since Homeowner may recover under a negligence theory, (B) is not the best answer.

169. **(D)** Under **Restatement of Torts 2d,** Section 402A, which states that "One who sells any product in a defective condition unreasonably dangerous to the user or consumer, or to his property, is subject to liability for physical harm thereby caused if (1) the seller is engaged in the business of selling such a product, and (2) it is expected to and does reach the user or consumer without substantial change in the condition in which it is sold." Clearly, if plaintiff Crum's car left the manufacturer's plant in a defective condition, then strict liability would be imposed on the manufacturer for all harm proximately caused by the defect. Choice (D) is correct. Choice (C) is incorrect because not only is contributory negligence no defense in a products liability action, but the facts state that Crum was on his way back to Cougar Motors because he realized there was still a problem. He was not contributorily negligent. Choice (A) is incorrect because the negligence of a third party is not the basis for strict liability of the defendant. Choice (B) is close, but addresses only the ***present*** defective condition and not the key issue of whether liability should still be imposed down the manufacturing chain to the original manufacturer.

170. **(A)** Cougar, the car dealer, will be liable under **Restatement 2d,** Section 402A to the same extent as the manufacturer for any defective conditions which existed at the time of sale. Choice (A) is correct. Choice (B) is incorrect because strict liability extends to defects existing at the time of sale, not to defective repairs. Choice (C) is incorrect because no matter how few or how many miles the car was driven the dealer's liability is based on defects existing at the time of the sale. Choice (D) is incorrect because a defendant's negligence is irrelevant if he is strictly liable. Hint: When the question states the plaintiff "asserts a claim" against defendant, look at the status of the defendant to determine if he has potential liability as a commercial seller under **Restatement 2d,** Section 402A.

171. **(B)** Another repetively tested Multistate area deals with tortious deceit. The elements of deceit consist of: 1) a false representation made by the defendant; (2) knowledge or belief on the part of the defendant that the representation is false (i.e., "scienter"); (3) an intention to induce the plaintiff to act or to refrain from action in reliance upon the misrepresentation; (4) justifiable reliance upon the representation on the part of the plaintiff; and (5) damage to the plaintiff, resulting from such reliance. Quit often on the MBE, a difficult problem arises as to whether mere silence, or a passive failure to disclose facts of which the defendant has knowledge, can serve as the foundation of a deceit action. As a general rule, an action for deceit will *not* lie for such tacit nondisclosure. Refer to Question 29 in the Torts Section of the **PMBR Workbook** for such an illustration. To this general rule, however, the courts have developed a number of exceptions. For instance, where the parties stand in some confidential or fiduciary relation to one another, such as that of principal and agent, executor and beneficiary of an estate, bank and investing depositor, majority and minority stockholders, there is a duty of full and fair

disclosure of all material facts. Prosser, pp. 696-697. Therefore, choice (B) is correct because Agnes, as a fiduciary, owed Deke a duty of disclosure since she was aware that he was acting under a misapprehension as to the true value of the misprinted $5 bill.

172. **(B)** This Multistate question is based on **Restatement of Torts 2d,** Section 359, which provides: "A lessor who leases land for the purpose which involves the admission of the public is subject to liability for physical harm caused to persons who enter the land for that purpose by a condition of the land existing when the lessee takes possession if the lessor (1) knows or by the exercise of reasonable care could discover that the condition involves an unreasonable risk of harm to such person, and (2) has reason to expect that the lessee will admit them before the land is put in safe condition for their reception, and (3) fails to exercise reasonable care to discover or to remedy the condition, or otherwise to protect such persons against it." Since Stubbs, as lessor, had a duty to exercise reasonable care to remedy the unsafe condition of the parking lot, choice (B) is correct.

173. **(A)** Senator Harrison would only be entitled to recover for invasion of privacy if he were able to prove malice on the part of *The Planet.* In *Times vs. Hill,* 385 U.S. 374 (1967), the United States Supreme Court applied the New York *Times-Sullivan* rule to the tort of invasion of privacy. In other words, the Court extended the constitutional privilege (the guarantee of freedom of speech and of the press) to invasion of privacy cases where the published matter in question was in the public interest *unless* the plaintiff establishes that the defendant acted with "malice". Thus, the misstatements of fact by the newspaper defendant are privileged unless Senator Harrison can prove that the misstatements were made with (1) knowledge of falsity or (2) in reckless disregard of the truth. Students should note that the two branches of invasion of privacy which turn on publicity, (placing the plaintiff in a false light and public disclosure of private facts about the plaintiff) are both encompassed within the constitutional privilege.

174. **(B)** In his defamation action against the *Washington Planet*, Senator Harrison, as a public official, must prove malice on the defendant's part to sustain a prima facie case. In accordance with *New York Times vs. Sullivan*, 376 U.S. 254 (1946), The United States Supreme Court held that the First Amendment guarantees of freedom of speech and freedom of press conferred a privilege on news media defendants which extended to false statements of facts about public official-plaintiffs, provided however, that the statements were made without malice. Malice was further defined by the court as (1) knowledge of falsity and (2) reckless disregard of the truth. Therefore, a public official or public figure may not recover for defamatory remarks relating to his official conduct in the absence of proof that the defendant made the statement with malice. Choice (A) is incorrect since the qualified privilege is lost if the defendant newspaper published the statement maliciously. Choice (D) is also wrong since an absolute privilege did not exist in the facts presented. An absolute privilege exists only in the following cases (1) judicial proceedings, (2) legislative proceedings (Speech and Debate Clauses), (3) executive proceedings, and (4) compelled broadcast situations, where the news media is compelled to allow a speaker to use the air or to print notices in a newspaper.

175. **(A)** Where a written statement is defamatory on its face (referred to as libel *per se*), the majority of American courts take the position that the injury to the plaintiff's reputation is presumed by law. Moreover, libel *per se* is actionable without pleading or proving special damages. If the libelous statement falls within one of the four *per se* categories, imputing (1) criminal conduct, (2) loathsome disease, (3) unchastity, or (4) improper conduct in business, trade, or profession, the plaintiff need not prove special damages. In the present hypothetical, the information contained in the letters which Buddy gave to Bob Bernfield would constitute libel *per se* since the letters imputed criminal conduct to Senator Harrison in soliciting illegal campaign contributions. Please note that choice (B) is incorrect since libel *per se* denotes a statement defamatory on its face. Alternative (C) is wrong since slander is the spoken word.

MIG 1 INTENTIONAL TORTS: PERSONAL AND EMOTIONAL INJURY

- **BATTERY**
  - **ACT** — must be volitional act
  - **INTENT** — to cause a harmful or offensive contact to someone (*Note:* For all intentional torts, intent includes (1) conscious desire that result occur, (2) knowledge that result will occur, and (3) knowledge that result is substantially likely to occur)*
  - **HARM** — act must result in contact of a harmful or offensive nature
  - **DEFENSES**
    - **CONSENT**
      - **Informed Consent** — P must know all relevant facts for consent to be valid
      - **Scope of Consent** — D must not cause a touching different in kind than which P could reasonably expect
    - **SELF-DEFENSE (same rules as in Criminal Law)**
      - D must not be initial aggressor
      - D must reasonably conclude that force is necessary to protect himself from imminent bodily harm
      - Amount of force used must be reasonable; in some jurisdictions, D must retreat before using *deadly* force
    - **DEFENSE OF OTHERS**
      - **Majority** — D stands in the shoes of person defended (that person must have had right to use force in self-defense)
      - **Minority** — D must reasonably believe that person defended was privileged to use force
    - **DEFENSE OF PROPERTY**
      - Must make prior demand that D cease (or show that demand would be futile) before using force
      - May never use deadly force
- **ASSAULT**
  - **ACT** — must be volitional act
  - **INTENT** — to cause someone to be apprehensive of receiving a harmful or offensive contact*
  - **HARM** — resulting apprehension of an imminent harmful or offensive contact
  - **DEFENSES** — all battery defenses
- **FALSE IMPRISONMENT**
  - **ACT** — must be volitional act
  - **INTENT** — to confine someone
  - **RESULT** — actual confinement of P; reasonable means of escape does *not* include
    - Having to leave property
    - Dangerous means of escape
    - Unreasonably embarrassing means of escape
  - **HARM** — knowledge of confinement *or* injury resulting from confinement
  - **DEFENSES**
    - All battery defenses
    - Lawful arrest
    - **Shopkeepers Privilege** — merchant may detain a suspected shoplifter for a reasonable time if he has probable cause that P is stealing and the shopkeeper does not use excessive force (Shopkeeper is still liable for actual injuries)
- **INTENTIONAL INFLICTION OF EMOTIONAL DISTRESS**
  - **ACT** — extreme and outrageous conduct
  - **INTENT** — to cause severe emotional upset to P or recklessness with regard to P's upset
  - **HARM** — resulting emotional distress of a significant nature
  - **DEFENSES**
    - All battery defenses
    - D's lack of knowledge of P's unusual susceptibility to emotional upset

**NOTE: If D has the intent to commit (1) battery, (2) assault, (3) false imprisonment, (4) trespass to land, or (5) trespass to chattels and ends up causing an injury protected by any other of these five torts, the intent requirement is satisfied.*

MIG 2 INTENTIONAL TORTS: INJURY TO PROPERTY

TRESPASS TO LAND
- **ACT** — must be volitional act
- **INTENT** — to do act which results in trespass*
- **HARM** — invasion of P's right to use and enjoy her land; no damages need be proven, and once D has committed a trespass he is strictly liable for all injuries to P's land, buildings, and chattels
- **DEFENSES**
  - Consent of person in lawful possession
  - Entry to reclaim D's own property on P's land
  - Entry under public or private necessity
  - Entry to abate public or private nuisance

TRESPASS TO CHATTELS
- **ACT** — must be volitional act
- **INTENT** — to do act which results in trespass*
- **HARM** — interference with P's use and enjoyment of his personal property
  - Injury to chattel
  - Denying P possession
- **REMEDY** — diminution of value (or cost of repair) and/or reasonable rental value
- **DEFENSES** — all battery defenses

CONVERSION
- **ACT** — must be volitional act
- **INTENT** — to assert rights of ownership over chattel which in fact belongs to P
- **HARM** — substantial interference with P's rights to use and enjoy his chattel
- **REMEDY** — P may require D to pay full market value of chattel instead of returning it along with damages
- **DEFENSES**
  - Consent
  - Necessity

**NOTE: If D has the intent to commit (1) battery, (2) assault, (3) false imprisonment, (4) trespass to land, or (5) trespass to chattels and ends up causing an injury protected by any other of these five torts, the intent requirement is satisfied.*

MIG 3 DEFAMATION

DEFAMATORY STATEMENT — one which subjects P to hatred, contempt, or ridicule (1st Restatement) or which lowers the esteem in which P is held by third parties (2nd Restatement)

OF OR CONCERNING P — someone must recognize that the statement is about this particular P
- P must be a living human being
- Group defamation
  - **Small group (less than 25)** — all members may have action even if statement is not all-inclusive
  - **Medium group (between 25 and 150)** — may give each member a cause of action if all-inclusive
  - **Large group (over 150)** — no member may sue even if statement is all-inclusive

PUBLICATION — at least one third party must hear the statement and understand its defamatory nature; D must be at least negligent with regard to the publication

PROOF OF SPECIAL DAMAGES OR EXCEPTION (a prima facie case requirement, *not* a rule of damages)
- **Special Damages** — pecuniary loss resulting from a third party's response to the defamatory statement
- **Exceptions**
  - **Slander per se** — oral statements relating to: (1) incompetence in trade or profession, (2) present loathsome disease, (3) commission of serious crime, *or* (4) lack of chastity of a woman
  - **Libel (written statements)** — in some states all libel is actionable without proof of special damages, but common law required special damages unless libel is
    - **On its face** — (no innuendo or external knowledge is required to understand the statement's defamatory nature) *or*
    - **Per quod** — (innuendo or external knowledge is required to understand the statement's defamatory nature) *if* defamation relates to a slander per se category

DEFENSES
- **Truth** must go to defamatory sting
- **Absolute Privileges (not defeated by even spite or knowledge of falsity)** — (1) legislative proceeding, (2) judicial proceedings, (3) other official statements of governmental officials, (4) equal time broadcasts, and (5) communications between spouses
- **Common Law Qualified Privileges (defeated by spite or ill will, knowledge of falsity or reckless disregard of truth, and, perhaps, negligence)** — (1) statements in D's own interest, (2) statements in the interest of third persons, (3) statements in the interest of the public, (4) reports of public proceedings, and (5) fair comment opinions
- **First Amendment Qualified Privileges**
  - **Public Officials, Candidates for Public Office, and Well-Known Public Figures** — must prove "malice" as defined by *NY Times v Sullivan* (that D knew statement was false or acted in reckless disregard of truth)
  - **Limited Public Figures** — ordinary persons who *voluntarily* inject themselves into a public controversy are treated as public figures if alleged defamation relates to their position in the controversy but are treated as private persons if defamation concerns other matters
  - **Private Persons** — must prove negligence with regard to truth when defendant is a member of the media; jurisdictions split when D is a private person

DAMAGES (once prima facie case, including existence of some special damages or exceptions, is made)
- All special damages (defined above), including lost customers and lost employment
- Damage to P's reputation
- Damage to P's feelings, including medical bills attributable to P's emotional distress
- Punitive damages (when appropriate)
- *Note:* When First Amendment qualified privilege applies, only actual damages (i.e., those proven with reasonable certainty by P) and not punitive damages may be recovered unless P proves *NY Times* malice

MIG 4 NEGLIGENCE

- **DUTY**
  - **Forseeable Plaintiff**
    - Cardozo — no duty owed to persons outside geographic zone of danger at the time of D's negligence
    - Andrews — if D has breached a duty to anyone, duty is owed to everyone
    - Rescuers are always foreseeable Ps
  - **Omission — as a general rule, there is not duty to act or aid another. The exceptions include:**
    - Duty to alleviate consequences of his own act endangers others (perhaps even if D's act was not even negligent)
    - Duty to control others (e.g., children)
    - Special relationship between P and D including:
      - contractual duty
      - innkeepers and guest
      - common carriers and passengers
      - school and pupils
    - Undertaking to act — may not abandon an attempted rescue if D leaves P's in a worse condition

    NOTE: Always consider cause-in-fact issue in all omission problems

- **STANDARDS OF CARE**
  - **Reasonable Person Standard — what would a reasonable person have done in those circumstances. Balance (1) likelihood of harm and (2) gravity of potential injury against (3) social utility of D's actual conduct and (4) burden of adequate precautions.** *Always state what D should have done.*
    - Mental characteristics of adult defendant irrelevant
    - Physical characteristics of adult defendant may be considered
    - Children must act as would children of the same age, experience, and intelligence except that they are measured by adult standards when they are engaged in adult activities
    - Emergency situation will lower D's standard if, but only if, D's own negligence did not cause emergency
    - Community custom is relevant to establishing what is reasonable, but it is not determinative
  - **Standards for Professionals (Malpractice) — the minimum common skill of members in good standing in the profession. Expert testimony is required except when negligence is obvious**
    - **Locality Rule** — at common law, conduct of general practitioners was measured by what others in the same or similar localities would do (today, locality rule is simply a factor in most states)
    - **Specialists** — held to national standard
  - **Statutes — if statute establishes *civil* liability, it conclusively establishes standard. If criminal statute ask (1) is P in a class that the statute was designed to protect (2) was he to be protected from this type of harm; if answer to both questions is "yes" then**
    - **Negligence Per Se (majority rule)** — D may not introduce evidence as to reasonableness, although she may argue for an implied exception (i.e., because of the unique circumstances of this case, what she did was inherently more reasonable than what the statute required)
    - **Presumption of Negligence** — D may argue that his conduct was nevertheless reasonable despite the statute, but has the burden of proving this
    - **Evidence of Negligence** — violation merely helps P establish his prima facie case (Note: Most jurisdictions follow this rule for violation of local ordinances.)
    - **Caveat** — under any of these views the issues of cause-in-fact, proximate cause, and compensible damage issues are the same as in any other negligence action. Contributory negligence and assumption of risk issues are also the same except when statute was designed to protect P from his own folly
  - **Special Standards**
    - **Automotive Guests** — under "guest statutes" existing in many states, an automobile driver is liable to a non-paying guest only if the driver was reckless
    - Owners and Occupiers of Land
    - Innkeepers and Common Carriers — owe "highest" duty of care

(continued below)

MIG 4 NEGLIGENCE *(continued)*

- **BREACH**
  - **Normally, simply a question of fact**
  - **Res Ipsa Loquitur — circumstantial evidence of negligence arises when**
    - Accident is one that normally does not occur in the absence of negligence
    - Instrumentality causing injury is under D's exclusive control or D is responsible for all others in control
    - P must introduce evidence removing any inference of his own fault
  - **Concurrent Conduct — even conduct which is not negligent by itself will be actionable if it combines with similar conduct of others if the other's conduct was foreseeable**

- **CAUSE-IN-FACT (Actual Cause)**
  - **"But for" Test — normally, ask if injury would have occurred but for that aspect of D's conduct which was negligent**
  - **Substantial Factor Test (or Superabundant Cause) — when two or more causes concur to cause an event but either alone would have been sufficient to cause injury, each is a cause-in-fact if it is a substantial factor in causing the injury**
  - **When two or more Ds are negligent but P cannot prove whose negligence caused the injury, court may shift burden of disproving causation to Ds**
  - **Look for cause-in-fact issues in all omission problems**

- **PROXIMATE CAUSE (Legal Cause)**
  - **Spotting the Issue — look for**
    - Minor negligence causing tremendous injury
    - Freakish results
    - Multiple persons or factors contributing to the injury
  - **Basic Rules**
    - **Direct Injury Cases (i.e., there are no intervening causes between D's negligence and P's injury)**
      - Injury to Persons — all direct causes are proximate
      - Injury to Property
        - Traditional View — all direct causes are proximate
        - Trend — was this injury a foreseeable result of D's conduct?
    - **Indirect Injury Cases — was this injury a foreseeable result of D's conduct (even if the exact way in which the injury occurred was unforeseeable)?**
  - **Decided Cases**
    - Subsequent negligence, including medical malpractice, is always foreseeable
    - Subsequent criminal acts or intentional tortious conduct are not normally foreseeable, but may be foreseeable if that risk is what made D's conduct negligent in the first place
    - An attempted rescue is always foreseeable
    - Acts of nature are generally unforeseeable
    - Suicide is unforeseeable unless it was the result of an uncontrollable impulse caused by D's negligence

- **DAMAGES**
  - **Emotional Injury — recoverable only if there is some accompanying physical injury**
    - Only a few states (including Florida) still require impact
    - Trend is to allow recovery even if emotional injury was not caused by P's concern for her own safety
  - **Pure economic injury not protectible by negligence cause of action**

MIG 5 DEFENSES TO NEGLIGENCE

- **CONTRIBUTORY NEGLIGENCE**
  - **Normally, the issue of P's contributory negligence is controlled by the same rules as those governing D's negligence, except that the mental defects of an adult P may be considered**
  - **Imputed Contributory Negligence — as a general rule, the negligence of a third party will be imputed to P only if P would have been vicariously liable for the third party's negligence if P had been the defendant**
  - **Effect of a finding of contributory negligence**
    - **Traditional View — P's action is *totally* barred except that**
      - P's ordinary negligence will be ignored if D's conduct was *willful and wanton* or *reckless*
      - Last Clear Chance — P's negligence may be irrelevant if D had the last clear chance to avoid the danger created by P's prior negligence (including the actual ability to avoid the accident)
        - If D sees a helpless P, D had the last clear chance
        - If D sees a negligently inattentive P and should have known that P was unaware of the danger, D has the last clear chance
        - If D should have seen a helpless P, D has the last clear chance under the Restatement, but not in states following the doctrine of discovered peril
        - If D should have seen a negligently inattentive P but doesn't, D does not have the last clear chance
    - **Comparative Negligence —most states now simply reduce P's recovery by the percentage that his own negligence contributed to the injury. Apply comparative negligence on the MBE unless the facts state otherwise.**
      - Pure (including Alaska, California, Florida, Michigan, and New York) — P always collects something from a negligent D
      - Restricted (including Massachusetts, Minnesota, and Pennsylvania) — P can collect only if D was at least as negligent as P
      - "Willful and wanton" rule and Last Clear Chance doctrine (as discussed above) are inapplicable

- **ASSUMPTION OF RISK — when P actually understands the risk to his safety and voluntarily subjects himself to it**
  - Traditional View — a complete defense
  - Comparative Negligence Jurisdictions — assumption of risk is normally treated as an aspect of contributory negligence (and is thus only a partial bar), but may still be a total bar when D's only duty was to warn (as in certain landowner and products liability cases)

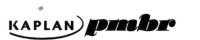

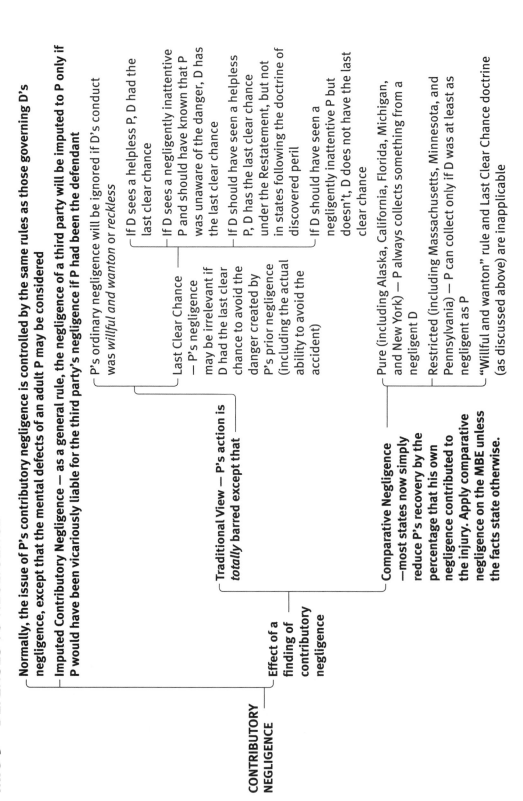

MIG 6 PRODUCTS LIABILITY

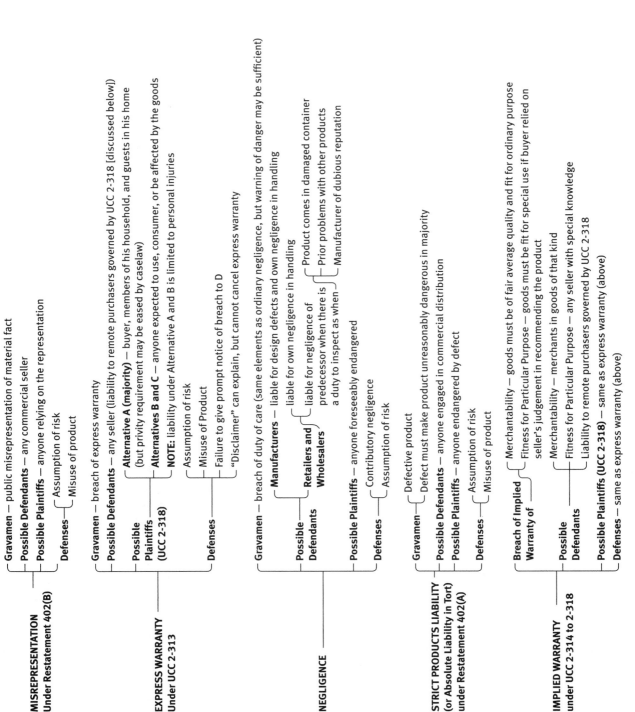

MISREPRESENTATION Under Restatement 402(B)

- **Gravamen** — public misrepresentation of material fact
- **Possible Defendants** — any commercial seller
- **Possible Plaintiffs** — anyone relying on the representation
- **Defenses**
  - Assumption of risk
  - Misuse of product

EXPRESS WARRANTY Under UCC 2-313

- **Gravamen** — breach of express warranty
- **Possible Defendants** — any seller (liability to remote purchasers governed by UCC 2-318 [discussed below])
- **Possible Plaintiffs (UCC 2-318)**
  - **Alternative A (majority)** — buyer, members of his household, and guests in his home (but privity requirement may be eased by caselaw)
  - **Alternatives B and C** — anyone expected to use, consumer, or be affected by the goods
  - **NOTE:** liability under Alternative A and B is limited to personal injuries
- **Defenses**
  - Assumption of risk
  - Misuse of Product
  - Failure to give prompt notice of breach to D
  - "Disclaimer" can explain, but cannot cancel express warranty

NEGLIGENCE

- **Gravamen** — breach of duty of care (same elements as ordinary negligence, but warning of danger may be sufficient)
- **Possible Defendants**
  - **Manufacturers** — liable for design defects and own negligence in handling
  - **Retailers and Wholesalers**
    - liable for own negligence in handling
    - liable for negligence of predecessor when there is a duty to inspect as when
      - Product comes in damaged container
      - Prior problems with other products
      - Manufacturer of dubious reputation
- **Possible Plaintiffs** — anyone foreseeably endangered
- **Defenses**
  - Contributory negligence
  - Assumption of risk

STRICT PRODUCTS LIABILITY (or Absolute Liability in Tort) under Restatement 402(A)

- **Gravamen**
  - Defective product
  - Defect must make product unreasonably dangerous in majority
- **Possible Defendants** — anyone engaged in commercial distribution
- **Possible Plaintiffs** — anyone endangered by defect
- **Defenses**
  - Assumption of risk
  - Misuse of product

IMPLIED WARRANTY under UCC 2-314 to 2-318

- **Breach of Implied Warranty of**
  - Merchantability — goods must be of fair average quality and fit for ordinary purpose
  - Fitness for Particular Purpose — goods must be fit for special use if buyer relied on seller's judgement in recommending the product
- **Possible Defendants**
  - Merchantability — merchants in goods of that kind
  - Fitness for Particular Purpose — any seller with special knowledge
  - Liability to remote purchasers governed by UCC 2-318
- **Possible Plaintiffs (UCC 2-318)** — same as express warranty (above)
- **Defenses** — same as express warranty (above)

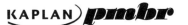